ROUTLED[illegible]

Volume 55

OBJECT AND ABSOLUTIVE IN HALKOMELEM SALISH

OBJECT AND ABSOLUTIVE IN HALKOMELEM SALISH

DONNA B. GERDTS

Routledge
Taylor & Francis Group
LONDON AND NEW YORK

First published in 1988

This edition first published in 2014
by Routledge
2 Park Square, Milton Park, Abingdon, Oxon, OX14 4RN

Simultaneously published in the USA and Canada
by Routledge
711 Third Avenue, New York, NY 10017

Routledge is an imprint of the Taylor & Francis Group, an informa business

First issued in paperback 2016

British Library Cataloguing in Publication Data
A catalogue record for this book is available from the British Library

ISBN13: 978-0-415-72748-8 (hbk)
ISBN13: 978-1-138-99456-0 (pbk)

Publisher's Note
The publisher has gone to great lengths to ensure the quality of this reprint but points out that some imperfections in the original copies may be apparent.

Disclaimer
The publisher has made every effort to trace copyright holders and would welcome correspondence from those they have been unable to trace.

Object and Absolutive in Halkomelem Salish

Donna B. Gerdts

Garland Publishing, Inc. ■ New York & London
1988

Library of Congress Cataloging-in-Publication Data

Gerdts, Donna B.
Object and absolutive in Halkomelem Salish / Donna B. Gerdts. p. cm. — (Outstanding dissertations in linguistics) Thesis (Ph.D.)—University of California, San Diego, 1981. Bibliography: p.
ISBN 0–8240–5183–1
1. Stalo language—Syntax. 2. Relational grammar. I. Title. II. Series.
PM2381.S81G4 1988
497'.3—dc19 88–16513

Printed on acid-free, 250-year-life paper
Manufactured in the United States of America

FOR XVŪNUTHUT

ACKNOWLEDGEMENTS

I would very much like to thank the native speakers of Halkomelem who served as my language consultants. I would especially like to thank Arnold Guerin for being my teacher and my friend.

I would also like to thank the other scholars of Halkomelem who have shared their expertise with me--Brent Galloway, Tom Hukari, and especially Wayne Suttles. Other Salishanists, including Larry Thompson and Dick Demers, have also shared their knowledge and have provided comments and criticism of earlier versions of this work. I greatly appreciate the leg up I got on Halkomelem from a field methods course taught by Dale Kinkade, who I also thank for showing continuing interest in my work.

Most importantly, I would like to thank my professors and fellow students at UCSD. I especially thank Margaret Langdon for making me clarify my analysis and presentation of data and David Perlmutter for his demands of theoretical and stylistic preciseness.

I gratefully acknowledge the various funding agencies which have made my fieldwork on Halkomelem possible--the Melville and Elizabeth Jacobs' Research Fund, The Phillips Fund (American Philosophical Society), the Canadian Ethnology Service, National Museum of Man, Ottawa, the Society of Sigma Xi, the National Science Foundation through grant No. BNS78-17490 to the University of California, and the Public Affairs Division of the Canadian Embassy, Washington, D.C.

PREFACE

This study treats aspects of the syntax of Halkomelem, a Salish language spoken in southwestern British Columbia, specifically those constructions which involve objects. Working in the theory of Relational Grammar, I find evidence for the following constructions: advancements to object -- indirect object, benefactive, causal, and directional to object advancements; object resignations -- antipassives, reflexives, reciprocals, and object cancellations; and passives. Evidence for the above constructions is based on several rules which I have formulated for Halkomelem: Nominal Case, Pronominal Case, 3rd Person Agreement, and Transitive Marking. Also, data involving conditions on extractions, possessor extraction, quantifier extraction, causative clause union, and raising provide evidence for the structure of the above constructions.

There are several interesting results of this investigation apropos the description of Halkomelem and the theory of Relational Grammar. First, I point out that several phenomena -- 3rd Person Agreement, One-Nominal Interpretation, possessor extraction, quantifier extraction, and a surface constraint on proper nouns -- make reference to the distinction ergative/absolutive. This is the first evidence that this distinction is necessary for the syntactic description of Salish languages.

Second, although 3-2 and Ben-2 advancement clauses have no corresponding constructions without advancement, I am able to provide evidence for advancement. I argue that conditions on four constructions -- reflexives, limited control marking, antipassives, and object cancellations -- distinguish initial from non-intial objects, thus providing evidence for advancement.

Third, I provide evidence from raising that passives in Halkomelem involve the advancement of object to subject; thus, they do not, as has been claimed, constitute a counterexample to the universal formulation of passive. Furthermore, the ability of passive agents to raise argues for their initial subjecthood and thus provides support for the Relational Grammar view of passives over analyses which posit that passive agents are prepositional phrases in initial structure.

Finally, giving evidence based on a condition on causative clause union, I argue for the initial unaccusativity for some clauses in Halkomelem. In discussing passives of clauses involving clausal to object advancement, I point out that such constructions violate a law proposed as a universal in Relational Grammar -- the 1-Advancement Exclusiveness Law.

This study seeks to accomplish two goals. First, it provides natural language fodder for the debate concerning the nature of grammatical relations and their place in syntactic theory. Second, by showing that Halkomelem draws from a familiar class of universal constructions and organizes its syntax around some simple and common parameters, I have brought Salish languages, which due to their phonological and morphological complexity seemed particularly fearsome, into cross-linguistic perspective. Nevertheless, I hope this study conveys, that despite its being so revealed, Halkomelem, like all natural languages, remains mysterious and wonderful.

TABLE OF CONTENTS

Page

LIST OF ABBREVIATIONS

These abbreviations are used in the glosses of the Halkomelem data:

act	activity
adv	advancement marker
aux	auxiliary
cn	connective
cont	continuative
cs	causative
det	determiner
emph	emphatic pronouns
erg	ergative
evid	evidential
imp	imperative
int	interrogative
intr	intransitive
l.c.	limited control
lnk	linker
neg	negative
nom	nominalizer
obj	objective pronominal suffixes
obl	oblique marker
pas	passive person markers
pl	plural
pos	pronominal possessive affixes
pst	past tense
rec	reciprocal
ref	reflexive
ser	serial
sub	subjective pronominal clitics
sup	suppositive
st	stative
tr	transitive
1	1st person
2	2nd person
3	3rd person

LIST OF MAPS

INTRODUCTION

0 Introduction

This study treats aspects of the syntax of Halkomelem, a Salish language spoken in southwestern British Columbia. Until quite recently, descriptive work on Halkomelem was unavailable. For this reason, I have chosen a topic which allows the presentation of analyses for constructions comprising a significant portion of the syntax of Halkomelem.

The data on which this study is based are from my fieldwork with speakers on Vancouver Island and from the area of Vancouver, B.C. Largely, the data are from Arnold Guerin, Musqueam Reserve, Vancouver, B.C., but most aspects of the data have been checked with other speakers on Vancouver Island and in the Vancouver area.

0.1 Focus of the Investigation

This study focuses on constructions which involve objects. Working in the theory of Relational Grammar, I find evidence for the following constructions: <u>advancements to object</u> -- indirect object, benefactive, causal, and directional to object advancements; <u>object resignations</u> -- antipassives, reflexives, reciprocals, and object cancellations; and <u>passives</u>. For each construction, I give:

a. evidence for the changes of grammatical relations

b. conditions on the construction

c. verbal morphology correlated with the construction.

I discuss these constructions with respect to the rules of Nominal Case, Pronominal Case, 3rd Person Agreement, and Transitive

Marking. I also discuss the interaction of these constructions with nominalizations, causatives, extractions, possessor extraction, and quantifier extraction.

Not only do these constructions and rules comprise a significant portion of Halkomelem syntax, but these are certainly some of the most common syntactic processes in the language.

Because of the focus of this thesis, many topics of interest have been set aside. These include: aspect, auxiliaries, particles, coordination, deixis, word order, modals, adverbs, and the discourse uses of constructions. Furthermore, certain issues of importance to linguists working on Salish languages--such as control, the validity of the noun/verb distinction, and the peripheralness of noun phrases -- are not addressed here. I hope the careful treatment given to the constructions and rules I do consider will justify my exclusion of these important topics.

0.2 Why Relational Grammar?

I show below that the constructions and rules dealt with in this study are best treated by referring to the grammatical relations of the nominals (i.e., subject, object, oblique) and not to linear order or semantic role. For this reason, I chose to write in a framework which takes subject, object, and certain other grammatical relations as central concepts -- Relational Grammar. Also, I discuss certain rules of Halkomelem which do not make reference to subject and object but rather to ergative and absolutive. Because nominal case in Halkomelem does not distinguish ergative and absolutive, I needed a framework, such as Relational Grammar, that provided a definition of these concepts independently of case marking.

Since many readers interested in this study primarily for the discussion of the Halkomelem data are unfamiliar with Relational Grammar, I use a slightly modified version of the framework (cf. §0.3.5). I rely on evidence internal to Halkomelem and avoid basing arguments upon universals and laws proposed within the theory. I also discuss areas such as nominalization which are important to the grammar of Halkomelem but which have not been given characterizations in Relational Grammar. I feel justified that the loss of some theoretical preciseness is offset by the accessibility gained.

0.3 Outline of Relational Grammar

I present here a summary of the basic concepts of Relational Grammar (RG) needed to comprehend the analyses presented below. For a more thorough discussion and justification of these concepts, cf. Perlmutter and Postal (1977, to appear c) and Perlmutter (1980).

The basic claim of RG is that the following information is needed in the syntactic characterization of a clause:

(i) the grammatical relations which each element bears in the clause (cf. §0.3.1)

(ii) the level at which each element bears grammatical relations to the other elements.

This information is represented in RG by means of a relational network (cf. §0.3.2).

The use of relational networks (RNs) to characterize clauses has an immediate consequence; because RNs reference grammatical relations rather than word order, case marking, etc., it is possible to compare grammatical constructions in different languages. Linguistic theory can be conceived of as the task of characterizing the set of well-formed RNs for natural languages. The task of grammars of individual languages is to state which subset of the set of well-formed RNs are well-formed in that language. In addition, a grammar of a language must stage various language particular rules and generalizations, e.g., case marking, word order.

0.3.1 Grammatical Relations

Among the grammatical relations (GRs) used in RG are: predicate (P), subject (1), object (2), indirect object (3), Oblique [locative (Loc), benefactive (Ben), instrument (Instr), etc.], and chomeur (Cho). The chomeur relation (from the French 'unemployed') is borne by nominals that bear no other nominal-clausal relation at that level. For further discussion of the chomeur relation and its importance to linguistic theory, see Perlmutter (1980).

The GRs are organized into classes; of relevance here are two classes: <u>nuclear terms</u>, consisting of 1s and 2s, and <u>non-terms</u>, consisting of chomeurs and Obliques.

The nominal-clausal GRs are also conceived of as being organized hierarchically, as follows:

(1) 1 > 2 > 3 > non-terms

Although it is not entirely clear what principles would determine the assignment of the GRs at initial level, Perlmutter and Postal (1977, p. 402) suggest the following:

(2) Our ultimate claim is that the justification for [the assignment of GRs at initial level] is universally determined by principles referring to the semantic role of the nominal. Thus, as traditionally recognized, agent nominals are initially 1s, (although, of course not <u>all</u> 1s represent agents), patients 2s, etc.

In the present study, I use semantic role as an expedient means for introducing the data in a way that is not biased towards my solution. I make no claims as the the usefulness or definability of such notions. However, I have found it possible to present analyses which are consistent with the claim in (2). In several instances (cf. §3.3, §5.5, §5.6.2) I give evidence for initial grammatical relations which is independent of any assumptions concerning semantic role. In each case, this independent evidence confirms the initial grammatical relation assigned by a principle such as (2).

0.3.2 Relational Networks

The relational networks involves three types of primitive elements:

(i) a set of nodes, which represent linguistic elements of all sorts, including morphemes and abstract elements such as clauses or phrases.

(ii) a set of R-signs, which are the names of the grammatical relations that elements bear to other elements.

(iii) a set of coordinates, $c_1 \ldots c_n$, which indicate the level at which the elements bear grammatical relations to other elements.

The information that an element bears a grammatical relation at a certain level can be captured by means of an <u>arc</u>, as in (3).

(3)

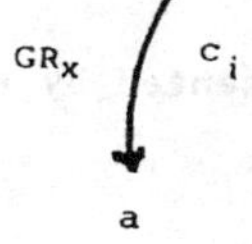

The arc in (3) is interpreted to mean that element a bears relation GR_x with respect to element b at the c_i level.

A relational network is a set of arcs meeting certain conditions. A clause (d) with 3 elements (a,b,c) bearing grammatical relations (x,y,z respectively) at the c_1 level can be represented by the following relational network.

(4)

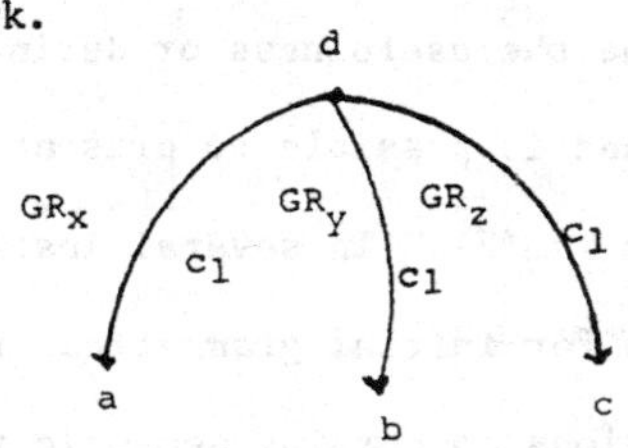

In some grammatical constructions, a nominal bears different relations at different levels of the same clause. Speaking informally and figuratively, I say that such constructions involve 'changes in grammatical relations.' For example, in advancements, a nominal bearing a GR at the c_i level, bears a GR that is higher on the hierarchy given in (1) at the c_{i+1} level. For example, passive has been universally characterized by Perlmutter and Postal in terms of the following sub-network:

(5)

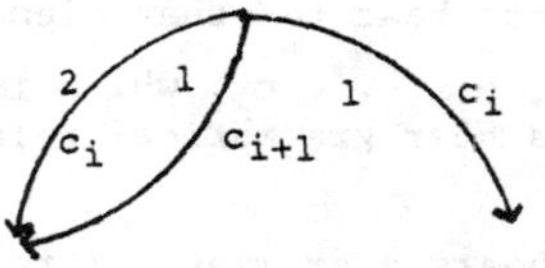

That is, a nominal bearing the 2-relation in the c_i stratum, in which there is also a nominal bearing the 1-relation, bears the 1-relation in the c_{i+1} stratum.

The passive clause in (6) is represented by the relational network in (7):

(6) Sally was criticized by Marcia.

(7)

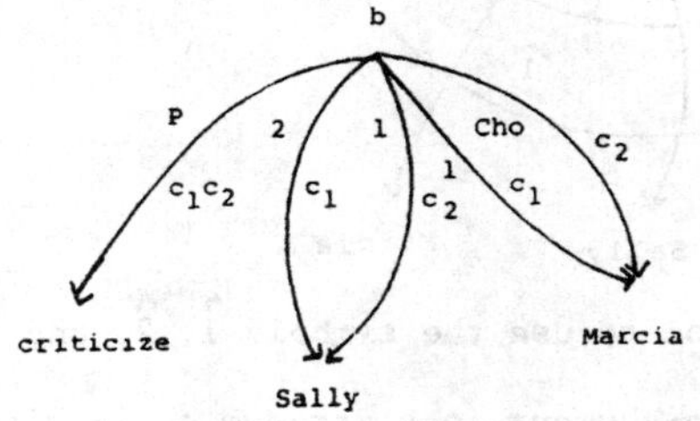

As can be observed in (7), (6) has two levels of structure (c_1 and c_2). The notion of level can be re-stated formally in terms of the concept of stratum, exemplified as follows: the c_{ith} or i^{th} stratum of b, where b is a node and c_i is an arbitrary coordinate, is the set of all arcs with tail b and coordinate c_i.

Thus, in the c_1 stratum of (6), 'criticize' heads a P-arc, 'Marcia' heads a 1-arc, and 'Sally' heads a 2-arc, as represented in (8).

(8)

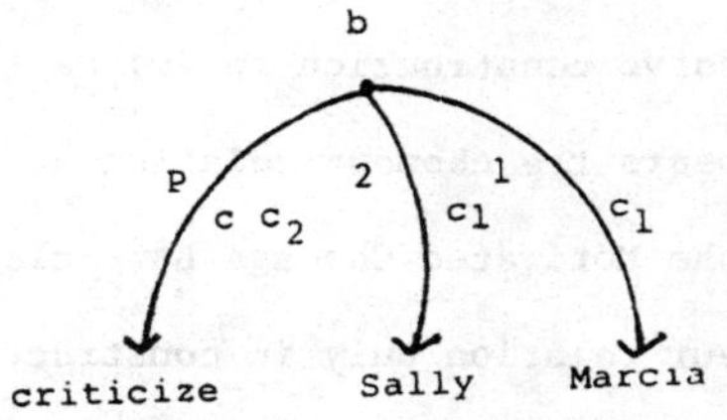

In the c_2 stratum of (6), 'criticize' heads a P-arc, 'Sally' heads a 1-arc, and 'Marcia' heads a Cho-arc, as represented in (9).

(9)

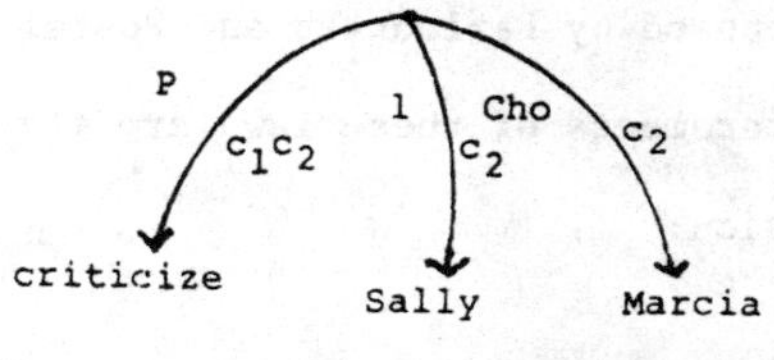

The strata are more clearly seen in an alternative representation of the relational network--the stratal diagram. The stratal diagram of (6) is given in (10).

(10)

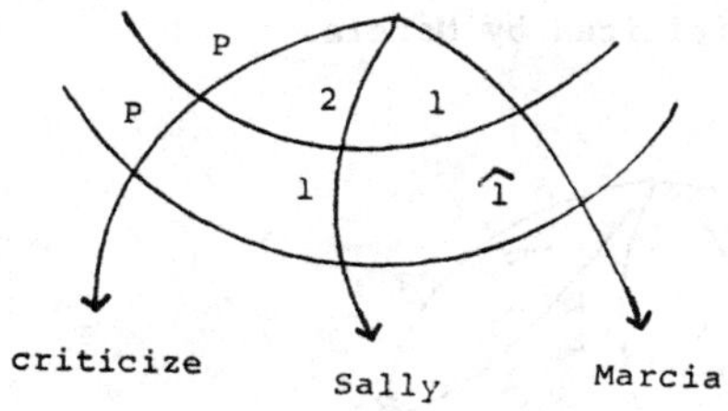

In stratal diagrams, it is common to use the symbols $\hat{1}$, $\hat{2}$, and $\hat{3}$ to represent 1-chomeurs, etc. An n-chomeur in a stratum c_i is a nominal heading a Cho-arc in the c_i stratum and an n-arc in the stratum immediately before the first stratum in which it heads a Cho-arc.

0.3.3 Laws in Relational Grammar

Perlmutter and Postal (1977, to appear a,b,c) have proposed a number of laws stated in terms of grammatical relations. These laws, make falsifiable empirical claims about the class of possible natural languages.

For example, in the passive construction in (6) as represented in (7) and (10) the initial 1 bears the chomeur-relation at final level. A proposed universal--the Motivated Chomage Law--claims that a nominal N_i can bear the chomeur relation only in constructions in which some other nominal N_j assumes N_i's relation. In English passives, the initial 2 assumes the 1-relation at final level; thus this construction obeys the Motivated Chomage Law.

Several other laws proposed by Perlmutter and Postal are referred to in this paper. Statements of these laws are given as they become relevant to the discussion.

0.3.4 Some Defined Concepts

Finally, some other concepts used in this paper are given

formal definitions in RG. These are:

(i) transitive--a transitive stratum is one containing both a 1-arc and a 2-arc.

(ii) intransitive--an intransitive stratum is one that is not transitive.

(iii) ergative arc--a 1-arc in a transitive stratum is an erg-arc in that stratum.

(iv) absolutive arc--a 2-arc in a transitive stratum or the nuclear term-arc in an intransitive stratum is an abs-arc in that stratum.

0.3.5 Modifications in the Framework

In Relational Grammar, there is frequently a formal and an informal way of expressing constructs. For example, it is said formally that a nominal 'heads a 1-arc' and informally that a nominal 'bears the 1 relation.' Throughout this study, I refer to nominals which head 1-arcs as subjects, nominals which head erg-arcs as ergatives, etc.

Furthermore, as seen in §0.3.4 and §1.2 below, transitive and intransitive are technically defined in terms of strata and not in terms of clauses. In Chapter 2, some rules are initially formulated with reference to the transitivity of the clause; these are made precise with respect to strata in subsequent chapters as additional data are given.

0.4 Notational Devices Used in Citing Data

As is traditional, I use * to mark sentences which are ungrammatical to native speakers and ! to mark forms which are structurally grammatical but semantically anomalous. In addition, forms that speakers are not sure about are marked by ? and forms which are disagreed about, where some speakers accept them and some reject them, are marked by @. Elements which may be present optionally are given in parentheses. More precisely, (X) indicates that the form is grammatical whether or not X is present; *(X) indicates that the form is grammatical only if X is present; and (*X) indicates that the form is grammatical only if X is absent.

English glosses as translated by native speakers are given for the grammatical Halkomelem forms. Sometimes I give a literal translation as well. English equivalents of ungrammatical sentences are given in parentheses; these glosses were volunteered by me. Finally, a * before an English gloss indicates that it is not an acceptable translation.

Chapter 1

INTRODUCTION TO HALKOMELEM

1.0 Introduction

In this short introduction to Halkomelem, I discuss the genetic classification, location, and dialects of Halkomelem, and the relationship of this study to previous ones. I also give a brief outline of phonology and structure.

1.1 Genetic Classification, Location, and Dialects

Halkomelem is a member of the Salishan family which includes languages of southern British Columbia and the northwestern United States. According to Thompson (1979b, p. 692-3), the 23 Salishan languages are genetically classified into two major divisions: Bella Coola and the main body of languages, which is further divided into Interior, Tsamosan, and Coast. The Coast division, to which Halkomelem belongs, includes Tillamook and the Central Salish languages, which are listed in (1). Major dialects are given in parentheses.

(1) Central Salish:

Comox
  (Sliammon)
Sechelt
Pentlatch
Squamish
Halkomelem
Nooksack
Straits
  (Northern Straits:
    Songish
    Sooke
    Saanich
    Lummi)
  (Clallam)
Lushootseed [Puget Salish]
Twana

The aboriginal territory of the Halkomelem people stretched from Nanoose to Malahat on Vancouver Island, from Tsawwassen north to Vancouver on the mainland, and from Vancouver 105 miles up the Fraser River to a point north of Yale.

As seen in Map 1, Halkomelem is bounded to the south and north by other Central Salish languages, to the northeast by two Interior Salish languages, Lillooet and Thompson, and to the west, by Nootkan, a Wakashan language unrelated to Salishan.

As discussed in Elmendorf and Suttles (1960) and Gerdts (1977), phonological and lexical evidence points to the division of Halkomelem into three major dialect areas: Island, Downriver, and Upriver. These dialects and the major sub-dialects are given in Map 2. The data in this study are largely from the Island dialect of Halkomelem. Some data from Musqueam, a Downriver dialect, is included; it is indicated by [Ms].

At present, a couple hundred people speak Halkomelem; many of the fluent speakers are over 50 years old, and children and young adults generally do not speak the language. There are several language projects which teach Halkomelem to school children and adults.

1.2 The Relationship of this Study to Previous Research

When I first began fieldwork on Halkomelem in 1975, little information was available on the language. Modern studies consisted of Elmendorf and Suttles (1960), which briefly outlined phonological, morphological, and lexical differences of the three major dialects and included a 600-word list, and two M.A. theses, Harris (1966) and Kava (1969), on phonology. Since that time, important work on Halkomelem has become available: Galloway (1977) treats the phonology, morphology,

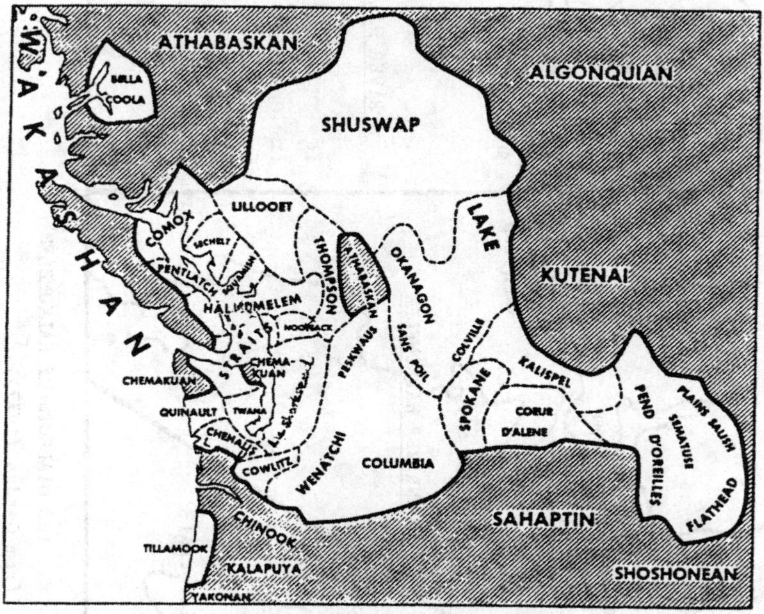

Map 1: **MAP OF THE SALISH LANGUAGE AREA**

(adapted from Kuipers (1967))

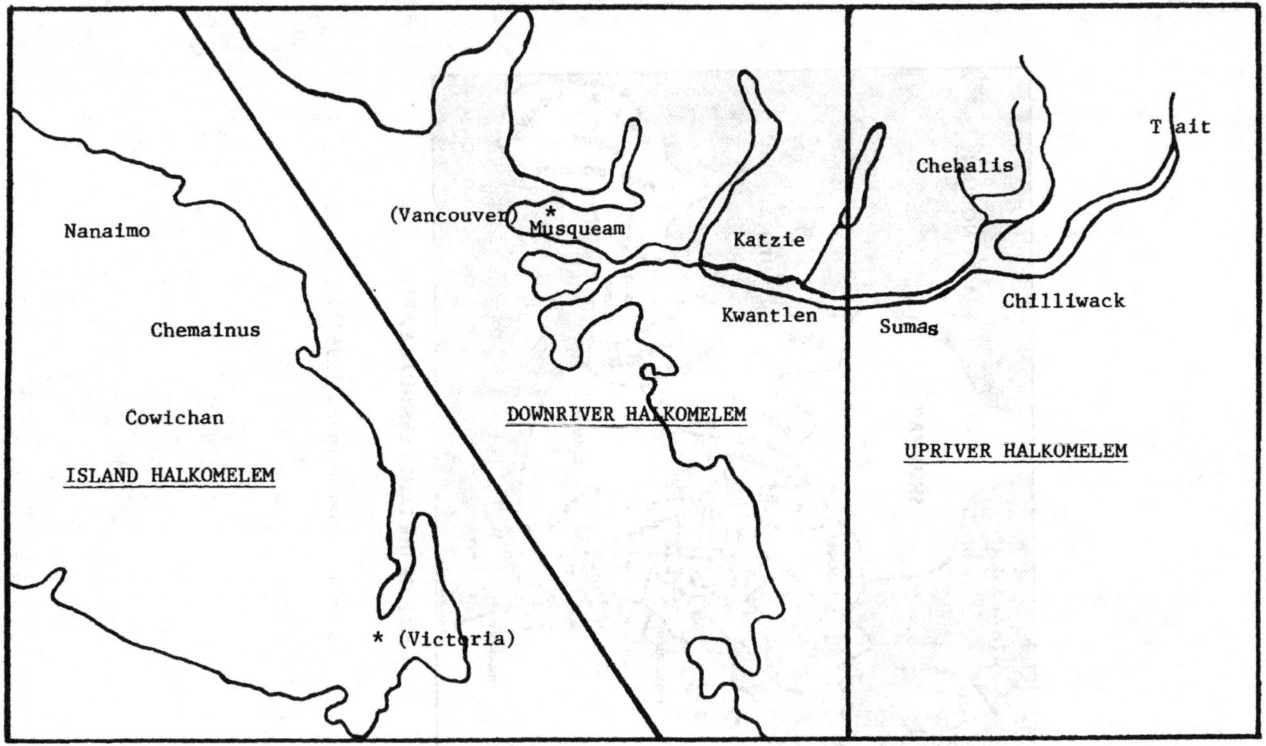

Map 2: THE DIALECTS OF HALKOMELEM
(from Gerdts (1977))

syntax, and semantics of Upriver Halkomelem, Leslie (1979) deals with the morphology and syntax of Island Halkomelem, Hukari, Peter and White (1977) give a brief grammatical sketch and a text in Island Halkomelem, and Hukari in various papers discusses theoretical aspects of the phonology, morphology, and syntax of Island Halkomelem. In addition, two extensive works on Downriver Halkomelem are in preparation: a grammar by Suttles and a dictionary by A. Guerin, of the Musqueam Reserve.

The various scholars of Halkomelem (and other Central Salish languages) have worked largely independently of one another and have made little attempt to integrate their frameworks, terminology, or even transcriptions. Differences in framework are due in part to differences in purpose and focus of the studies. For these reasons, it is difficult, and perhaps unfair, to contrast the present work to other studies on Halkomelem. However, there are three points of comparison that should be discussed.

First, Galloway (1977), Leslie (1979), and Suttles (in preparation) place priority on the general and thorough description of the language and their discussions on morphology include copious examples. In contrast, this study focusses on certain syntactic constructions and limits morphological analysis to generalizations relevant to those constructions. In discussing morphology, I do not reference points of analysis stemming from my own research which are duplicated in other studies. Rather I reference particularly insightful discussions or important points of disagreement.

Secondly, different assumptions are made concerning the relationship of morphology and syntax. For example, a point of contrast is the treatment of transitivity. Galloway (1977) and Leslie (1979), writing in structuralist frameworks, assume a distinction between derivational and inflectional affixation. Although neither defines this distinction, both agree that inflectional processes include transitive (i.e. transitivizing and detransitivizing) suffixes, non-enclitic person markers, and aspect. Further, it is implied that the transitivity of a verb (and thus the clause) is determined by its inflectional status. (cf. Leslie, p. 14, and Galloway, p. 227)

In contrast, this study adopts the assumption made in Relational Grammar that transitive and intransitive are universal notions which can be defined with respect to strata, as given in §0.3.4 above. These concepts, since they are defined in terms of subject and object and not in terms of language specific morphology, are equally available to English and Halkomelem. I assume that transitive morphology neither determines nor is determined by the transitivity of the stratum but the two correlate. This correlation is captured in the grammar by a rule for transitive marking which gives conditions with respect to the transitivity of the strata of the clause; if these conditions are met, then the clause, if it is to be grammatical, must have transitive marking.

A third and more serious difference between this study and others is the range of phenomena which are considered to be syntactic. Since this is a study in Relational Grammar, constructions such as passives, reflexives, and relative clauses are all considered to be syntactic. This contrasts with structuralist grammars (Galloway and Leslie) which limit syntax to the discussion of constituency, order, and complex clauses. Phenomena like passives and reflexives are treated as inflectional processes.

Galloway's treatment of passive is typical of this framework; he says: 'The passive voice can be defined as a verb with an object pronoun being acted upon by an unspecified subject pronoun.' (1977, p. 272) Leaving aside questions concerning the empirical adequacy of this definition, such a definition, which focusses on language-particular features, makes it difficult to contrast Halkomelem passives with those in other languages. According to Perlmutter and Postal (1977), a fruitful line of research involves characterizing constructions such as passives in language-independent terms by making use of the syntactic concepts (subject, object, stratum, etc.) available in Relational Grammar. By defining the aspects common to passives in various languages, they are able to propose a universal characterization of passive, which is available for the description of individual languages. As with transitive morphology, language specific features (word order, case, verbal morphology, etc.) may correlate to aspects of syntactic constructions such as passive. The rules in the grammar of a particular language capture these correlations.

Recently, there has been a trend among theoretical linguists to treat constructions involving changes of grammatical relations (e.g., passives, advancement to object, causatives) within the lexical component of the grammar. Various frameworks have been proposed which analyze some (Jackendoff (1975), Wasow (1977), Aissen and Hankamer (1980)) or all (Bresnan (1978)) such constructions as lexical. In fact, the possibility of a lexical analysis has been proposed for Halkomelem. Writing in a transformational framework, Hukari (1977) points out the semantic similarity of certain nominals in the oblique case with objects of transitives and concludes: 'Obviously these facts must be accounted for in the grammar, however this need not be a function of syntactic description. It seems equally, if not more, plausible to account for such case or thematic relations in the lexicon by lexical redundancy rules along the lines of Jackendoff (1975).' In a brief discussion in Relational Grammar of the same phenomena, Hukari concludes by expressing reservations concerning 'the apparent indifference of relational grammarians to the distinction between syntactic and lexical relations.' (1979, p. 12) However, at present Hukari has not offered an explicit lexical account of any aspect of Halkomelem, and although I assume it is possible to do so, positing a lexical alternative and contrasting it to the present analysis is not within the scope of this study.

1.3 Phonology

In this section, I outline the phonemic inventory of Island Halkomelem and briefly exemplify some phonological processes manifested in later examples.

1.3.1 Phonemic Inventory

In (2), I have listed the consonant phonemes in the transcription used in this study:

(2)

	bilabial	dental	alveolar	lateral	palatal	velar	labialized velar	uvular	labialized uvular	laryngeal
voiceless stop	p	t				(k)	kʷ	q	qʷ	
glottalized stop	p'	t'				(k')	k'ʷ	q'	q'ʷ	ʔ
voiceless affricate		t^{θ}	c		č					
glottalized affricate		θ'	c'	ƛ'	č'					
voiceless fricative		θ	s	ɬ	š		xʷ	x̌	x̌ʷ	h
voiced resonants	m	n		l	y		w			
glottalized resonants	mˀ	nˀ		lˀ	yˀ		wˀ			

The transcriptions used here are standard for northwest languages with the exceptions that I use /x̌/ rather than /χ/ or /x̣/ for the uvular fricative and /θ'/ rather than /t'$^{\theta}$/ for the glottalized dental affricate. Also, I use /ˀ/ and not /'/ to represent glottalization of resonants.

As can be seen in (2), Halkomelem, like other northwest coast languages, has a distinction between velar and uvular stops and fricatives, between plain and labialized velars and uvulars, and between plain and glottalized stops and affricates. In addition, Suttles (in preparation) argues for the inclusion of glottalized resonants in the phonemic inventory.[2]

The phonemes /k/ and /k'/ are marginal; the former occurs mainly in borrowings and the latter in borrowings and in baby talk. The phonemes /č/ and /š/, although common in Island Halkomelem, also arise as alternatives of /c/ and /s/ before /xʷ/. Also, the non-glottalized affricate /tθ/ is limited in occurrence, appearing only in determiners. (cf. §1.44)

The vowel phonemes are: /i,e,ə,u,a/. Also, vowel length is phonemic.

1.3.2 Some Phonological Processes

Stress, which is a complicated phenomenon in Halkomelem, has not been adequately treated to date. Basically, roots and suffixes are assigned a degree of stress lexically. Within a word, the strongest stress is realized as primary stress, the second strongest as secondary stress, and others as unstressed. Vowels in unstressed syllables are frequently reduced to /ə/, as seen in the examples in (3):

(3)	a.	słéniʔ	'woman'	słəniʔ-áłł woman-offspring	'girl infant'
	b.	lém-ət look-tr	'look at it'	ləm-əθ-ámʔš look-tr-1obj	'look at me'

Many instances of schwa may be epenthetic. Observe the following examples; it is not clear whether the schwa in the transitive suffix is epenthesized in the (a) examples or deleted in the (b) examples.

(4) a. q'ʷáqʷ-ət kʷə́n-ət
club-tr take-tr

b. séwq'-t ʔám-əs-t
look for-tr give-advA-tr

If the schwas are epenthetic, then the problem of segmentation arises.[3] I have arbitrarily assigned all schwas of uncertain status to the following segment.

Many speakers delete certain /n/'s, especially in less formal speech. Basically, this occurs in cən 1st person singular subjective clitic, and ʔən- 2nd person singular possessive prefix.

Contraction is possible in some cases where a word ending in a vowel is followed by a word beginning with a glottal stop vowel, as seen in (5):

(5) a. kʷθə ʔən kʷθənʔ
det 2pos det-2pos

b. ní ʔəɬ ní.ɬ [4]
be pst be-pst

I point out other less common phonological processes in footnotes to appropriate examples.

1.4 Basic Structure

The Halkomelem clause consists minimally of a predicate, which, as seen in (6-8), occurs in initial position; this may be followed by one or more nominals (cf. § 1.5).[5]

(6) ʔíməš ce? 'He will walk.'
walk fut

(7) ʔíyəs ɬə sɬéniʔ 'The woman is happy.'
happy det woman

(8) θéʔwən kʷθə scé.ɬtən 'The coho is a salmon.'
coho det salmon (literally: "A salmon is the coho.")

In the above examples, several types of predicates are illustrated; in (6) the predicate is a verb and a particle, in (7) a predicate adjective, and in (8) a predicate nominal. Verbs are frequently preceeded by auxiliaries, discussed in §1.4.1.[6] Verbal morphology is discussed in §1.4.2 and nominal morphology in §1.4.3. I briefly discuss determiners and pronominals, as well.

1.4.1 Auxiliaries

There are four auxiliaries in two classes; each occurs as a main verb as well.

(9)

	auxiliaries		verbs	
A	ʔi	'here (and now)'	ʔí	'be located here'
	ni	'there (and then)'	níʔ	'be located there'
B	mʔi	'come'	ʔəmʔí	'come'
	nemʔ	'go'	némʔ	'go'

Auxiliaries are extremely frequent although not obligatory, as seen in (6) above. A predicate can contain an auxiliary from either class or one from each class, as represented in (10):

(10) (auxA) (auxB) verb

I illustrate various patterns of auxilliaries in (11-15):

(11) ni ʔíməš
aux walk
'He walked.'

(12) ʔi ʔíʔməš
aux walk (cont.)
'He's walking.'

(13) nemʔ ʔíməš
go walk
'He went and walked.'

(14) m'i ʔéwə
come come here
'Come here.'

(15) ʔi ɬe nemʔ ckʷə́mləxʷ
aux imp go get roots
'Let's go get roots.'

The syntactic status of Halkomelem auxiliaries is unclear at present. Here, I have treated them as adjuncts to verbs within a single predicate, although it may be possible to analyze them as predicates themselves. This question requires further study.[7]

1.4.2 Verbal Morphology

I analyze the verb complex as consisting of a stem--the root, aspect marking, and various frozen affixes--and affixes, as outlined in (16):[8]

(16)

-1	0	+1	+2	+3	+4
prefixes	root + aspect	advancement markers lexical suffixes	transitivity suffixes	object suffixes reflexive suffixes reciprocal suffixes	subject suffixes

Most roots in Halkomelem have the shape CVC or CVCC, where the second consonant is a resonant. The root is internally modified to indicate aspect. This is a complicated subject which I discuss only briefly here; Suttles (in preparation) presents a detailed analysis of the morphological and semantic characteristics of Halkomelen aspect. Briefly, the completive/continuative aspect is always indicated. The completive is marked by lack of modification of the root. The continuative, used for events happening over a period of time, is indicated in a number of ways: infixation of a glottal stop (as in (17)), reduplication (as in (18)), vowel lengthening (as in (19)), a change in vowel (as in 20)), or a combination of these.

	completive	continuative	
(17)	ˀíləqət	ˀílˀəqət	'buy it'
	ˀíx̌ʷəθət	ˀíˀx̌ʷəθət	'sweep'
(18)	kʷé.l	kʷəkʷé.lˀ	'hide'
	t'íləm	t'ít'ələmˀ	'sing'
	ɬák'ʷ	ɬáɬək'ʷ	'fly'
(19)	héyˀ	hé.yˀ	'build a canoe'
	qáˀqaˀ	qá.ˀqaˀ	'drink'

	completive	continuative	
(20)	qʷə́l'st	qʷál'st	'boil it'
	θə́yt	θéy'tt	'make it'
	ɬə́yx̌t	ɬéy'x̌t	'eat it'

As can be seen in the above examples, glottalization of resonants in the stem frequently occurs in the continuative.

Stative, durative, and other aspects have been recognized but these will not be discussed here.

Verb prefixes, which are far less numerous and frequent than suffixes, occur rarely in the data in this study. One prefix that appears in discussions of directionals is yə-, which, following Leslie (1979), I refer to as 'serial'. This suffix, illustrated in (21), seems to indicate that the motion is extended through time or space or that something is accompanying the motion.

(21) ʔéwə 'come to' yəʔéʔwə 'coming towards' /'coming along'

The first suffixes that occur after the stem are the advancement markers and lexical suffixes. Advancement markers are suffixed to verbs in clauses involving advancement to object (cf. Chapter 3). I recognize four such suffixes, which I label adv A-D; these are illustrated below:

(22)	adv A[9]	-əs		
	ʔéʔəm	'give'	ʔám-əs-t [10]	'give it to him/her'
	xʷáyəm	'sell'	xʷáyem-əs-t	'sell it to him/her'
			ʔíw-əs-t	'show it to him/her'
			yə́θ-əs-t	'tell him/her about it'

(23)	adv B	-ɬc		
	q'ʷə́l	'bake'	q'ʷə́l-əɬc-ət	'bake it for him/her'
	θə́y-t	'fix it'	θə́y-əɬc-ət	'fix it for him/her'
	x̌ə́lʔ-t	'write it'	x̌ə́lʔ-əɬc-ət	'write it for/to him/her'

(24)	adv C	-meʔ		
	ɬcíws	'tired'	ɬciws-méʔ-t	'tired of him/her'
	q'élʔ	'believe'	q'elʔ-méʔ-t	'believe him/her'
	síwəl	'sense'	sìwəl-méʔ-t	'sense him/her'
	síʔsiʔ	'afraid'	sìʔsiʔ-méʔ-t	'afraid of him/her'
	x̌íʔx̌iʔ	'embarrassed'	x̌íʔx̌iʔ-mə-t	'embarrassed on account of him/her'

(25)	adv D	-n		
	ʔəmʔí	'come'	ʔəmʔí-ns	'come to him/her'
	némʔ	'go'	nəʔém-n-əs	'go to him/her'

I briefly discuss the distribution of these suffixes in §3.8.

Lexical suffixes, verbal suffixes with the meaning of a lexical item, are not discussed here. In Gerdts (1981b) and (1981c) I have presented an analysis of lexical suffixes.

There are several suffixes correlated with transitivity. Two intransitive suffixes, which play an important part in the discussion in Chapter 4, are -əm 'intransitive' and -els 'activity', illustrated below.[11]

(26)   q'ʷə́l-ət   'bake it'   q'ʷə́l-əm   'bake'

pə́n-ət   'plant it'   pə́nʔ-əm   'plant'

(27)   k'ʷɬé-t   'pour it'   k'ʷɬé-ls [12]   'pour'

c'ə́k ʷx̌-t   'fry it'   c'ək ʷx̌-éls   'fry'

The transitive suffixes which are discussed in this study are: -t 'transitive', -nəxʷ 'limited control transitive', and -staxʷ 'causative'. Their distribution is correlated to syntactic factors, which I discuss later. [13]

One semantic factor determining the choice of transitive marker is 'control'. [cf. Thompson (1979a, 1979b, ms), Thompson and Thompson (in press), Saunders and Davis (n.d.), and Galloway (1978)] The limited control transitive suffix is used in clauses where the action performed was out of the control of the agent. That is, the agent had difficulty performing the action or unintentionally or accidentally performed it. The other transitive suffixes do not imply limited control. In (28-30), I give examples contrasting the suffixes -t and -nəxʷ.

(28) a. ni q'ʷáqʷ-ət-əs   ɬə sɬéniʔ   ʔə kʷθə   sqə́məlʔ
aux club-tr-3erg   det woman   obl det   paddle
'He clubbed the woman with the paddle.' [on purpose]

b. ni q'ʷə́qʷ-nəxʷ-əs   ɬə sɬéniʔ   ʔə kʷθə   sqə́məlʔ
aux club-l.c.tr-3erg det woman obl det paddle
'He [accidentally] clubbed the woman with the paddle.'

(29) a. ni lém-ət-əs   θə sɬéniʔ
aux see-tr-3erg det woman
'He looked at the woman.'

b. ni lə́m-nəxʷ-əs   θə sɬéniʔ
aux see-l.c.tr-3erg det woman
'He saw the woman.'

(30) a. ni sq'é-t-əs
aux tear-tr-3erg

'He tore it [on purpose].'

b. ni səq'-néxʷ-əs
aux tear-l.c.tr-3erg

'He tore it [unintentionally] .'

Control marking will be discussed further in §3.3.

The causative suffix, occurring on verbs in causative constructions (cf. §4.2) basically means 'cause', 'make', 'have', or 'let', as illustrated in (31):

(31)	ʔíməš 'walk'		ʔíməš-stəxʷ	'have walk'/ 'let walk'/ 'take for a walk', etc.
	qáʔqaʔ	'drink'	qáʔqaʔ-stəxʷ	'give him/her a drink'
	némʔ	'go'	nəʔémʔ-əstəxʷ	'let go'/ 'bring'
	t'íləmʔ	'sing'	t'íləmʔ-stəxʷ	'make sing'/ 'have sing'

However, there are a few verbs with causative suffixes deviating from this pattern; I regard these as exceptional and do not try to integrate these into the account of causatives given in §4.2:

(32)	qʷál	'speak'	qʷə́l-stəxʷ	'speak to him/her/it'
	ʔə́yʔ	'good'	ʔə́y-stəxʷ	'like him/her/it'
	qə́l	'bad'	qə́l-stəxʷ	'hate him/her/it'
	tátəl-	'understand'	státəl-stəxʷ	'know him/her/it'
	(as in tátəl-ʔəθən 'understand a language')			

Following the transitive suffixes are the objective suffixes, which are discussed in §1.4.5 below, the reflexive suffixes, or the reciprocal suffix.

There are two reflexive suffixes: -θət, which I have glossed as 'self', and -namət, marking limited control.[14]

Both suffixes are used in reflexive constructions, i.e., clauses in which the subject and object are coreferential (cf. §2.4). As with the transitive suffixes, the limited control suffix is used in cases where the action is performed accidentally, unintentionally, or with great difficulty. The two suffixes are contrasted in (33-34):

(33) a. ni kʷə́ləš-θət
aux shoot-self
'He shot himself.' [on purpose]

b. ni kʷələš-námət
aux shoot-l.c.ref
'He managed to shoot himself.' [accidentally]

(34) a. ni x̌íq'-əθət
aux scratch-self
'He scratched himself.' [on purpose]

b. ni x̌əq'-námət
aux scratch-l.c.ref
'He scratched himself.' [accidentally]

In addition to appearing in reflexive constructions, reflexive suffixes are used in constructions where no action of an agent on a patient seems to be implied. These are sometimes inchoative in meaning.[15] I illustrate this use of the reflexive suffixes in (35); I do not discuss these constructions here, limiting my attention to reflexive constructions:

(35)	xʷá-θət	'come down'/'get off'
	x'ə́lc'-θət	'roll over'
	θ'ə́θ'q'ʷəmˀ-θət	'be rotting'
	θə́y-θət	'get well'
	nəqʷ-námət	'oversleep'

The reciprocal suffix -təl appears in reciprocal constructions, which express the action of two entities on each other; this is illustrated in (36).[16]

(36) θ'íq'ʷ-ətəl 'punch each other'
ləmá?-təl 'kick each other'
tíq'ʷ-təl 'collide'
ɬiɬq'á?əlcəp-təl? 'living on opposite sides of the fire in a long house'

Apparently, there is no special reciprocal suffix indicating limited control.

The final suffixes in the verb complex are the subjective suffixes. These are discussed in §1.4.5 below.

1.4.3 Nominal Morphology

The internal morphology of nominals is an extremely complicated topic which is irrelevant to the present study. For this reason, I do not indicate glosses and segmentation to indicate internal structure of nominals.

One obvious characteristic of Halkomelem nominals is that they frequently consist of verb roots prefixed with the nominalizers s- or š- (šxʷ- before vowels or glottal stop vowel), as illustrated in (37) and (38):

(37)
?əɬtən	'eat'	s-?əɬtən	'food'
nét	'be late'	s-nét	'night'
qʷál	'talk'	s-qʷál	'speech'/'language'
t'íləm	'sing'	s-t'íləm	'song'

(38) θíqʷels 'dig' š-θáy?qʷəl?s 'shovel'
k'ʷíc' 'clean fish/animals' š-k'ʷík'ʷəc' 'butchering tool'
ƛ'p'í?wənəm 'pull in rear end' š-ƛ'p'í?wən? 'shirt'

These nominalizers also occur in sentential nominalizations, as discussed in Chapter 2-4. (cf. §2.6.2.2 and §3.2.2)

1.4.4 Determiners

Nominals are usually preceded by one of a set of determiners. I give the articles in (39):

(39)

	plain	feminine (sg.)
proximal	t^{θ}ə	θə
non-proximal	kʷθə	ɬə
remote	k'ʷə	kʷsə
indefinite	k'ʷ, kʷ	

The feminine articles are used only with singular nominals referring to females. The plain articles are used elsewhere. The proximal articles are used for nominals in the view of the speaker. Remote articles are used when referring to distant, ancient, mythological, or deceased entities. The indefinite article is used for an unspecified nominal; it is also used in a partitive sense. The use of these articles is illustrated in (40).[17]

(40) t^{θ}ə swə́y?qe? 'the man' (visible)
kʷθə sɬənɬéni? 'the women' (invisible)
θə sɬéni? 'the woman' (visible)
ɬə sɬéni? 'the woman' (invisible)
k'ʷə nə-sí?lə 'my late grandfather'
kʷsə nə-sí?lə 'my late grandmother'
k'ʷ šúkʷa 'some sugar'

In addition, the determiner <u>ƛ'</u> occurs preceding proper nouns (personal and place names, etc.) and independent pronouns (cf. §1.4.5), but only in the oblique case, discussed in §2.1, §2.4.1. This determiner is illustrated in (41):

(41)	ʔə-ƛ̓	Bill	'to/by Bill'
	ʔə-ƛ̓	nə́wə	'to you'
	ʔə-ƛ̓	qəwʔə́cən	'to Cowichan'

The articles in (39) serve as roots for a large series of demonstratives, which can be used preceding a nominal or alone. I give some of these in (42):

(42) a. plain, singular:

tənʔá	'this (very near)'
tiʔí	'this here'
$t^{θ}$éyʔ	'that'
tøníʔ	'that, over there'

b. feminine, singular:

θənʔá	'this (very near)'

c. plural:

$t^{θ}$éliʔ	'those visible'
kʷθéliʔ	'those invisible'

d. indefinite:

k'ʷənʔá	'this one invisible'
k'ʷiʔí	'over here/there invisible'

1.4.5 Pronominals

Pronominals are expressed by various affixes and particles. As pointed out above, subjective and objective pronominal suffixes are part of the verb complex. The subjective suffixes for 1st and 2nd person are given in (43):

(43) subjective pronominal suffixes:

	singular	plural
1st	-ˀenˀ	-ət
2nd	-əxʷ	-ələp

These suffixes are only used in subordinate clauses. In main clauses, subject clitics, which are 2nd position particles (cf. §1.4.6), are used. These clitics consist of the prefix <u>c-</u> and a reduced form of the suffixes in (44), as follows:[18]

(44) subjective pronominal clitics:

	singular	plural
1st	cən (~ cə)	ct
2nd	č	ce.p

The objective suffixes, illustrated in (45), follow the transitive suffixes in the verb complex.

(45) objective pronominal suffixes:

	singular	plural
1st	-amˀš	-ˀalˀxʷ
2nd	-amə	-alə

Note that the transitive marker <u>-t</u>, when preceding the 1st and 2nd person singular objective suffixes, has the form <u>-θ</u>.[19]

I discuss subject and object marking for 3rd person in §2.4.2-4.

There is also a set of emphatic pronouns, as given in (46):

(46) emphatic pronouns

	singular	plural
1st	ʔe.nʔθə	ɬníməɬ
2nd	nə́wə	ɬwə́ləp
3rd	níɬ	nə́ʔəlɬ

These pronouns can be used as appositions to a clause to emphasize a person; in this case the pronoun is preceded by a determiner, as illustrated in (47):

(47) ni ʔíməš θuʔníɬ
aux walk det-3emph
'That (feminine) one walked.'

Also the emphatic pronouns are used in the oblique case (cf. §2.4); here they are always preceded by the determiner ƛ̓, as illustrated in (48):

(48) ʔə-ƛ̓ nə́wə 'to you'
obl-det 2emph

Possession is expressed by means of possessive affixes, given in (49):

(49)

	singular	plural
1st	nə-	-ct
2nd	ʔən-	-ən . . . -ələp
3rd	-s	-s

In a possessive phrase the possessed nominal is preceded by a determiner, as seen in (50):

(50) t^{θ}ə nə-mə́n'ʔə 'my (male) child'

θə nə-tén 'my mother'

kʷθə scé.ɬtən-ct 'our salmon'

For a discussion of possessive nominals, see §2.1.[20]

FOOTNOTES TO CHAPTER 1

[1]In recent times, the Halkomelem language is also spoken in the Nooksack Valley in northern Washington.

[2]Glottalized resonants are phonetically realized as Rʔ, ʔR, or R', depending upon position and environment. Cf. Suttles (in preparation) for discussion.

[3]One reason for supposing that schwa is not epenthetic, at least in some cases, is the contrast between -ǝs 3rd ergative and -s 3rd possessive, as seen in the following examples.

i) ni ʔám-ǝs-t-ǝs 'He/she gave it to him/her.'
aux give'advA-tr-3erg

ii) s-ʔám-ǝs-t-s 'his/her giving it to him/her'
nom-give-advA-tr-3pos

[4]Note that ní.ɬ 'be-past' contrasts with níɬ the 3rd emphatic pronoun with respect to vowel length.

[5]I am using predicate as a cover term for verbs, predicate adjectives, and predicate nominals and the auxiliaries and particles which occur with them. As I use predicate, it does not mean verb phrase.

[6]By verb, I mean words describing actions or changes of state.

[7]Cf. Demers (1980) for a treatment of the category AUX in Lummi.

[8]I have simplified the order of affixes somewhat for the sake of exposition. This chart would be slightly modified to handle data involving passives, cf. Chapter 5.

[9]I have no examples of the roots /yǝ́θ/ or /ʔíw/ occuring without the advancement A suffix.

[10]Certain suffixes, e.g. /-ǝs/ 'advA' and /-stǝxʷ/ 'causative' and /-θǝt/ 'reflexive', discussed below trigger umlaut in the root; see Suttles (in preparation) for discussion.

[11] See Hukari (1979b) for an interesting discussion contrasting these suffixes.

[12] In cases like /k'ʷé-ls/ the vowel of the root and the vowel of the suffix coalesce.

[13] The transitive suffixes /-stəxʷ/ and /-nəxʷ/ have that form when the object is 3rd person but they have the form /-st/ and /-n/ when the object is 1st or 2nd persons. See Suttles (in preparation) for a discussion of this.

[14] The reflexive suffixes doubtedly contain the transitive suffixes /-t/ and /-n/. For another example of /-t/ ∿ /-θ /, see §1.4.5.

[15] Galloway (1977) suggests that the inchoative use of /-θət / might be a semantic extension of the reflexive meaning.

[16] The reciprocal suffix /- təl/ may contain /-t/ the transitive suffix thus paralleling reflexives (cf. f.n. 14).

[17] There are some unexpected uses of the feminine articles in texts. See Suttles (in preparation) for discussion.

[18] There are several verbal prefixes with the form c-. See Suttles (in preparation) for discussion.

[19] An alternative account for the occurrence of /-θ / in the object pronominal prefixes would posit that the 1st and 2nd person singular objective suffixes began with /s-/. Under this analysis, the initial /s-/ coalesceses with /-t/ to give /-θ /. After /-n/, this initial /s-/ is deleted.
Although this analysis is certainly more accurate historically, it is rather cumbersome for a synchronic description.

[20] Possessives also occur in sentential nominalizations which are discussed below.

Chapter 2

SOME BASIC PHENOMENA OF HALKOMELEM

2.0 Introduction

This chapter presents some basic rules of Halkomelem which will be used as evidence for constructions discussed in subsequent chapters. First, I give examples of clauses which I assume do not involve any change of grammatical relations. These exemplify several concepts important in the grammar of Halkomelem--subject, object, ergative, absolutive, oblique, transitive, and intransitive. These concepts were defined in §0.3. Giving further data, I formulate several rules or conditions on rules. I conclude the chapter with a summary of the distinctions referred to in the rules in this chapter.

I have given examples of what I assume to be intransitive clauses in (1-4) and transitive clauses in (5-7):[1]

(1) ni ʔíməš ɬə sɬéniʔ
aux walk det woman
'The woman walked.'

(2) ni ʔə́ɬtən tᶿə sqʷəméyʔ
aux eat det dog
'The dog ate.'

(3) ni t'ák'ʷ ɬə nə tén
aux go home det 1pos mother
'My mother went home.'

(4) ni cám kʷθə nikʷ ʔə kʷθə smént
aux go up det uncle obl det mountain
'Uncle went up into the mountains.'

(5) ni q'ʷə́l-ət-əs θə sɬéniʔ tθə scé.ɬtən
aux bake-tr-3erg det woman det salmon
'The woman baked the salmon.'

(6) ni q'ʷáqʷ-ət-əs tᶿə swə́yʔqeʔ tᶿə spéʔəθ ʔə tᶿə šápəl
aux club-tr-3erg det man det bear obl det shovel
'The man clubbed the bear with the shovel.'

(7) ni ɬíc'-ət-əs ɬə sɬéniʔ kʷθə səplíl
aux cut in two-tr-3erg det woman det bread
'The woman cut the bread.'

I assume that these clauses do not involve any change of grammatical relations: the first nominals in (1-4), which are semantically 'actors', and in (5-7), which are semantically 'agents', are initial and final subjects; the second nominals in (5-7), which are semantically 'patients' are both initial and final objects; and, the last nominals in (6) and (4), which are semantically 'instrumental' and 'directional', are oblique relations (Instr) and (Dir) at both initial and final level.

In the subsequent discussion I will make the point that the distinction ergative vs. absolutive is important in Halkomelem. These concepts are exemplified above: the first nominal in (5-7), since they are subjects in transitive strata, are ergatives; the first nominals in (1-5), since they are subjects in intransitive strata, and the second nominals in (5-7), since they are objects in transitive strata, are absolutives.

2.1 Nominal Case

Halkomelem distinguishes two cases for nominals: the straight case, in which the nominal is preceded only by a determiner as in (8a), and the oblique case, in which the nominal is preceded by the oblique marker and a determiner as in (8b):

(8) a. ɬə sɬéniʔ b. ʔə ɬə sɬéniʔ
det woman obl det woman

The form of the oblique marker is always ʔə. The determiners, as discussed in §1.4.4, vary according to such factors as the gender, definiteness, and proximity of the nominal.

Note that in the intransitive and transitive clauses above the subject is in the straight case. Also, as can be observed in (5-7), the object is in the straight case. Thus, a rule for straight case can be formulated as in (9):

(9) Nuclear terms, i.e. subjects and objects, are in the straight case.

In (10-12), nuclear terms are in the oblique case and the clauses are ungrammatical, thus supporting (9).

(10) ni ˀíməš ˀə ɬə sɬéniˀ
aux walk obl det woman
*(The woman walked.)
/irrelevantly: 'He walked to get something from the woman.'

(11) * ni q'ʷə́l-ət-əs ˀə θə sɬéniˀ t$^{\theta}$ə scé.ɬtən
aux bake-tr-3erg obl det woman det salmon
(The woman baked the salmon.)

(12) * ni q'ʷə́l-ət-əs θə sɬéniˀ ˀə t$^{\theta}$ə scé.ɬtən
aux bake-tr-3erg det woman obl det salmon
(The woman baked the salmon.)

In contrast, nominals bearing oblique relations, e.g. the instrument in (3) and the directional in (4), are in the oblique case.[2] Thus, a rule for oblique case can be formulated as follows:[3]

(13) Obliques are in the oblique case.

These case distinctions are also involved in the marking of possessive phrases; there are two case patterns as follows:

(14) kʷθə sqʷəméyʔ-s ɬə sɬéniʔ
aux dog-3pos det woman

'the woman's dog'

(15) kʷθə púkʷ-s ɬə sɬéniʔ
aux book-3pos det woman

'the woman's book'

(16) kʷθə sqʷəméyʔ ʔə-ƛ̓ John
det dog obl-det

'John's dog'

(17) kʷθə púkʷ ʔə-ƛ̓ John
det book obl-det

'John's book'

As can be seen in (14-15), when the possessor is a common noun, the possessed nominal (the <u>head</u>) is suffixed with a possessive marker (cf. §1.4.5) and the possessor is in the straight case. Oblique case is not possible for common noun possessors, as is seen in (18-19):[4]

(18) *kʷθə sqʷəméyʔ (-s) ʔə ɬə sɬéniʔ
det dog -3pos obl det woman

(the woman's dog)

(19) * kʷθə púkʷ(-s) ʔə ɬə sɬéniʔ
det book-3pos obl det woman

(the woman's book)

However, as can be seen in (16-17), when the possessor is a proper noun, the head is not suffixed with a possessive marker and the possessor is in the oblique case; straight case is not possible, as seen in (20-21):

(20) *kʷθə sqʷəméyʔ (-s) kʷθə John
det dog -3pos det

(John's dog)

(21) *kʷθə púkʷ (-s) kʷθə John
det book-3pos det

(John's book)

Thus, the rule for case must distinguish common and proper noun possessors, as follows:[5]

(22) a. Common noun possessors are in the straight case.

b. Proper noun possessors are in the oblique case.

To summarize the above discussion, I give the rule for Nominal Case as follows:

(23) a. Nuclear terms and common noun possessors are in the straight case.

b. Obliques and proper noun possessors are in the oblique case.

2.2 Word Order

Although both subject and object nominals are in the straight case, there is little confusion between them. This is partly due to word order tendencies in Halkomelem. As can be seen above, the predicate is initial in simple clauses. In transitive clauses, e.g. (5-7), subject nominals tend to precede objects. However, as Hukari (1980) has pointed out, for some speakers this is not a fixed order and the alternative order, where objects precede subjects, is also possible. Therefore, clauses like (24) can have two meanings.

(24) ni c'ə́w-ət-əs kʷθə swə́yʔqeʔ ɬə sɬéniʔ
aux help-tr-3erg det man det woman
'The man helped the woman.'
/'The woman helped the man.'

In addition, word order is fairly flexible in clauses with nominals in both the straight and oblique cases. Thus, the nominals in clauses like (25) can occur in either order, although (25b) where the directional precedes the subject seems to be preferred.

(25) a. ni ném? kʷθə swə́y?qe? ?ə ɬə sɬéni?
aux go det man obl det woman
'The man went to the woman.'

b. ni ném? ?ə ɬə sɬéni? kʷθə swə́y?qe?
aux go obl det woman det man
'The man went to the woman.'

Factors such as person and animacy appear to affect word order, and, although it may be possible to account for variation in terms of a basic word order and stylistic inversion, such an analysis is outside the scope of this study. For that reason, I will not use word order as the basis of any arguments.

2.3 Transitive Marking

Contrasting (1-4) and (5-7) above, we note that verbs in transitive clauses bear the suffix -t while verbs in intransitive clauses lack this suffix. In fact, intransitive clauses such as (1-4) are ungrammatical if the verb is suffixed with -t, as seen in (26-27):

(26) ni ?íməš-(*ət) ɬə sɬéni?
aux walk-tr det woman
'The woman walked.'

(27) ni cám-(*ət) kʷθə níkʷ ?ə tθə smé.nt
aux go up-tr det uncle obl det mountain
'Uncle went up into the mountains.'

Likewise, transitive clauses are ungrammatical if a transitive suffix is not present, as seen in (28-29):

(28) ni q'ʷə́l-*(ət)-əs θə sɬéni? tθə scé.ɬtən
aux bake-tr-3erg det woman det salmon
'The woman baked the salmon.'

(29) ni q'ʷáqʷ-*(ət)-əs tθə swə́y?qe? tθə spé?əθ
aux club-tr-3erg det man det bear
'The man clubbed the bear.'

On the basis of these data, the rule for Transitive Marking can be formulated as follows:

(30) Transitive marking is required in transitive clauses.

As further data are presented in Chapter 3-5, this rule will be refined.

2.4 Person Marking

In this section, I discuss pronominal case for 1st and 2nd persons and 3rd person agreement. I briefly discuss split ergativity, showing that of three common types of split ergativity--based on person, clause-type, and aspect--Halkomelem exhibits the first two types. Lastly, I discuss reflexives and reciprocals.

2.4.1 Pronominal Case

In contrast with nominals, which distinguish two cases, pronominals distinguish four cases--subjective, objective, oblique, and possessive, as discussed in §1.4.5. Pronominal subjects of intransitive and transitive clauses are in the subjective case, as seen in (31-36):

(31) ni cən ʔíməš
aux 1sub walk
'I walked.'

(32) ni č ʔə́ɬtən
aux 2sub eat
'You ate.'

(33) ni ct nə́mʔ
aux 1plsub go
'We went.'

(34) ni cən q'ʷə́l-ət $t^{θ}$ə scé.ɬtən
aux 1sub bake-tr det salmon
'I baked the salmon.'

(35) ni č q'ʷáqʷ-ət tᶿə spéʔəθ
aux 2sub club-tr det bear

'You clubbed the bear.'

(36) ni ct kʷə́n-ət ɬə sɬéniʔ
aux 1plsub grab-tr det woman

'We grabbed the woman.'

In contrast, pronominal objects are in the objective case, as seen in (37-40).

(37) ni kʷən-əθ-ámʔš-əs
aux grab-tr-1obj-3erg

'He grabbed me.'

(38) ni cən kʷən-əθ-ámə
aux 1sub grab-tr-2obj

'I grabbed you.'

(39) ni č ʔà.-t-álʔxʷ
aux 2sub call-tr-1plobj

'You called us.'

(40) ni ct lem-ət-álə
aux 1plsub look-tr-2plobj

'We looked at you pl.'

Pronominals bearing oblique relations, as in (41-44), are in the oblique case:

(41) ʔi yə-ʔéʔwə ʔə-ƛ̓ ʔé.nʔθə
aux ser-come obl-det 1emph

'He's coming to me.'

(42) ʔi yə-ʔéʔwə ʔə-ƛ̓ nə́wə
aux ser-come obl-det 2emph

'He is coming to you.'

(43) ʔi yə-ʔéʔwə ʔə-ƛ̓ ɬníməɬ
aux ser-come obl-det 1plemph

'He's coming to us.'

(44) ʔi yə-ʔéʔwə ʔə-ƛ̓ ɬwə́ləp
aux ser-come obl-det 2plemph

'He is coming to you pl.'

Pronominal possessors are in the possessive case, as seen in (45-48):

(45) kʷθə nə-sqʷəméyʔ
aux 1pos-dog

'my dog'

(46) kʷθə ʔən-lélǝmʔ
det 2pos-house

'your house'

(47) kʷθə scé.ɬtən-ct
det salmon-1plpos

'out salmon'

(48) tᶿə ʔən-méʔmənʔə ʔələp
det 2pos-children 2pl

'you pl.'s children'

On the basis of the above data, the rule for Pronominal Case can be stated as follows:

(49) Pronominal Case (1st and 2nd person)

a. Subjects are in the subjective case.
b. Objects are in the objective case.
c. Possessors are in the possessive case.

It is interesting to compare Pronominal Case (49) and Nominal Case, repeated here as (50).

(50) Nominal Case

a. Nuclear terms and common noun possessors are in the straight case.
b. Obliques and proper noun possessors are in the oblique case.

There is an important difference in the two systems: nominal subjects and objects are marked alike while pronominal subjects and objects are marked differently. Thus, data involving pronominal case will be important evidence for distinguishing subject and object in Halkomelem.

2.4.2 3rd Person Agreement

The non-emphatic form of the 3rd person pronoun is Ø for both subject and object. Contrast clauses (1-2) and (5-6) above, which contain a nominal subject or object, with the following clauses, which have a 3rd person pronominal subject or object.

(51) ni ʔíməš
aux walk
'He/she/it walked.'

(52) ni ʔə́łtən
aux eat
'He/she/it ate.'

(53) ni cən q'ʷə́l-ət
aux 1sub bake-tr
'I baked it.'

(54) ni cən q'ʷáqʷ-ət
aux 1sub club-tr
'I clubbed him/her/it.'

(55) ni q'ʷə́l-ət-əs
aux bake-tr-3erg
'He/she baked it.'

(56) ni q'ʷáqʷ-ət-əs
aux club-tr-3erg
'He/she clubbed him/her/it.'

(57) ni kʷən-əθ-ám̓ʔš-əs
aux grab-tr-1obj-3erg
'He/she grabbed me.'

(58) ni q'ʷàqʷ-əθ-ám̓ʔš-əs
aux club-tr-1obj-3erg
'He/she clubbed me.'

However, as can be seen by contrasting (51-54) with (55-58) there is a verbal suffix -$\underline{^{\text{əs}}}$ marking 3rd person agreement in the latter clauses. When the subject is not 3rd person, as in (53-54), this suffix is not possible as seen in (59-60).

(59) *ni cən q'ʷə́l-ət-əs
aux 1sub bake-tr-3erg
(I baked it.)

(60) *ni cən q'ʷáqʷ-ət-əs
aux 1sub club-tr-3erg
(I clubbed it.)

Notice that the agreement suffix is not possible even though the object is 3rd person. Thus, agreement is not marked for 3rd person objects. Furthermore, in clauses like (55-58), where the subject is 3rd person, the agreement suffix is obligatory, as seen in (61-62).

(61) *ni q'ʷə́l-ət
aux bake-tr
(He baked it.)

(62) * ni q'ʷàqʷ-əθ-ámˀš
aux club-tr-1obj
(He clubbed me.)

However, in clauses like (51-52), where the subject is 3rd person, agreement is not possible, as seen in (63-64):

(63) *ni ˀíməš-əs
aux walk-3erg
(He walked.)

(64) *ni ˀə́ɬtən-əs
aux eat-3erg
(He ate.)

There is a crucial difference between clauses like (51-52) which do not have agreement and those like (55-58) which do have agreement: while the former are intransitive, the latter are transitive.

These data concerning the occurrence versus the absence of the agreement suffix can be summarized in (65):

(65) 3rd person agreement:

a. -<u>əs</u> -- subjects of transitives

b. ∅ -- objects of transitives
subjects of intransitives

It is clear that the notions subject and object will not be sufficient for the formulation of a rule of 3rd person agreement. Rather, the concepts <u>ergative</u> and <u>absolutive</u> are needed. As discussed in §0.3 an ergative is the subject of a transitive stratum while an absolutive is the subject of an intransitive stratum or the object of a transitive stratum. Using these concepts, we can summarize the data concerning 3rd person agreement as follows:

(66) 3rd person agreement:

a. -<u>əs</u> -- ergatives

b. ∅ -- absolutives

Thus, a rule for 3rd Person Agreement can be stated as follows:

(67) Agreement is marked only for ergatives.

It is interesting to note that 3rd Person Agreement and Pronominal Case (49) operate on different parameters. In the latter, the distinction is subject vs. object, while in the former the relevant distinction is ergative vs. absolutive. Thus, person marking in Halkomelem is a split system with 1st and 2nd persons behaving in one manner and 3rd person behaving in another.

2.4.3 Subordinate Person Marking

In subordinate clauses, unlike main clauses as exemplified above, all persons distinguish subject vs. object, regardless of the transitivity of the clause. As discussed in §1.4.5 subjects in subordinate clauses are expressed by verbal suffixes, and, as can be seen in (68-71), the suffix is the same in intransitive ((68) and (70)) and transitive ((69) and (71)) subordinate clauses.

(68) lə́ʔləmʔ ʔə č ceʔ ʔu t'ìləm-ʔə́.nʔ
look(cont) int 2sub fut lnk sing-1ssub
'Will you be watching when/if I sing?'

(69) lə́ʔləmʔ ʔə č ceʔ ʔu q'ʷàqʷ-ət-ʔə́.nʔ
look(cont) int 2-sub futlnk club-tr-1ssub
'Will you be watching when/if I club him?'

(70) lə́ʔləmʔ cən ceʔ ʔu t'íləm-əxʷ
look(cont) 1sub fut lnk sing-2ssub
'I will be watching when/if you sing.'

(71) lə́ʔləmʔ cən ceʔ ʔu q'ʷáqʷ-ət-əxʷ
look(cont) 1sub fut lnk club-tr-2ssub
'I will be watching when/if you club him.'

In (72-75), I have given examples of subordinate clauses with 3rd person subjects. Although the subordinate clauses in (72-73) are intransitive and those in (74-75) are transitive, 3rd person agreement is marked in each case.

(72) lə́ʔləmʔ ʔə č ceʔ ʔu x̌čénəm-ʔəs
look(cont) int 2sub fut lnk run-3ssub
'Will you be watching when/if he runs?'

(73) lə́ʔləmʔ ʔə č ceʔ ʔu t'íləm-ʔəs
look(cont) int 2sub fut lnk sing-3ssub
'Will you be watching when/if he sings?'

(74) lé?ləm? ?ə č ce? ?u q'ʷàqʷ-əθ-ám?š-əs
look(cont) int 2sub fut lnk club-tr-1obj-3ssub
'Will you be watching when/if he clubs me?'

(75) lé?ləm? ?ə č ce? ?u kʷən-əθ-ám?š-əs
look(cont) int 2sub fut lnk grab-tr-1obj-3ssub
'Will you be watching when/if he grabs me?'

Objects in subordinate clauses are marked with the same set of suffixes as objects in main clauses, as can be seen in (74-75) above and (76-77) below:

(76) lé?ləm? ce? ?u q'ʷàqʷ-əθ-am-?é.n?
look(cont) fut lnk club-tr-2obj-1ssub
'He will be looking when/if I club you.'

(77) lé?ləm? ce? ?u kʷənə-θam-?é.n?
look(cont) fut lnk grab-2obj-1ssub
'He will be looking when/if I grab you.'

Furthermore, 3rd person objects in subordinate clauses, like 3rd person absolutives in main clauses, are unmarked, as can be seen in (69) and (71) above.

Therefore, the rule formulated for Pronominal Case in (49) above is sufficient for 1st and 2nd person case in subordinate clauses: subjects are in the subjective case and objects are in the objective case. However, the rule for 3rd Person Agreement in (67) does not account for 3rd person agreement in subordinate clauses. As we have seen in (72-75) above, agreement is marked for all 3rd person subjects in subordinate clauses, regardless of the transitivity of the clause. Thus, the rule for 3rd Person Agreement must be modified as follows:

(78) a. Agreement is marked only for ergatives in main clauses.
b. Agreement is marked only for subjects in subordinate clauses.

In other words, the relevant distinction for 3rd Person agreement is ergative/absolutive in main clauses while it is subject/object in subordinate clauses.

2.4.4 Aspect and Person Marking

In the preceding sections, we have seen that Halkomelem exhibits two types of split ergativity--lst and 2nd person pronominal case distinguishes subject/object while 3rd person agreement distinguishes ergative/absolutive; 3rd person agreement in main clauses distinguishes subject/object. Thus, Halkomelem has two common types of split ergativity--based on person and clause type.

In this section, I show that Halkomelem does not exhibit a third common type of split ergativity--that based on tense or aspect (cf. §1.4.2).

In the following examples, the clauses in a) are in the completive aspect while the clauses in b) are in the continuative aspect. Notice that a subjective pronominal clitic is used in each case.

(79) a. ni cən ˀə́ɬtən
aux lsub eat
'I ate.'

b. ˀi cən ˀí ˀɬtən
aux lsub eat(cont)
'I am eating.'

(80) a. ni cən ɬə́yx̌-t kʷθə scé.ɬtən
aux lsub eat-tr det salmon
'I ate the salmon.'

b. ˀi cən ɬéyˀx̌-t tᶿə scé.ɬtən
aux lsub eat(cont)-tr det salmon
'I am eating the salmon.'

(81) a. ni č ʔə́ɬtən
aux 2sub eat
'You ate.'

b. ʔi č ʔí ʔɬtən
aux 2sub eat(cont)
'You are eating.'

(82) a. ni č ɬə́yx̌-t kʷθə scé.ɬtən
aux 2sub eat-tr det salmon
'You ate the salmon.'

b. ʔi č ɬéyʔx̌-t tᶿə scé.ɬtən
aux 2sub eat-tr det salmon
'You are eating the salmon.'

Thus, the completive/continuative aspectual distinction has no effect on Pronominal Case as formulated in (49) above.

Likewise, aspect has no effect on 3rd Person Agreement as formulated in (78) above. In (83-84), the a) clauses are completive while the b) clauses are continuative:

(83) a. ni ʔə́ɬtən ɬə sɬéniʔ
aux eat det woman
'The woman ate.'

b. ʔi ʔí ʔɬtən ɬə sɬéniʔ
aux eat(cont) det woman
'The woman is eating.'

(84) a. ni ɬə́yx̌-t-əs ɬə sɬéniʔ kʷθə scé.ɬtən
aux eat-tr-3erg det woman det salmon
'The woman ate the salmon.'

b. ʔi ɬéyʔx̌-t-əs ɬə sɬéniʔ kʷθə scé.ɬtən
aux eat(cont)-tr-3erg det woman det salmon
'The woman is eating the salmon.'

As predicted by (78), 3rd Person Agreement is marked in the transitive clauses in (84) but not in the intransitive clauses in (83).

We can conclude from the above examples that the completive/

continuative aspectual distinction has no effect on the patterning of person marking with respect to the subject/object and the ergative/absolutive distinctions.[6]

2.4.5 Reflexives

When the subject and the object of a clause are co-referential, a special reflexive construction is used. Here, 1st and 2nd person subjects are in the subjective case; there are no object suffixes, but a reflexive marker -θət , undifferentiated for person, is suffixed to the verb, as exemplified in (85-88):

(85) ni cən lə̂x̌ʷ-əθət
aux 1sub blanket-self
'I covered myself with a blanket.'

(86) ni cən x̌íq'-əθət
aux 1sub scratch-self
'I scratched myself.'

(87) ni ʔə č q'ə́ləc'-θət
aux int 2sub shelter-self
'Did you shelter yourself?'

(88) ʔi ʔə č lá'ʔləmʔ-əθət
aux int 2sub look(cont)-self
'Are you looking after yourself?'

(89) ni lə̂x̌ʷ-əθət
aux blanket-self
'He covered himself with a blanket.'

(90) ni x̌íq'-əθət
aux scratch-self
'He scratched himself.'

Notice that in (89-90), where the subject is 3rd person, agreement is not marked; this will be discussed further in §4.3.

Of relevance here are two restrictions placed on reflexives. First, a reflexive construction is possible only if the subject and

and object are co-referential. In the examples in (91) and (92), the subject is coreferential with an oblique and a possessor. As is seen in the b) clauses, reflexives are not possible in these cases.

(91) a. ni cən čxʷənə́mʔ ʔə-ƛ̓ ʔé.nʔθə
aux 1sub speak obl-det lemph
'I spoke about me.'

b. * ni cən čxʷnə́.mʔ-θət
aux 1sub speak-self
(I spoke about myself.)

(92) a. ni cən q'ʷál ʔə kʷθə nə- tél̓ə
aux 1sub speak obl det 1pos money
'I spoke about my money.'

b. *ni cən qʷál-θət ʔə kʷθə (nə-) tél̓ə
aux 1sub speak-self obl det 1pos-money
(I spoke about my(self's) money.)

Furthermore, in (93) and (94), the object is coreferential with a locative and a possessor, and, as seen in the b) clauses, reflexives are not possible.

(93) a. ?ni yəθ-əs-θ-ámʔš-əs ʔə-ƛ̓ ʔé.nʔθə
aux tell-advA-tr-1obj-3erg obl-det lemph
'He told me about myself.'

b. *ni yə́θ-əs-θət ʔə-ƛ̓ ʔé.nʔθə
aux tell-advA-self obl-det lemph
(He told me about myself.)

(94) a. ni cən yə́θ-əs-t ʔə kʷθə sq'áq'iʔ-s
aux 1sub tell-advA-tr obl det illness-3pos
'I told him$_i$ about his$_i$ illness.'

b. *ni cən yə́θ-əs-θət ʔə kʷθə sq'áq'iʔ-s
aux 1sub tell-advA-self obl det illness-3pos
(I told him$_i$ about his$_i$ illness.)

Second, reflexives in Halkomelem are clause-bounded (i.e., the subject and the object must be in the same clause). Although the subject of a matrix clause is coreferential with an object of an embedded clause, reflexives are not possible, as can be seen in (95) and (96):

(95) a. cse-t-álə cə ce? ?u ləx̌ʷ-əθ-ám?š-?ələp
tell-tr-2plobj 1sub fut lnk blanket-tr-1obj-2plssub
'I will tell you pl. to cover me with a blanket.'

b. cse-t-álə cə ce? ?u lə́x̌ʷ-əθət-?ələp
tell-tr-2plobj 1sub fut lnk blanket-self-2plssub
*'I will tell you pl. to cover me with a blanket.'
/'I will tell you pl. to cover yourselves with a blanket.'

(96) a. cse-t-álə cə ce? ?u la?ləm?-əθ-ám?š-?ələp
tell-tr-2plobj 1sub fut lnk look(cont)-tr-1obj- 2plssub
'I will tell you pl. to look after me.'

b. ces-t-álə cə ce? ?u là?ləm?-əθət-?ə́ləp
tell-tr-2plobj 1sub fut lnk look(cont)-self- 2plssub
*'I will tell you pl. to look after me.'
/'I will tell you pl. to look after yourselves.'

In the b) sentences, the reflexives are unambiguously interpreted as marking the coreference of the subject and the object of the embedded clause, and not coreference of the matrix subject and embedded object. Thus, reflexives in Halkomelem are clause-bounded.

To summarize, there are several conditions on reflexives in Halkomelem:

(97) i. The antecedent must be a subject.
ii. The nominal coreferent to the antecedent must be an object.
iii. Reflexives are clause-bounded; the antecedent and the coreferent nominal must be clausemates.

2.4.6 Reciprocals

Parallel to the reflexive construction, there is a reciprocal construction for cases when the subject and object are performing actions on each other. This construction is marked with a reciprocal suffix -tәl, which is undifferentiated for person, as illustrated in (98-101):

(98) ni ct lәmáʔ-tәl
aux 1plsub kick-rec
'We kicked each other.'

(99) ni ʔә ce.p q'ʷáqʷ-әtәl
aux int 2plsub club-rec
'Did you club each other.'

(100) ni θ'íq'ʷ-әtәl
aux punch-rec
'They punched each other.'

(101) ni tíq'ʷ-tәl
aux bump-rec
'They collided.'

In (100-101), even though the subject is 3rd person, there is no agreement. This problem is addressed in §4.3.

In all of the reciprocals that I have recorded or observed in the literature, the reciprocal relation stands between subjects and objects.

2.5 One-Nominal Interpretation

As shown in §2.1, nominal subjects and objects are not differentiated by case and as discussed in §2.2, both subjects and objects follow the verb. Furthermore, it was pointed out in §2.4.2 that non-emphatic 3rd person pronominal subjects and objects are ∅. A question arises: in clauses where only one nominal is expressed, is that nominal interpreted as the subject or the object?

First, in intransitive clauses, e.g. (102-103), only one interpretation is available for the nominal, i.e. subject.

(102) ni ʔíməš ɬə sɬéniʔ
aux walk det woman
'The woman walked.'

(103) ni ʔə́ɬtən kʷθə sqʷəméyʔ
aux eat det dog
'The dog ate.'

In transitive clauses, however, where a single nominal could be interpreted as either subject or object, the nominal is unambiguously interpreted as object, as in (104-107).

(104) ni q'ʷáqʷ-ət-əs kʷθə swə́yʔqeʔ
aux club-tr-3erg det man
'He clubbed the man.'
/*'The man clubbed him.'

(105) ni kʷə́n-ət-əs ɬə sɬéniʔ
aux grab-tr-3erg det woman
'He grabbed the woman.'
/*'The woman grabbed him.'

(106) ni q'ʷə́l-ət-əs tᶿə scé.ɬtən
aux bake-tr-3erg det salmon
'He baked the salmon.'
/*'The salmon baked it.'

(107) !!ni q'ʷə́l-ət-əs ɬə sɬéniʔ
aux bake-tr-3erg det woman
!! 'He baked the woman.'
/*'The woman baked it.'

Summarizing the data for both intransitive and transitive clauses, in intransitive clauses, a single nominal is interpreted as subject and, intransitive clauses, it is interpreted as object. Making use of the notion <u>absolutive</u>, the following generalization is possible.

(108) In the absence of marking for other persons, a single 3rd person nominal is interpreted as the absolutive.

2.6 Extractions

In this section I discuss constructions involving extraction in Halkomelem. In §2.6.1, I illustrate four construction involving extraction and briefly discuss the structure that I posit for each. In §2.6.2, I give examples where subjects, objects, obliques, possessors, and quantifiers are extracted and discuss the conditions on these constructions. In §2.6.3, I discuss person marking and extraction.

2.6.1 Constructions Involving Extraction

In Halkomelem, there are four constructions involving extraction--relative clauses, cleft sentences, pseudo-cleft sentences, and WH-questions.[7]

In relative clauses, a head (underlined) is modified by an embedded clause (in brackets), as illustrated in (109-113b); the corresponding simple clauses are given in (109-113a).

(109) a. ni ʔíməš ɬə sɬéniʔ
aux walk det woman
'The woman walked.'

b. státəl-stəxʷ cən <u>ɬə sɬéniʔ</u> [ni ʔíməš]
know-cs 1sub det woman aux walk
'I know the woman who walked.'

(110) a. ni t'íləm tᶿə swə́yʔqeʔ
aux sing det man
'The man sang.'

b. ni cən lem-ət <u>tᶿə swə́yʔqeʔ</u> [ni t'íləm]
aux 1sub look at-tr det man aux sing
'I looked at the man who sang.'

(111) a. ni qʷál kʷθə xʷənítəm
aux speak det white man

'The white man spoke.'

b. ni q'á y kʷθə xʷənítəm [ni ʔəɬ qʷál]
aux die det white man aux pst speak

'The white man who spoke died.'

(112) a. ni č xʷmə́kʷəθ-ət kʷθə swíwʔləs
aux 2sub kiss-tr det boy

'You kissed the boy.'

b. státəl-stəxʷ cən kʷθə swíwʔləs [ni xʷmə́kʷəθ-ət-əxʷ]
know-cs 1sub det boy aux kiss-tr-2ssub

'I know the boy who you kissed.'

(113) a. ni cən lə́m-ət ɬə sɬéniʔ
aux 1sub look at-tr det woman

'I looked at the woman.'

b. státəl-stəxʷ č ɬə sɬéniʔ [ni ləm-ət-ʔé.nʔ]
know-cs 2sub det woman aux look at-tr-1ssub

'You know the woman who I looked at.'

Extraction is not a well-developed area in Relational Grammar, but I will assume a structure for relative clauses like that given in (114) for (113b):[8]

(114)

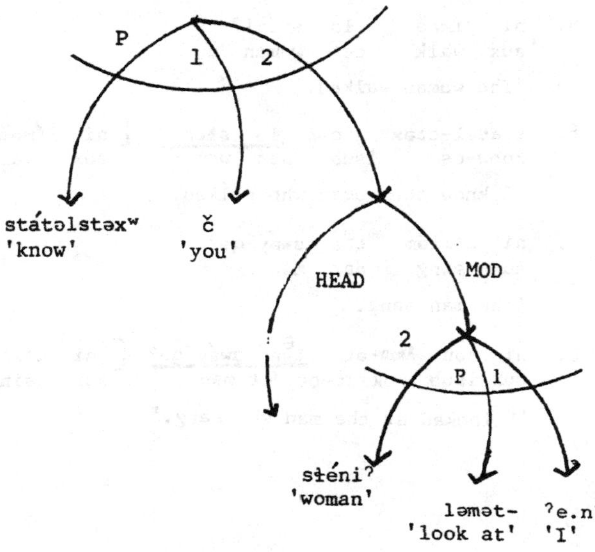

As represented in (114), the extraction nominal <u>sɬéniʔ</u> 'woman') bears two relations: it is a head and also the object of the embedded clause.[9,10]

In the above examples, the head was a nominal preceded by a determiner. However, a nominal head is not necessary, as seen in (115-117).

(115) statəl-stəxʷ cən kʷθə [ni xʷmə́kʷəθ-ət-əxʷ]
know-cs 1sub det aux kiss-tr-2ssub
'I know the one that you kissed.'

(116) státəl-stəxʷ č ɬə [ni ləm-ət-ʔé.nʔ]
know-cs 2sub det aux look at-tr-1ssub
'You know the one (feminine) that I looked at.'

(117) státəl-stəxʷ-əs kʷθə [ni t'íləm]
know-cs-3erg det aux sing
'He knows the one who sang.'

Leslie (1979, p. 173f.) and Hukari (1980) have referred to such constructions as <u>headless</u> relative clauses. However, a headless relative clause is characterized not only by the lack of a nominal head but also by the appearance of the nominal semantically understood to be the head in the embedded clause. (cf. Gorbet (1977), p. 270)[11] But in Halkomelem relative clauses like (115-117), the occurrence of the nominal within the embedded clause is not possible, as seen in (118-119):[12]

(118) *státəl-stəxʷ cən [ni ʔíməš ɬə sɬéniʔ]
know-cs 1sub aux walk det woman
(I know the woman who walked.)

(119) *ni q'áy [ni q'ʷal kʷθə xʷənítəm]
aux die aux speak det white man
(The white man who spoke died.)

For this reason, I do not analyze constructions like (115-117) as headless relative clauses.

Furthermore, a determiner conveying information concerning gender, number, and proximity appears in the position preceding the empty head. I assume that the determiner agrees with some understood nominal which does not appear on the surface; I will refer to this nominal as an <u>eclipsed</u> nominal and represent it as <u>(nom)</u>. Thus (117) can be represented as follows:

(120)

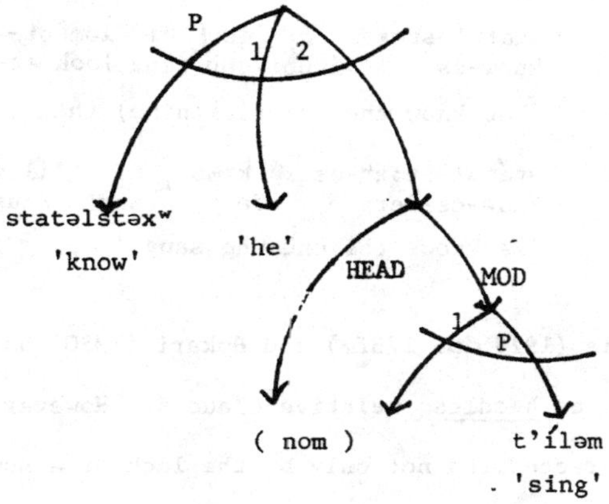

Cleft sentences consist of the 3rd person emphatic pronoun <u>níɬ</u> followed by a relative clause. In (121-125b) I give cleft sentences corresponding to the clauses in (121-125a).

(121) a. ni t'íləm ɬə sɬéniʔ
aux sing det woman
'The woman sang.'

b. níɬ ɬə sɬéniʔ [ni t'íləm]
3emph det woman aux sing
'It's the woman who sang.'

(122) a. ni wəwá'ʔəs kʷθə sqʷəméy̓ʔ-s
aux bark det dog-3pos

'His dog barked.'

b. níɬ kʷθə sqʷəméy̓ʔ-s [ni wəwá'ʔəs]
3emph det dog-3pos aux bark

'It's his dog that barked.'

(123) a. ni qʷál kʷθə swə́yʔqeʔ
aux speak det man

'The man spoke.'

b. níɬ kʷθə swə́yʔqeʔ [ni qʷál]
3emph det man aux speak

'It's the man who spoke.'

(124) a. ni cən kʷə́n-ət kʷθə swíwʔləs
aux 1sub grab-tr det boy

'I grabbed the boy.'

b. níɬ kʷθə swíwʔləs [ni kʷən-ət-ʔé.nʔ]
3emph det boy aux grab-tr-1ssub

'It's the boy that I grabbed.'

(125) a. ni č lə́m-ət kʷθə swə́yʔqeʔ
aux 2sub look at-tr det man

'You looked at the man.'

b. níɬ kʷθə swə́yʔqeʔ [ni lə́m-ət-əxʷ]
3emph det man aux look at-tr-2ssub

'It's the man that you looked at.'

The structure I posit for cleft sentences, like that represented in (126) for (125), is that of a predicate nominal: the emphatic pronoun is predicate and the nominal head and embedded clause serve as subject.

(126)

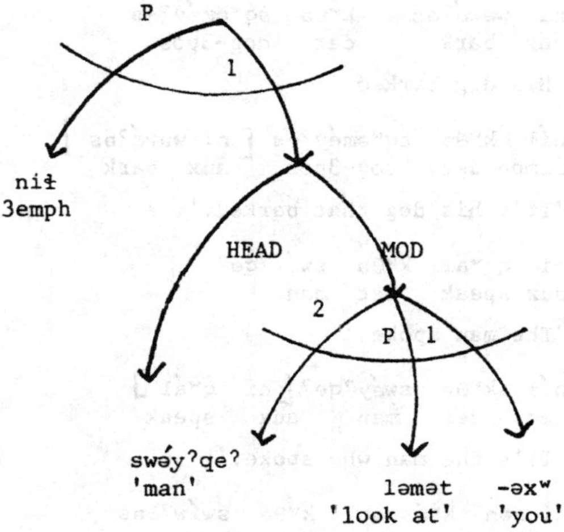

I will not justify this structure here, but note that the emphatic pronoun is in initial position, like other predicates, and that it is not preceded by a determiner, a property of other predicate nominals.

I posit a similar analysis for pseudo-cleft sentences; I give examples of this construction in (127-131b).[13]

(127) a. ni t'íləm ɬə sɬéniˀ
aux sing det woman
'The woman sang.'

b. sɬéniˀ ɬə [ni t'íləm]
woman det aux sing
'The woman is the one who sang.'

(128) a. ni qʷál kʷθə swíwˀləs
aux speak det boy
'The boy spoke.'

b. swíwˀləs kʷθə [ni qʷál]
boy det aux speak
'A boy was who spoke.'

(129) a. ni q'áy kʷθə sqʷəméyʔ
aux die det dog
'The dog died.'

b. sqʷəméyʔ kʷθə [ni q'áy]
dog det aux die
'A dog is what died.'

(130) a. ni cən q'ʷə́l-ət kʷθə scé.łtən
aux 1sub bake-tr det salmon
'I baked the salmon.'

b. scé.łtən kʷθə [ni q'ʷəl-ət-ʔé.nʔ]
salmon det aux bake-tr-1ssub
'Salmon is what I baked.'

(131) a. ni č lə́m-ət kʷθə sqʷəméyʔ
aux 2sub look at-tr det dog
'You looked at the dog.'

b. sqʷəméyʔ kʷθə [ni lə́m-ət-əxʷ]
dog det aux look at-tr-2ssub
'A dog is what you looked at.'

I assume that pseudo-cleft sentences are predicate nominal constructions, with the first nominal, which occurs in initial position and is not preceded by a determiner, as predicate. However, in this case, the head of the relative clause is an eclipsed nominal and the relative clause has a structure as represented in (120) above. Thus, pseudo-cleft sentences like (131b) can be represented as in (132).

(132)

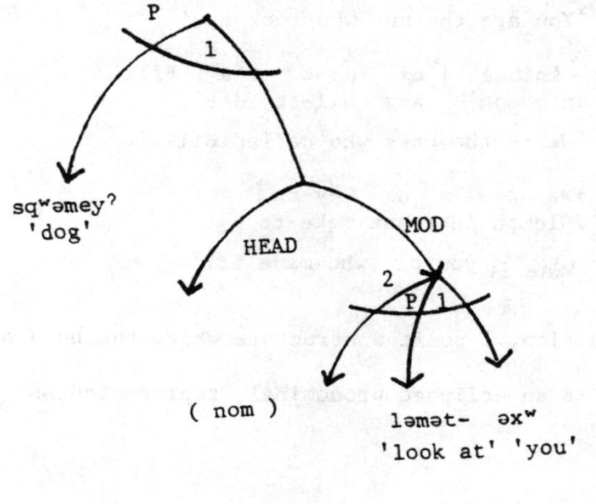

However, pseudo-cleft sentences are different from other predicate nominal constructions: the predicate nominal in pseudo-clefts and the eclipsed nominal head of the relative clause are the same nominal. Thus, in each case, the determiner agreeing with the eclipsed head also would agree with the predicate nominal; for example, the determiner must be in the right gender, as seen by comparing (127-128b) with (133-134) below:

(133) *sɬéniʔ kʷθə [ni t'íləm]
woman det aux sing
(A woman is the one who sang.)

(134) *swíwʔləs ɬə [ni qʷál]
boy det aux speak
(A boy is the one who spoke.)

A common construction, which I assume to be a type of pseudo-cleft, has as its predicate an emphatic pronoun, as illustrated in (135-138):

(135) ʔé.nʔθə [ni t'íləm]
1emph aux sing
'I am the one who sang.'

(136) nə́wə [ni kʷə́n-ət]
2emph aux grab-tr
'You are the one who took it.'

(137) ɬníməɬ [ni ʔá.-t tᶿə Bill]
1plemph aux call-tr det
'We're the ones who called Bill.'

(138) ɬwə́ləp ʔə [ni θə́y-t]
2plemph intr aux make-tr
'Was it you pl. who made it?'

For this construction, I posit a structure where the head of the relative clause is an eclipsed pronominal, represented as (<u>pro</u>).

Thus, the structure of (138) is given in (139).

(139)

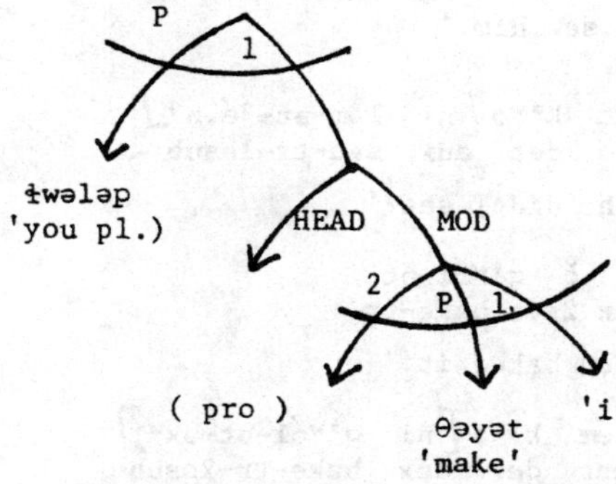

As with other pseudo-cleft sentences, a condition must be stated to assure that the pronoun in predicate position is coreferent with the eclipsed pronominal.

WH-questions, illustrated in (140-144b), are parallel in structure to pseudo-cleft sentences.

(140) a. ni ʔíməš
aux walk

'He walked.'

b. wét k'ʷə [ni ʔíməš]
who det aux walk

'Who walked?"

(141) a. ni q'áy
aux die

'He died'

b. wét k̓ʷə [ni q'áy]
who det aux die

'Who died?'

(142) a. ni lə́kʷ
aux break

'It broke.'

b. stém k'ʷə [ni lə́kʷ]
what det aux break

'What broke?'

(143) a. ni cən lə́m-ət
aux 1sub see-tr

'I saw him.'

b. wə́t k'ʷə [ni ləm-ət-ʔə́.nʔ]
who det aux see-tr-1ssub

'Who did I see?'

(144) a. ni č q'ʷə́l-ət
aux 2sub bake-tr

'You baked it.'

b. stə́m k'ʷə [ni q'ʷə́l-ət-əxʷ]
what det aux bake-tr-2ssub

'What did you bake.'

The WH-pronoun is the predicate, appearing in initial position, and is followed by a relative clause with an eclipsed nominal as its head. Thus, (144) would be represented as in (145).

(145)

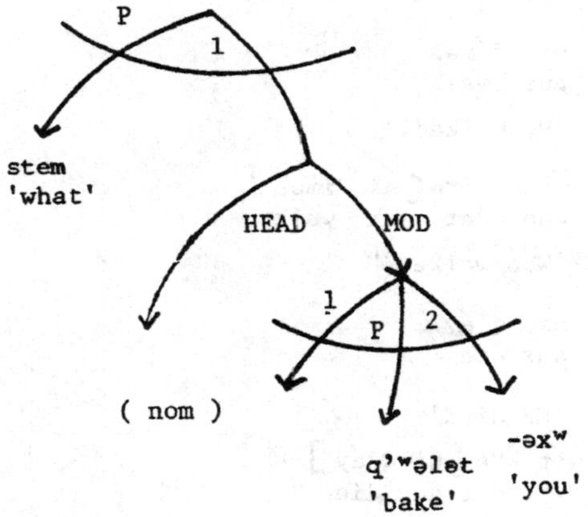

The determiner following the predicate in the above examples agrees with the eclipsed nominal. Although this determiner is usually hypothetical (cf. §1.4.4) as in (146), some speakers appear to allow other determiners, as in example (147) given in Hukari (1980).

(146) ɬwə́t kʷsə[niʔ k'ʷíc'-ət tᶿə sməýəθ]
who det aux butcher-tr det deer

'Who (feminine) butchered the deer?'

(147) ɬwə́t θə [niʔ k'ʷíc'-ət tᶿə sməýəθ]
who det aux butcher-tr det deer

'Who (feminine) butchered the deer?'

2.6.2 Conditions on Extraction

In this section, I give examples of extractions where the extracted nominals bear the grammatical relation of subject, object, oblique, possessor, and quantifier in the embedded clause. I formulate conditions on extraction.

2.6.2.1 Extraction of Subjects and Objects

In all of the above examples, the extracted nominals bear the grammatical relations of subject or object in the embedded clause. In each case, the verb of the embedded clause is the same as the verb in the corresponding simple clause; i.e., the verb is not affected. I call this process of extraction--with no effect on the verb--<u>direct extraction</u>.

We have seen examples of the direct extraction of subject and object. However, when the nominal which is extracted bears an oblique relation in the corresponding simple clause, direct extraction is not possible, as seen in (148-149).

(148) a. ni ɬíc'-ət-əs ʔə kʷθə šə́ptən
aux cut-tr-3erg obl det knife

'He cut it with the knife.'

b. * (ʔə) šə́ptən kʷθə [ni ɬíc'-ət-əs]
obl knife det aux cut-tr 3ssub

(A knife is what he cut it with.)

(149) a. ni ɬcíws ʔə kʷθə sqʷál
aux tired obl det talk
'He's tired of the talk.'

b.* (ʔə) stém k'ʷ[ni ɬcíws]
obl what det aux tired
(What is he tired of?)

Thus, a condition on direct extraction can be formulated as follows:

(150) Only nuclear terms can be directly extracted.

2.6.2.2 Extraction of Obliques

As Hukari (1977a) has pointed out, in order to extract obliques, the embedded clause must be a nominalization.[14] In (151-153), I give examples of simple clauses and their corresponding nominalizations.

(151) a. ni cən q'ʷáqʷ-ət ʔə kʷθə ʔənʔ-šápəl-ʔəɬ
aux 1sub club-tr obl det 2pos-shovel-pst
'I hit him with your shovel.'

b. ni nə- š-q'ʷáqʷ-ət kʷθə ʔənʔ-šápəl-ʔəɬ
aux 1pos-nom-club-tr det 2pos-shovel-pst
'I hit him with your shovel.'
[literally: 'your shovel was my hitting him with.']

(152) a. yáθ ʔu yə-x̌ʷánčənəm ʔə tənʔá šé.ɬ
always lnk ser-run obl det road
'He always ran on that road.'

b. yáθ ʔu š-x̌ʷánčənəm-s tənáʔ šé.ɬ
always lnk nom-run-3pos det road
'He always ran on that road.'
[literally: 'This road was always his running on.']

(153) a. ni č wəɬ ɬcíws ʔə kʷθə qʷə́lmən-s
aux 2sub already tired obl det talk-3pos

'You are already tired of his talk.'

b. ni wəɬ ʔən-š-ɬcíws kʷθə qʷə́lmən-s
aux already 2pos-nom-tired det talk-3pos

'You are already tired of his talk.'
[literally: His talk was your tiring.']

Although I will not treat nominalization in detail, I will briefly point out some of the features of nominalizations in Halkomelem.

Nominalizations can stand as complete sentences, as seen in the (b) examples above. I assume, following Hukari (1977a), that nominalizations such as (151-153b) are predicate nominal constructions; that is, the nominal which corresponds to the oblique in the (a) sentences is the subject in the nominalization (i.e., the (b) sentences) and the nominalized clause (i.e., the rest of the (a) sentence) is the predicate. I have underlined the subjects in the nominalizations given above.[15] In the nominalized clause, the nominal corresponding to the subject of the simple clause is expressed as possessor; other nominals appear to have the same grammatical relations in both the (a) and (b) sentences.[16]

A distinctive feature of nominalizations in Halkomelem, is the presence of a nominalizer prefix. In (151-153b), the element corresponding to the verb of simple clauses (a) is prefixed with the nominalizer š-, which is used in nominalizations with an instrument (as in (151), a locative (as in 152)), or a causal (as in 153)) is the subject in the corresponding nominalization.

In (154-156), I give examples of constructions involving extractions; these correspond to the sentences in (151-153) above.

Notice that in each case, the embedded clause is nominalized.

(154) níɬ kʷθə ˀənˀ-šápəl-ˀəɬ ni nə-š-q'ʷáqʷ-ət
3emph det 2pos-shovel-pst aux 1pos-nom-club-tr
'It's your shovel that I clubbed it with.'

(155) níɬ təhˀá šé.ɬ yaθ ˀu š-x̌ʷánčənəm-s
3emph det road always lnk nom-run-3pos
'It's this road that he always runs on.'

(156) stém k'ʷə ni ˀə-š-ɬcíws
what det aux 2pos-nom-tired
'What are you tired of?'

Apparently, the embedded clauses in (154-156) correspond to the nominalizations in (151-153).

As was pointed out in (148-149) above, nominals which are obliques cannot be directly extracted. Thus, in order to have extraction constructions involving clauses with obliques, the corresponding nominalization is used. As discussed above, the nominal corresponding to the oblique is the subject in the nominalization. This process of extracting the subject of nominalizations I will refer to as <u>extraction through nominalization</u>.

It should also be pointed out that nominals corresponding to subjects and objects in simple clauses cannot be subjects in nominalizations, as seen in (157-158).[17]

(157) a. ni t'íləm ɬə sɬéniˀ
aux sing det woman
'The woman sang.'

b. *ni š-t'íləm ɬə sɬéniˀ
aux nom-sing det woman
(The woman sang.)

(158) a. ni pə́n-ət-əs kʷθə sqéwθ
aux plant-tr-3erg det potato
'He planted potatoes.'

b. *ni š-pə́n-ət-s kʷθə sqéwθ
aux nom-plant-tr-3pos det potato
(He planted potatoes.')

Since subjects and objects in simple clauses cannot be subjects in corresponding nominalizations, they are not extracted through nominalization, as is seen in (159-160):

(159) * níɬ ɬə sɬéniʔ ni š-t'íləm
3emph det woman aux nom-sing
(It's the woman who sang.)

(160) *sqéwθ kʷθə ni š-pə́n-ət-s
potato det aux nom-plant-tr-3pos
(Potatoes is what he planted.)

In summary, there are two types of extraction in Halkomelem: Direct extraction, which is used for the extraction of only subjects and objects, and extraction through nominalization, which is used for obliques (which are subjects in the corresponding nominalizations). Thus, conditions for extraction can be given as follows:

(161) a. Only nuclear terms are directly extracted.
b. Only obliques are extracted through nominalization.

2.6.2.3 Possessor Extraction

It is also possible to extract possessors, as seen below; in the (b) sentences, a nominal corresponding to the possessor in the (a) clauses is extracted: [18]

(162) a. ni x̌č́énəm kʷθə sqé?əq-s ɬə sɬéni?
aux run det y.brother-3pos det woman

'The woman's younger brother ran.'

b. stáṫəl-stəxʷ cən ɬə sɬéni? ni x̌č́énəm kʷθə sqé?əq-s
know-cs 1sub det woman aux run det y.brother-3pos

'I know the woman whose younger brother ran.'

(163) a. ni t'íləm kʷθə sqé?əq-s ɬə sɬéni?
aux sing det y.brother-3pos det woman

'The woman's younger brother sang.'

b. stáṫəl-stəxʷ cən ɬə sɬéni? ni t'íləm kʷθə sqé?əq-s
know-cs 1sub det woman aux sing det y.brother-3pos

'I know the woman whose younger brother sang.'

(164) a. ni q'áy kʷθə nə-sqʷəméy?
aux die det 1pos-dog

'My dog died.'

b. ?é.n?θə ni q'áy kʷθə nə-sqʷəméy?
1emph aux die det 1pos-dog

'I'm the one whose dog died.'

Not all possessors can be extracted, however, as seen in the following examples:

(165) a. ni q'ʷél-ət-əs kʷθə sqé?əq-s ɬə sɬéni? kʷθə scé.ɬtən
aux bake-tr-3erg det y.brother-3pos det woman det salmon

'The woman's younger brother baked the salmon.'

b. *stáṫəl-stəxʷ cən ɬe sɬéni? ni q'ʷél-ət-əs kʷθə sqé?əq-s
know-cs 1sub det woman aux bake-tr-3ssub det y.b.-3pos
kʷθə scé.ɬtən
det salmon
(I know the woman whose younger brother baked the salmon.)

(168) a. ni q'á.y-t-əs kʷθə sqé?əq-s ɬə sɬéni? kʷθə sqʷəméy?
aux kill-tr-3erg det y.b.-3pos det woman det dog
'The woman's younger brother killed the dog.'

b. *stáṫəl-stəxʷ cən ɬə sɬéni? ni q'á.y-t-əs kʷθə sqé?əq-s
know- cs 1sub det woman aux kill-tr-3ssub det y.b.-3pos

kʷθə sqʷəméy?
det dog
(I know the woman whose younger brother killed the dog.)

(167) a. ni ʔà.-θ-ámʔš-əs θə ʔən-stáʔləs
aux call-tr-1obj-3erg det 2pos-spouse
'Your wife called me.'

b. *nə́wə ni ʔà.-θ-ámš-əs θə ʔən-stáʔləs
2emph aux call-tr-1obj-3ssub det 2pos-spouse
(You're the one whose wife called me.)

The crucial difference between cases where possessor extraction is possible and where it is not possible is the transitivity of the embedded clause; it is intransitive in (162-164b) but transitive in (165-167b).

However, extraction of possessors from transitive clauses is possible, as is seen in (168-170):

(168) a. ni q'ʷə́l-ət-əs kʷθə scé.łtən-s łə słéniʔ
aux bake-tr-3erg det salmon-3pos det woman
'He baked the woman's salmon.'

b. státəl-stəxʷ cən łə słéniʔ ni q'ʷə́l-ət-əs
know-cs 1sub det woman aux bake-tr-3ssub
kʷθə scé.łtən-s
det salmon-3pos
'I know the woman whose salmon he baked.'

(169) a. ni č q'á.y-t kʷθə sqéʔəq-s łə słéniʔ
aux 2sub kill-tr det y.b.-3pos det woman
'You killed the woman's younger brother.'

b. státəl-stəxʷ cən łə słéniʔ ni q'á.y-t-əxʷ
know-cs 1sub det woman aux kill-tr-2ssub
kʷθə sqéʔəq-s
det y.b.-3pos
'I know the woman whose younger brother you killed.'

(170) a. ni cən ʔá.-t θə ʔən-stáʔləs
aux 1sub call-tr det 2pos-spouse
'I called your wife.'

b. nə́wə ni ʔá.-t-ʔe.nʔ θə ʔən-stáʔləs
2emph aux call-tr-1ssub det 2pos-spouse
'You are the one whose wife I called.'

In the above examples, the possessive phrase from which the possessor is extracted is the object of a transitive clause.

I summarize the distribution of possessive extraction in (171):

(171) a. Possessor extraction is possible if the possessive phrases are: objects of transitives or subjects of intransitives.

b. Possessor extraction is impossible if the possessive phrases are: subjects of transitives.

Clearly, the relevant distinction for formulating a condition on possessor extraction is not subject vs. object but rather absolutive vs. ergative. The condition on possessor extraction can be formulated as follows:

(172) A possessor can be extracted only if the possessive phrase from which it is extracted is an absolutive.

Condition (172) interacts with extraction through nominalization to provide interesting evidence that obliques in simple clauses bear the subject relation in corresponding nominalizations. In the following examples the possessive phrase from which the possessor is extracted is an oblique:

(173) a. ni cən ném? ?ə kʷθə lélem?-s ɬə sɬéni?
aux 1sub go obl det house-3pos det woman
'I went to the woman's house.'

b. *níɬ ɬə sɬéni? ni nem?-é.n?θə kʷθə lélәm?-s
3emph det woman aux go-1ssub obl det house-3pos
(It's the woman whose house I went to.)

(174) a. ni cən q'ʷáqʷ-ət ?ə kʷθə ?ən?-šápəl-?əɬ
aux 1sub club-tr obl det 2pos-shovel-pst
'I hit him with your shovel.'

b. *nə́wə ni q'ʷàqʷ-ət-?é.n? ?ə kʷθə ?ən?-šápəl-?əɬ
2emph aux club-tr-1ss7b obl det 2pos-shovel-pst
(You're the one whose shovel I clubbed him with.)

Possessor extraction, as predicted by (169) is not possible in these cases. However, possessor extraction is possible if the embedded clause is a nominalization. Observe the nominalizations in (172-173a) which correspond to the simple clauses in (173-174a); possessor extraction is possible, as is seen in (175-176b):

(175) a. ni nə-š-ném? kʷθə lélәm?-s ɬə sɬéni?
aux 1pos-nom-go det house-3pos det woman
'I went to the woman's house.'
[literally: 'The woman's house was my going to.']

b. níɬ ɬə sɬéni? ni nə-š-ném? kʷθə lélәm?-s
3emph det woman aux 1pos-nom-go det house-3pos
'It's the woman whose house I went to.'

(176) a. ni nə-š-q'ʷáqʷ-ət kʷθə ?ən?-šápəl-?əɬ
aux 1pos-nom-club-tr det 2pos-shovel-pst
'I hit him with your shovel.'
[literally: 'Your shovel was my hitting him with.']

b. nə́wə ni nə-š-q'ʷáqʷ-ət kʷθə ?ən?-šápəl-?əɬ
2emph aux 1pos-nom-club-tr det 2pos-shovel-pst
'You're the one whose shovel I hit him with.'

That possessor extraction is possible in these cases follows from the structure for nominalizations that I have assumed above and from the constraint on possessor extraction formulated in (172). Since the possessive phrases (which are semantically obliques) in (175-176) are subjects of nominalizations, these phrases are absolutives; hence possessors can be extracted from them.

2.6.2.4 Quantifier Extraction

In this section, I discuss constructions involving the extraction of the quantifier m<u>ə́k'ʷ</u> 'all'. Quantifiers, like other modifiers, appear preceding the nominal they modify, as exemplied in (177-178); in this case the quantifier, determiner, and nominal constitute a nominal phrase which I refer to as the quantified nominal.

(177) mə́k'ʷ kʷθə qá?
all det water
'all the water'

(178) mə́k'ʷ kʷθə səwwə́y?qe?
all det men
'all the men'

The quantifier <u>mə́k'ʷ</u> 'all' can occur in other positions as well.[19] For example, in certain cases, it can follow the nominal it modifies, as in (179-180):

(179) ni wəwá?əs kʷθə sqʷəmqʷəmə́y? mə́k'ʷ
aux bark det dogs all
'The dogs all barked.'

(180) ni ?ə́ɬtən tθə sɬənléni? mə́k'ʷ
aux eat det women all
'The women all ate.'

This construction is rare and I will not be dealing with it here.

There are two constructions where <u>mə́k'ʷ</u> appears in initial position in the sentence. First, the quantified nominal can be extracted and, thus, is in initial position followed by an embedded clause, as illustrated in (181-183):

(181) a. ni x̌ʷələnčénəm mə́k'ʷ kʷθə sƛ̓əl'íqəɬ
aux run(pl) all det children
'All the children ran.'

b. mə́k'ʷ kʷθə sƛ̓əl'íqəɬ ni x̌ʷələnčénəm
all det children aux run(pl)
'It was all the children who ran.'

(182) a. ni cən qá'qa'-t mə́k'ʷ kʷθə qá'
aux 1sub drink-tr all det water
'I drank all the water.'

b. mə́k'ʷ kʷθə qá' ni qà'qa'-t-'é.n'
all det water aux drink-tr-1ssub
'It's all the water that I drank.'

(183) a. ni nə́m' 'ə mə́k'ʷ kʷθə pú'əlt
aux go obl all det boats
'He went to all the boats.'

b. mə́k'ʷ kʷθə pú'əlt ni š-nə́m'-s
all det boats aux nom-go-3pos
'It's all the boats that he went to.'

The quantified nominal, like other extracted nominals, can bear the grammatical relations of subject (181), object (182), or oblique (i.e. subject of a nominalization) (183) in the clause from which it is extracted.

There is a second construction where only the quantifier is extracted. In this construction, the quantifier is in initial position followed by an embedded clause, as exemplified in (184-186b):[20]

(184) a. ni x̌ʷələnčénəm mə́k'ʷ kʷθə sƛ̓əl?íqəɬ
aux run(pl) all det children
'All the children ran.'

b. ni mə́k'ʷ ?u x̌ʷələnčénəm kʷθə sƛ̓əl?íqəɬ
aux all lnk run(pl) det children
'All the children ran.'

(185) a. ni wəwá?əs mə́k'ʷ kʷθə sqʷəmqʷəmə́y?
aux bark all det dogs
'All the dogs barked.'

b. ni mə́k'ʷ ?u wəwá?əs kʷθə sqʷəmqʷəmə́y?
aux all lnk bark det dogs
'All the dogs barked.'

(186) a. ni ?ə́ɬtən mə́k'ʷ tθə sɬənɬéni?
aux eat all det women
'All the woman ate.'

b. ni mə́k'ʷ ?u ?ə́ɬtən tθə sɬənɬéni?
aux all lnk eat det women
'All the women ate.'

In (184-186), the quantifier is extracted from quantified nominals which are subjects of intransitives. The quantifier can also be extracted from quantified nominals which are objects of transitives as seen in (187-189b).

(187) a. ni q'ʷə́l-ət-əs tθə sƛ̓əl?íqəɬ mə́k'ʷ kʷθə səplíl
aux bake-tr-3erg det children all det bread
'The children baked all the bread.'

b. ni mə́k'ʷ ?u q'ʷə́l-ət-əs tθə sƛ̓əl?íqəɬ kʷθə səplíl
aux all lnk bake-tr-3ssub det children det bread
'The children baked all the bread.'
*'All the children baked the bread.'

```
(188) a. ni qá?qa?-t-əs     kʷθə  səwwə́y?qe?  mək'ʷ  kʷθə  qá?
         aux drink-tr-3erg  det   men          all    det   water
         'The men drank all the water.'

      b. ni mə́k'ʷ ?u  qá?qa?-ət-əs      kʷθə  səwwə́y?qe?  kʷθə  qá?
         aux all  lnk  drink-tr-3ssub   det   men          det   water
         'The men drank all the water.'
         *'All the men drank the water.'

(189) a. ni ɬə́yx̌-t-əs   tθə  sɬənɬéni?  mə́k'ʷ  kʷθə  scé.ɬtən
         aux eat-tr-3erg det  women      all    det   salmon
         'The women ate all the salmon.'
      b. ni mə́k'ʷ ?u  ɬə́yx̌-t-əs     tθə  sɬənɬéni?  kʷθə  scé.ɬtən
         aux all  lnk  eat-tr-3ssub det  women      det   salmon
         'The women ate all the salmon.'
         *'All the women ate the salmon.'
```

However, the quantifier cannot be extracted from quantified nominals which are subjects of transitives as seen in (190-192):

```
(190) a. ni q'ʷə́l-ət-əs   mə́k'ʷ  tθə  sƛ̓əl?íqəɬ  kʷθə  səplíl
         aux bake-tr-3erg all    det  children   det   bread
         'All the children baked the bread.'

      b. ni mə́k'ʷ ?u  q'ʷə́l-ət-əs     tθə  sƛ̓əl?íqəɬ  kʷθə  səplíl
         aux all  lnk  bake-tr-3ssub  det  children   det   bread
         *'All the children baked the bread.'
         'The children baked all the bread.'

(191) a. ni qá?qa?-t-əs    mə́k'ʷ  kʷθə  səwwə́y?qe?  kʷθə  qá?
         aux drink-tr-3erg all    det   men          det   water
         'All the men drank the water.'

      b. ni mə́k'ʷ ?u  qá?qa?-t-əs      kʷθə  səwwə́y?qe?  kʷθə  qá?
         aux all  lnk  drink-tr-3ssub  det   men          det   water
         *'All the men drank the water.'
         'The men drank all the water.'
```

(192) a. ni ɬə́yx̌-t-əs mə́k'ʷ tᶿə sɬənɬéni? kʷθə scé.ɬten
aux eat-tr-3erg all det women det salmon

'All the women ate the salmon.'

b. ni mə́k'ʷ ?u ɬə́yx̌-t-əs tᶿə sɬənɬéni? kʷθə scé.ɬtən
aux all lnk eat-tr-3ssub det women det salmon

*'All the women ate the salmon.'
'The women ate all the salmon.'

Considering examples like the above, it is clear that the relevant distinction for formulating a condition on quantifier extraction is absolutive vs. ergative; that is, the quantifier can be extracted from subjects of intransitives or objects of transitives but not from subjects of transitives. Thus, a condition on quantifier extraction can be stated as follows:

(193) The quantifier mə́k'ʷ 'all' can be extracted only if the quantified nominal from which it is extracted is an absolutive.

2.6.3 Extraction and Person Marking

In this section I point out the features of person marking in the embedded clauses of extractions.

First, there are two types of extraction--extraction where there is person marking in the embedded clause which agrees with the extracted nominal and extraction where there is no such person marking. I deal with the former cases by assuming that the extracted nominal has a pronominal copy. In the latter cases, the extracted nominal does not have a pronomonal copy. As seen in (194-197), when objects or possessors are extracted, they have pronominal copies.

(194) ʔé.nʔθə ni q'ʷàqʷ-əθ-ám'š-əs
lemph aux club-tr-1obj-3ssub
'It's me who he clubbed.'

(195) nə́wə ni ləm-θ-amə-ʔé.nʔ
2emph aux look-tr-2obj-1ssub
'It's you that I looked at.'

(196) státəl-stəxʷ cən ɬə sɬéniʔ ni q'á.y-t-əxʷ kʷθə sqéʔəq-s
know-cs 1sub det woman aux kill-tr-2ssub det y.b.-3pos
'I know the woman whose younger brother you killed.'

(197) ʔé.nʔθə ni q'áy kʷθə nə-sqʷəméyʔ
lemph aux die det 1pos-dog
'I'm the one whose dog died.'

However, extracted subjects do not have pronominal copies, as seen in (198-199):

(198) a. ʔe.nʔθə ni q'ʷáqʷ-ət
lemph aux club-tr
'I'm the one who clubbed it.'

b. *ʔé.nʔθə ni q'ʷàqʷ-ət-ʔé.nʔ
lemph aux club-tr-1ssub
(I'm the one who clubbed it.)

(199) a. níɬ ɬə sɬéniʔ ni q'ʷáqʷ-ət
3emph det woman aux club-tr
'It's the woman who clubbed it.'

b. *níɬ ɬə sɬéniʔ ni q'ʷáqʷ-ət-əs
3emph det woman aux club-tr-3ssub
(It's the woman who clubbed it.)

Thus, while extracted objects and possessives have pronominal copies, extracted subjects do not.

Second, as seen in many examples above (e.g. (195) and (196)), person marking of subjects in the embedded clause is indicated by the subjective suffixes (cf. §1.4.5). As was pointed out in §2.4.3, person marking of subordinate clause subjects is indicated by these suffixes.

However, there is a difference between subordinate clauses and the embedded clauses in extractions. It was pointed out above that in subordinate clauses subject is marked for all 3rd persons regardless of ergativity. However, in the embedded clauses of extractions, this is not the case; here 3rd person agreement is indicated only for 3rd person ergatives. This can be seen in (200-201) below; in (200), the embedded clause is intransitive and 3rd person agreement is not possible, while in (201), the embedded clause is transitive and 3rd person agreement is necessary.

(200) státəl-stəxʷ cən ɬə sɬéniʔ ni t'íləm(*-əs) kʷθə sqéʔəq-s
know-cs 1sub det woman aux sing-3ssub det y.b.-3pos
'I know the woman whose brother sang.'

(201) státəl-stəxʷ cən ɬə sɬéniʔ ni q'ʷél-ət-əs kʷθə scé.ɬtən-s
know-cs 1sub det woman aux bake-tr-3ssub det salmon-3pos
'I know the woman whose salmon he baked.'

Thus, 3rd person agreement in the embedded clauses of extractions, as in main clauses, distinguishes ergative/absolutive, differing from subject marking in subordinate clauses which distinguishes subject/object.

2.7 Constraints on Clause Structure

There are some transitive clauses which are impossible in Halkomelem. I account for these by positing two constraints on structure.

The first, used by all speakers, prohibits transitive clauses with 3rd person subjects and 2nd person objects. Thus clauses like the following are ungrammatical:

(202) *ni q'ʷàqʷ-əθ-ám-əs ɬə sɬéniʔ
aux club-tr-2obj-3erg det woman
(The woman clubbed you.)

(203) *ni q'ʷàqʷ-ət-ál-əs
aux club-2plobj-3erg
(He clubbed you pl.)

The second constraint, limited to some speakers only, prohibits transitive clauses with subjects that are proper nouns; in other words, it prohibits proper noun ergatives. Thus, the following clauses are ungrammatical:

(204) *ni q'ʷə́l-ət-əs tᶿə Bob tᶿə scé.ɬtən
aux bake-tr-3erg det det salmon
(Bob baked the salmon.)

(205) *ni lə́m-ət-əs ɬə Mary kʷθə Joe
aux look-tr-3erg det det
(Mary looked at Joe.)

(206) *ni ləm-əθ-ám'š-əs ɬə Mary
aux look-tr-1obj-3erg det
(Mary looked at me.)

The status of the object is irrelevant to this constraint: it can be any person or it can be a proper or common noun; in all cases, the clauses are ungrammatical. Furthermore, this constraint is limited to ergatives; as seen in the following examples, subjects of intransitive clauses (i.e., absolutives) that are proper nouns are permitted.

(207) ni t'íləm kʷθə Arnold
aux sing det
'Arnold sang.'

(208) ni q'áy ɬə Mary
aux die det
'Mary died.'

2.8 Summary: Distinctions in Halkomelem

In this chapter, I have formulated several rules, conditions on constructions, and constraints in Halkomelem. Here I summarize these phenomena according to the distinctions they refer to.

First, two phenomena distinguish nuclear terms from obliques: Nominal Case (23) and extraction. While nuclear terms are directly extracted, obliques are extracted through nominalization.

Second, a few phenomena distinguish subjects from objects. Subjects and objects; when they are 1st or 2nd person, are in different pronominal cases (49). In addition, 3rd person agreement distinguishes subjects and objects in subordinate clauses, where agreement is marked only for subjects. Extraction also distinguishes subjects and objects: objects when they are extracted have pronominal copies, while subjects do not.

Lastly, several phenomena make reference to the distinction ergative/absolutive. Third Person Agreement (78) is marked only for ergatives in main and relative clauses, which thus differ from subordinate clauses. One Nominal Interpretation (108) limits the interpretation of a single 3rd person nominal (in the absence of marking for other persons) to absolutive. Also conditions on possessor extraction (172) and quantifier extraction (193) limit extractions of possessors or quantifiers to absolutives. Finally, for some speakers, there is a constraint against ergatives that are proper nouns.

The latter distinction, ergative/absolutive, is of particular interest. The phenomena I discuss here are the first providing evidence for the necessity of this as a syntactic distinction in Central Salish languages.[21]

FOOTNOTES TO CHAPTER 2

[1]Thompson (1979b, p. 740) points out that transitive sentences where both agent and patient are 3rd person nominals are atypical of many Salish Languages. In fact, Hess (1973) has noted the impossibility of such clauses in Lushootseed. Also, Hukari (1976b) has noted that such clauses are rare in texts. However, my informants seem to feel comfortable with these types of sentences and gave them freely. Suttles (in preparation) notes that he finds such sentences in texts.

[2]Temporals are not expressed in oblique phrases but rather by means of a subordinate clause.

[3]In Downriver Halkomelem, the oblique marker is apparently not obligatory. Whether or not it is present, all obliques relativize alike, through nominalization with /š-/ (cf. §2.6.2). In Upriver Halkomelem, the oblique marker has been lost altogether.

[4]There are instances where the oblique marker is used to form nominal compounds, e.g.:

i) lélәmʔ ʔә-ƛ̓ sqʷәméy̓ʔ
house obl-det dog
'dog house'

[5]For a discussion of ergativity, cf. Dixon (1979) and Silverstein (1976).

[6]I have concentrated on the major aspectual distinction in Halkomelem--continuative vs. completive. For a more thorough discussion of aspect, and also of tense and mode, see Suttles (in preparation).

[7]There is much previous research on Halkomelem and other Central Salish relative clauses; cf. Hukari (1977a), Leslie (1979), Suttles (in preparation), and Kuipers (1967).

[8]Relative clauses have not been extensively studied in Relational Grammar. Perlmutter and Postal (to appear c) propose an Overlay relation 'Rel'. Bell (to appear) employed this relation to her analysis of Cebuano relative clauses.

[9]I intend for this analysis to be neutral with respect to alternatives available for the initial structure of relative clauses. Relative clauses could have two coreferent NPs or one NP that heads two arcs. Other possibilities may exist as well.

[10] The embedded clauses in (109-113b) follow the head, but the opposite order, as follows, is also quite common.

i) státəl-stəxʷ-əs ɬə ni t'íləm sɬéniʔ
know-cs-3erg det aux sing woman

'He knows the woman who sang.'

[11] The following is an example of a headless relative clause from Diegueno: (Gorbet (1977) p. 270):

i) [tənay 'wai+∅ 'wu:w+pu+Lʸ] 'čiqawx
yesterday house+OBJ I-see-DEF+IN I-sing-IRREAL

'I'll sing in the house I saw yesterday.'

[12] The following are also ungrammatical:

i) *státəl-stəxʷ cən ɬə [ni ʔíməš sɬéniʔ]
know-cs 1sub det aux walk woman

(I know the woman who walked.)

ii) *ni q'áy kʷθə [ni q 'ál xʷənítəm]
aux die det aux speak white man

(The white man who spoke died.)

[13] Akmajian (1979, 104) discusses pseudo-cleft (i) and cleft (ii) sentences in English.

i) (The one) who Nixon chose was Agnew.

ii) It was Agnew who Nixon chose.

He points out that these 'express the same grammatical relations, share the same presuppositions, have the same focus, in short, ...are synonymous and are used interchangeably.'

In Halkomelem, there also appears to be little difference in meaning between cleft and pseudo-cleft sentences.

[14] Chamorro, according to Chung (to appear b) also extracts some nominals through nominalization.

[15] Note that the element posited to be predicate in nominalizations is, like other predicates, in initial position.

[16] Nominalizations in Halkomelem differ from sentential nominalizations in other languages because in Halkomelem the object of a simple clause is apparently an object (and not an oblique) in the corresponding nominalization.

[17] In Chapters 3 and 4 I point out that some nominals can be extracted from nominalizations with the prefix <u>s-</u>; however, such nominalizations would also be unagrammatical for examples like (157-158b).

[18] Besides extracting the possessor directly, as exemplified in the following discussion, it is also possible to express the possessor as subject of the predicate <u>cweˀ</u> 'to have, own' and, of course, it may be extractly directly. For example, compare (i) with (164b) below:

(i)	ˀé.nˀθə	cwéˀ	ˀu	kʷθə	ni	q'áy	sqʷəméyˀ
	lemph	own	lnk	det	aux	die	dog

'I'm the one who owns the dog that died.'

[19] Other quantifiers cannot appear in these alternative orders.

[20] The quantifier is a predicate in these constructions; thus it is introduced by an auxiliary and takes an embedded clause.

[21] Davis (1974) and Kuipers (1967, p. 173) make use of the term ergative with respect to 3rd person agreement in Sliammon and Squamish respectively, but neither develops this concept in the description of those languages.

Chapter 3

ADVANCEMENTS TO OBJECT

3.0 Introduction

In this chapter, I discuss constructions in which a nominal with the semantic role of 'recipient', 'benefactive', 'causal', or 'directional' is syntactically the object of the clause. Each type of construction is illustrated in (1-4):

(1) ni ˀám-əs-t-əs kʷθə sqʷəméyˀ ˀə kʷθə sθ'ámˀ
aux give-advA-tr-3erg det dog obl det bone
'He gave the dog the bone.'

(2) ni q'ʷə́l-əɬc-t-əs ɬə sɬéniˀ ˀə kʷθə səplíl
aux bake-advB-tr-3erg det woman obl det bread
'He baked the bread for the woman.'

(3) ni θ'eyˀk'ʷ-méˀ-t-əs kʷθə sqʷəméyˀ
aux startle-advC-tr-3erg det dog
'He was startled at the dog.'

(4) ˀi yə-ˀéˀwəˀ-n-əs-əs ɬə sɬéniˀ
aux ser-come-advD-tr-3erg det woman
'He's coming toward the woman.'

It is assumed that grammatical relations at the initial level of syntax correspond to the semantic role of the nominal, the initial grammatical relation of the 'recipient' in (1) would be indirect object [3], the 'benefactive', 'causal', and 'directional' in (2-4) respectively would be obliques [Ben, Causal, Dir].

In order to account for the behaviour of these nominals as objects, I propose that clauses like (1-4) should be analyzed as structures involving advancements to object: i.e., a nominal bearing an indirect object or oblique relation at the initial level bears the object relation at final level.[1] Thus, the advancements to object in (1-4) can be represented by the partial stratal diagrams given in (5-8) respectively:

(5) 

(6) 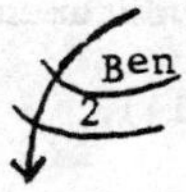

(7) 

(8) 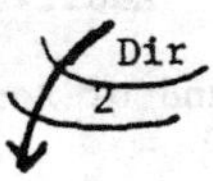

In arguing for an advancement analysis for the above clauses, I first consider indirect object to object advancement and benefactive to object advancement. In §3.1, I present evidence that the indirect object and benefactive are final objects. In §3.2, I discuss the status of the 'patient' in advancement clauses. In §3.3, I consider an alternative to an advancement analysis.

Second, I discuss causal to object advancement. In §3.4, I argue that the causal is the final object in clauses involving advancement. In §3.5, I consider an alternative to an advancement analysis.

Third, I briefly discuss directional to object advancement. In §3.6, I present evidence that the locative is the final object in advancement clauses.

Finally, in §3.7, I discuss conditions on advancements in Halkomelem, and, in §3.8, I briefly consider the verbal morphology associated with advancement. (cf. §1.4)

3.1 Indirect Object and Benefactive Advancement

In this section, I argue that the nominals bearing the semantic roles of 'recipient' and 'benefactive' in (1-2) respectively are objects at the final level of syntax.[2] Maintaining the assumption that initial grammatical relations correspond to semantic roles, I posit that the 'recipient' in (1) is an initial indirect object [3] and the 'benefactive' in (2) is an initial oblique relation [Ben]. 3-2 advancement and Ben-2 advancement, as represented in (5) and (6), are posited for these clauses. Additional examples of 3-2 advancement clauses are given in (9-11) and of Ben-2 advancement in (12-14).

(9) ni ʔám-əs-t-əs kʷθə swíwʔləs ʔə kʷθə púkʷ
aux give-advA-tr-3erg det boy obl det book
'He gave the boy the book.'

(10) ni cən xʷáyem-əs-t kʷθə Bob ʔə kʷθə nə-lélamʔ-əɬ
aux 1sub sell-advA-tr- det obl det 1pos-house-pst
'I sold Bob my house.'

(11) ni yə́θ-əs-t-əs ɬə Mary ʔə kʷθə-nʔ syays
aux tell-advA-tr-3erg det obl det-2pos work
'He told Mary about your job.'

(12) ni θə́y-əɬc- t-əs kʷθə swə̀yʔqeʔ ʔə kʷθə snə́xʷəɬ-s
aux fix-advB-tr-3erg det man obl det canoe-3pos
'He fixed the canoe for the man.'

(13) ni x̌ə́lʔ-əɬc- t-əs kʷθə-ənʔ mén ʔə kʷθə pípə-s
aux write-advB-tr-3erg det-2pos fater obl det letter-3pos
'He wrote the letter for your father.'

(14) ni cən ʔíləq-əɬc-ət ɬə nə-mə́nʔə ʔə kʷθə qʷɬə́yʔšənʔ
aux 1sub buy-advB-tr det 1pos-offspring obl det shoe
'I bought my daughter shoes.'

In this section, I present arguments that the 'recipients' and 'benefactives' in Halkomelem are final objects. I give two types of arguments. First, I give evidence based on Nominal Case, Pronominal Case and extraction, that the 'recipients' and 'benefactives' are objects. I argue that in order for the rules in Chapter 2 to account for these data, they must specify final level of structure. Second, I give evidence based on possessor and quantifier extraction that the 'recipients' and 'benefactives' are absolutives. That these nominals behave like absolutives, i.e. objects in a transitive clause, follows from an advancement analysis which posits that these nominals are indeed final objects.

Thus, in order for these rules to account for these data, they must specify final level of structure.

3.1.1 Nominal Case

The first argument that the 'recipient' and 'benefactive' are final objects is based on Nominal Case. As discussed above, nominal objects are in the straight case. Therefore, if the 'recipient' and 'benefactive' in the above examples are objects, as I propose, then they should be marked in the straight case. As can be seen in (9-14) above, this is so.

Interestingly, the 'recipient' or 'benefactive' <u>cannot</u> appear in the oblique case, as can be seen in (16-17):

(15) *ni ˀám(-əs)-t-əs (ˀə) kʷθə sθ'ámˀ ˀə kʷθə sqʷəméyˀ
aux give-advA-tr-3erg obl det bone obl det dog
(He gave the bone to the dog.)

(16) *ni q'ʷə́l(-ɬc)-t-əs (ˀə) kʷθə səplíl ˀə ɬə sɬéniˀ
aux bake-advB-tr-3erg obl det bread obl det woman
(He baked the bread for the woman.)

These sentences are ungrammatical regardless of the word order of the nominals, the case marking of the 'patient', or the presence or absence of the advancement suffix. That 'recipients' and 'benefactives' cannot occur in the oblique case can be accounted for if we assume that these nominals cannot bear the grammatical relations of indirect object and oblique respectively at final level of syntax. Thus, 3-2 advancement and Ben-2 advancement are obligatory in Halkomelem. This condition is discussed further in §3.7.[3]

If we maintain that the 'benefactive' is an initial oblique, but (as seen in (16)) cannot be in the oblique case, then the rule for Nominal Case as formulated in §2.1 is inadequate. Specifically, there is a difference between the obliques discussed in Chapter 2 and the 'benefactive' in the above example; while the former bear an oblique relation at final level, 'benefactives' do not. Thus, if we specified that the rule of Nominal Case only marks final relations, as in (17) then we can account for the oblique marking of the obliques discussed in Chapter 2 and also for the lack of oblique case marking of 'benefactives' in Ben-2 advancement clauses. Further justification of this modification is given in Chapter 4.

(17) Nominal Case

a. Final nuclear terms and common noun possessors are in the straight case.

b. Final obliques and proper noun possessors are in the oblique case.

As we proceed, we will see that other rules discussed in Chapter 2 must be modified to specify the level.

3.1.2 Pronominal Case

Pronominal Case (cf. §2.4) provides a second agrument for 3-2 and Ben-2 advancement. If the 'recipient' and 'benefactive' in the above clauses are objects, as I propose, then a 1st or 2nd person 'recipient' or 'benefactive' should be in the objective case. This prediction is correct, as seen in (18-21):

(18) ni ʔàm-əs-θ-ám̓ʔš-əs ʔə kʷθə púkʷ
aux give-advA-tr-lobj obl det book
'He gave me the book.'

(19) ni cən yəθ-əs-θ-ámə ʔə-ƛ̓ Bob
aux 1sub tell-advA-tr-2obj obl-det
'I told you about Bob.'

(20) ni θə̀y-əɬc-θ-ámʔš-əs ʔə kʷθə nə-snə́xʷəɬ
aux fix-advB-tr-1obj-3erg obl det 1pos-canoe
'He fixed my canoe for me.'

(21) ni cən θə̀y-əɬc-θ-ámə ʔə kʷθ-ənʔ snə́xʷəɬ
aux 1sub fix-advB-tr-2obj obl det-2pos canoe
'I fixed your canoe for you.'

The 'recipient' or 'benefactive' cannot be expressed in the oblique case, as can be seen in (22-23).

(22) *ni ʔam(-əs)-t-əs (ʔə) kʷθə púkʷ ʔə-ƛ̓ ʔe.nʔθə
aux give-advA-tr-3erg obl det book obl-det 1emph
(He gave the book to me.)

(23) *ni θə́y(-ɬc)-t-əs (ʔə) kʷθə snə́xʷəɬ ʔə-ƛ̓ ʔe.nʔθə
aux fix-advB-tr-3erg obl det canoe obl-det 1emph
(He fixed the canoe for me.)

Again, word order, the case of the 'patient', or the presence or absence of the advancement marker has no effect on the ungrammaticality of these clauses.

Therefore, that the 'recipient' and 'benefactive' in such sentences are expressed by object pronominal suffixes provides evidence that they bear the grammatical relation of object.

Again as with Nominal Case, the data involving 3-2 and Ben-2 advancement and Pronominal Case indicates that this rule should be specified for level. Since according to this analysis, 'benefactives' are initial but are not final obliques, the rule for oblique case should be limited to final level. Thus, Pronominal Case can be limited to final level as follows:

(24) Pronominal Case
   a. Final subjects are in the subjective case.
   b. Final objects are in the objective case.
   c. Final obliques are in the oblique case.

Further support for this modification is given in Chapter 4.

3.1.3 Extraction

Data involving the extraction of a 'recipient' or 'benefactive' provide a third argument for advancement to object of these nominals. As discussed in §2.6, nuclear terms are directly extracted, while obliques are extracted through nominalization. In (25-28), the 'recipient' or 'benefactive' is directly extracted.

(25) swíwˀləs kʷθə ni ˀám-əs-t-əs ˀə kʷθə púkʷ
 boy det aux give-advA-tr-3ssubobl det book
 'It's a boy that the gave the book to.'

(26) níɬ kʷθə Bob ni xʷàyəm-əs-t-ˀé.nˀ ˀə kʷθə nə-léləmˀ-ˀəɬ
 3emph det aux sell-advA-tr-1ssub obl det 1pos-house-pst
 'It's Bob who I sold the house to.'

(27) swə́yˀqeˀ kʷθə ni θə́y-əɬc-t-əs ˀə kʷθə snə́xʷəɬ
 man det aux fix-advB-tr-3ssub obl det canoe
 'It's a man that he fixed the canoe for.'

(28) wét k'ʷə ni q'ʷə̀l-əɬc-t-ə́xʷ ˀə kʷθə səplíl
 who det aux bake-advB-tr-2ssub obl det bread
 'Who did you bake the bread for?'

Furthermore, note that 'recipients' and 'benefactives' cannot be extracted through nominalization, as is seen in (29-30):

(29) *swíwˀləs kʷθə ni š-ˀám-əs-t-s kʷθə púkʷ
 boy det aux nom-give-advA-tr-3pos det book
 (His giving the book was to the boy.)

(30) *swə́yˀqeˀ kʷθə ni š-θə́y-əɬc-t-s kʷθə snə́xʷəɬ
 man det aux nom-fix-advB-tr-3pos det canoe
 (His fixing the canoe was for the man.)

That, the 'recipients' and 'benefactives' behave like objects and not like obliques with respect to extraction follows from an analysis which posits advancement to object for these nominals.

As with Nominal and Pronominal Case, these data also provide evidence that the rule for extraction should specify final level of syntax, as follows:

(31) a. Final nuclear terms are directly extracted.
b. Final obliques are extracted through nominalization.

3.1.4 Possessor Extraction

Data involving possessor extraction provide a fourth argument that the 'recipient' and 'benefactive' are objects. In §2.6, a condition on possessor extraction was formulated as follows:

(32) A possessor can be extracted only if the possessive phrase is an absolutive.

If the 'recipient' and 'benefactive' are final objects of the clause then they are absolutives at final level. Thus, the possessor in phrases which play the role of 'recipient' or 'benefactive' should extract, and indeed they do.

(33) státəl-stəxʷ cən ɬə sɬéniʔ ni ʔàm-əs-t-ʔé.nʔ kʷθə sqéʔəq-s
know-cs 1sub det woman aux give-advA-tr-1ssub det y.b.-3pos
'I know the woman whose younger brother I gave it to.'

(34) ʔé.nʔθə ni xʷáyəm-əs-t-əxʷ kʷθə nə-sqéʔəq ʔə kʷθə léləmʔ
lemph aux sell-advA-tr-2ssub det 1pos-y.b. obl det house
'I'm the one whose younger brother you sold the house to.'

(35) státəl-stəxʷ cən ɬə sɬéniʔ ni θə́y-əɬc-t-əxʷ kʷθə stáləs-s
know-cs 1sub det woman aux fix-advB-tr-2ssub det spouse-3pos
'I know the woman whose husband you fixed the canoe for.'

(36) nə́wə ni x̌ə́lʔ-əɬc-ət-əs kʷθə-ənʔ mén ʔə kʷθə pípə-s
2emph aux write-advB-tr-3ssub det-2pos father obl det letter-3pos
'You're the one whose father he wrote the letter for.'

According to the advancement analysis, 'recipients' and 'benefactives' are final objects although they are not initial objects. Thus, these nominals are absolutives at final level although they are not absolutives at initial level. The condition on possessor extraction is therefore limited to final absolutives, as follows:

(37) A possessor can be extracted only if the possessive phrase is a final absolutive.

I discuss this further in Chapter 4.

3.1.5. Quantifier Extraction

As discussed in §2.7, a condition on quantifier extraction is given as follows:

(38) The quantifier <u>mə́k'ʷ</u> can be extracted only from an absolutive.

Since under an advancement analysis, 'recipients' and 'benefactives' are objects and therefore absolutives, the quantifier should extract if the 'recipient' or 'benefactive' is a quantified phrase. This is the case, as seen in (39-42):

(39) ni mə́k'ʷ ʔu ʔám-əs-t-əs tᶿə sɬənɬéniʔ tᶿə sƛ'əlʔíqəɬ
aux all lnk give-advA-tr-3ssub det women det children
ʔə kʷθə púkʷ
obl det book
'He women gave all the children books.'

(40) ni mə́k'ʷ ʔu yə́θ-əs-t-ət kʷθə sɬənɬéniʔ ʔə-ƛ' nə́wə
aux all lnk tell-advA-tr-1plssub det women obl-det 2emph
'We told all the women about you.'

(41) ni mə́k'ʷ ʔu q'ʷə́l-əɬc-t-əxʷ kʷθə sɬənɬéniʔ ʔə kʷθə səplíl
aux all lnk bake-advB-tr-2ssub det women obl det bread
'You baked bread for all the women.'

(42) ni mə́k'ʷ ʔu ʔíləq-əɬc-t-ʔe.nʔ kʷθə nə-méʔmənʔə
aux all lnk buy-advB-tr-1ssub det 1pos-offspring
ʔə kʷθə qʷɬə́yʔšənʔ
obl det shoe
'I bought shoes for all my kids.'

Again, as with possessor extraction, that the quantifier is extracted from 'recipients' and 'benefactives', which are final absolutives but not initial absolutives, indicates that the condition on quantifier extraction may be limited to final absolutives, as follows:

(43) The quantifier <u>mə́k'ʷ</u> can be extracted only from a final absolutive.

This will be discussed further in Chapter 4.

3.2 The 'Patient' in Advancement Clauses

In the preceding section, I presented arguments that the 'recipient' and 'benefactive' are final objects in Halkomelem. In the examples discussed above, there was also a nominal with the semantic role of 'patient'. This raises the question: What grammatical relation does the 'patient' in 3-2 and Ben-2 advancement clauses bear? In this section, I give evidence pertaining to this question.

First, I give evidence that the 'patient' is not a final object nor an oblique. Second, I discuss two alternatives available within the theory of Relational Grammar for the final grammatical relation of the 'patient' in these clauses. In my discussion, I show that the Halkomelem data available at present provide no evidence for preferring one of these alternatives.

3.2.1 Arguments that the 'Patient' is not the Final Object

In proposing an advancement analysis for clauses with 'recipients' and 'benefactives', I maintained the assumption that initial grammatical relations correspond to semantic roles. If that assumption is to be consistently maintained, then the 'patient' in such clauses, like the 'patients' in the basic sentences discussed in Chapter 2, should be assigned the initial grammatical relation of <u>object</u>.

Since the 'patient' under this analysis is initial object, one possibility for the final grammatical relation of the 'patient' is <u>object</u>. Under such an analysis, the 'patient' does not change grammatical relations; the 'recipient' or 'benefactive' however, advances to object, as argued above. Under this analysis, a 3-2 advancement clause could be represented in the following stratal diagram.[4]

(44)

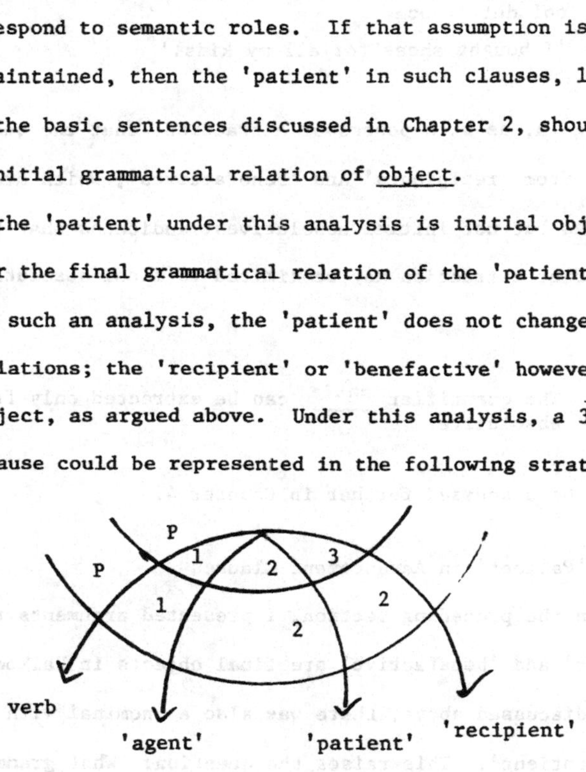

Such an analysis predicts that the 'patient' should behave like an object with respect to the rules making reference to object formulated in Chapter 2. I give arguments, based on Nominal Case and extraction, against this analysis.

As discussed in §2.1, object nominals are in the straight case.

However, in clauses with 3-2 or Ben-2 advancement, the 'patient' is always in the <u>oblique</u> case. This can be seen, for example, in (9-14). I repeat (9) and (13) here as (45) and (46).

(45) ni ʔám-əs-t-əs kʷθə swíwʔləs ʔə kʷθə púkʷ
aux give-advA-tr-3erg det boy obl det book
'He gave the boy the book.'

(46) ni x̌álʔ-əɬc-ət-əs kʷθə-enʔ mén ʔə kʷθə pípə-s
aux write-advB-tr-3erg det-2pos father obl det letter-3pos
'He wrote the letter for your father.'

Furthermore, the 'patient' nominal in 3-2 and Ben-2 advancement clauses cannot be expressed in the straight case, as is seen in (47) and (48):

(47) *ni ʔám-əs-t-əs kʷθə swíwʔləs kʷθə púkʷ
aux give-advA-tr-3erg det boy det book
(He gave the boy the book.)

(48) *ni x̌álʔ-əɬc-ət-əs kʷθə-enʔ mén kʷθə pípə-s
aux write-advB-tr-3erg det-2pos father det letter-3pos
(He wrote the letter for your father.)

Thus, Nominal Case provides an argument that the 'patient' in 3-2 and Ben-2 advancement clauses is <u>not</u> final object. In addition, the behaviour of 'patients' in these clauses with respect to Nominal Case indicates that this rule should refer to final level, as suggested in (17), since 'patients' are objects at initial level but are not in the straight case.

Data involving the extraction of the 'patient' in 3-2 and Ben-2 advancement clauses provide a second argument that the 'patient' is not the final object. In §2.6, the following condition on extraction was given:

(49) Final nuclear terms are directly extracted.

Thus, an analysis which proposed that the 'patient' in 3-2 and Ben-2 advancement clauses is a final object would predict that these nominals could be directly extracted. As can be seen in (50-52), this is not the case:

(50) *níɬ kʷθə púkʷ ni ʔám-əs-t-əs kʷθə swíwʔləs
3emph det book aux give-advA-tr-3ssub det boy
(It's a book that he gave the boy.)

(51) *niɬ kʷθə nə-léləm-ʔəɬ ni xʷàyəm-əs-t-ʔé.nʔ kʷθə Bob
3emph det 1pos-house-pst aux sell-advA-tr-1ssub det
(It's my house that I sold to Bob.)

(52) *səplíl kʷθə ni q'ʷə̀l-əɬc-θ-ámʔš-əs ɬə sɬéniʔ
bread det aux bake-advB-tr-1obj-3ssub det woman
(Bread is what the woman baded for me.)

(53) * snə́xʷəɬ kʷθə ni θə́y-əɬc-t-əs kʷθə swə́yʔqeʔ
canoe det aux fix-advB-tr-3ssub det man
(A canoe is what he fixed for the man.)

These data provide evidence that an analysis which proposes that the 'patient' in 3-2 and Ben-2 advancement clauses is the final object cannot be maintained.

Furthermore, since the 'patient' in these clauses is the initial although not the final object, the rule of extraction should refer to final object, as suggested in (31) above.

3.2.2 An Argument that the 'Patient' is not a Final Oblique

In the previous section, it was shown that 'patients' in 3-2 and Ben-2 advancement clauses are in the oblique rather than the straight case and that these nominals cannot be directly extracted. Thus, these nominals cannot be final objects.

The case of these nominals suggests a second alternative for their grammatical relation at final level--oblique, as represented in the stratal diagrams in (54) and (55):[3]

(54) 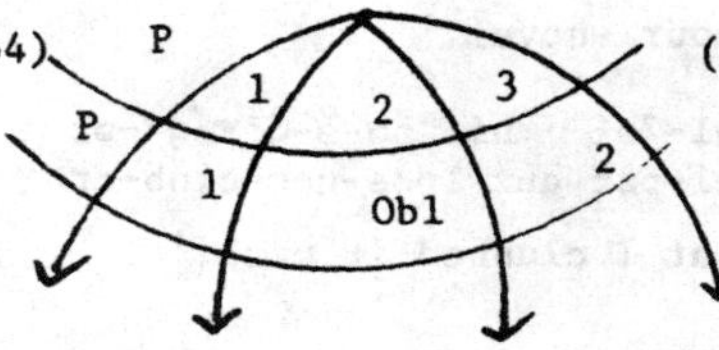

(55) 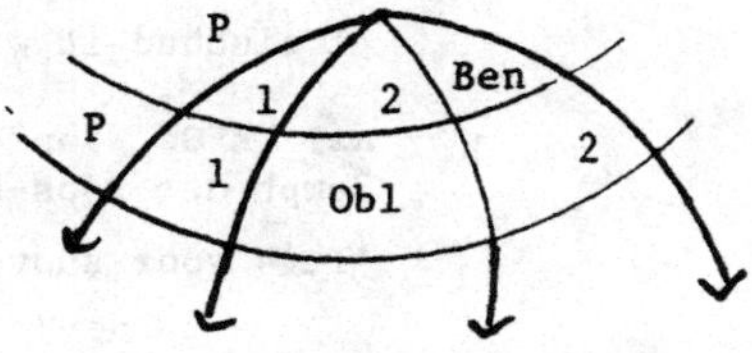

However, there is one argument, based on data involving extraction, against this analysis.

In (56-58) below, I have given examples involving the extraction of the 'patient' in 3-2 and Ben-2 advancement clauses (cf. 30-52)):

(56) níɬ kʷθə púkʷ ni s-ˀám-əs-t-s kʷθə swíwˀləs
3emph det book aux nom-give-advA-tr-3pos det boy
'It's a book that he gave the boy.'

(57) níɬ kʷθə nə-léləmˀ-əɬ ni nə-s-xʷáyəm-əs-t kʷθə Bob
3emph det lpos-house-pst aux lpos-nom-sell-advA-tr det
'It's my house that I sold to Bob.'

(58) səplíl kʷθə ni s-q'ʷəl-əɬc-θ-ámˀš-s ɬə sɬéniˀ
bread det aux nom-bake-advB-tr-lobj-3pos det woman
'Bread is what the woman baked for me.'

(59) snə́xʷəɬ kʷθə ni s-θə́y-əɬc-t-s kʷθə swə́yˀqeˀ
canoe det aux nom-fix-advB-tr-3pos det man
'A canoe is what he fixed for the man.'

As can be seen in the above examples, these nominals are extracted through nominalization. In §2.6.2.2, I pointed out that oblique nominals were also extracted through nominalization: e.g. the instrument in (60a) is extracted through nominalization in (60b):

(60) a. ni cən q'ʷáqʷ-ət ʔə kʷθə ʔənʔ-šápəl-ʔəɬ
aux 1sub club-tr obl det 2pos-shovel-pst
'I clubbed it with your shovel.'

b. níɬ kʷθə ʔənʔ-šápəl-ʔəɬ ni nə-š-q'ʷáqʷ-ət
3emph det 2pos-shovel-pst aux 1pos-nom-club-tr
'It's your shovel that I clubbed it with.'

This might suggest that 'patients' in 3-2 and Ben-2 advancement clauses, which are also extracted through nominalization, are also obliques. However, there is an important difference between the nominalizations in (56-59) and (60b). Notice that in (56-59) the nominalizer prefixed to the verb is <u>s</u>- while in (60b) it is <u>š</u>. As can be seen in (61-62), it is not possible to substitute the prefix <u>š</u>- in examples like (56-59):

(61) *níɬ kʷθə púk'ʷ ni š-ʔám-əs-t-s kʷθə swíwʔləs
3emph det book aux nom-give-advA-tr-3pos det boy
(It's a book that he gave the boy.)

(62) *snə́xʷəɬ kʷθə ni š-θə́y-əɬc-t-s kʷθə swə́yʔqeʔ
canoe det aux nom-fix-advB-tr-3pos det man
(A canoe is what he fixed for the man.)

Nor is it possible to substitute <u>s</u>- in examples like (60b):

(63) *níɬ kʷθə ʔənʔ-šápəl-ʔəɬ ni nə-s-q'ʷáqʷ-ət
3emph det 2pos-shovel-pst aux 1pos-club-tr
(It's your shovel that I clubbed it with.)

The nominalizers <u>s</u>- and <u>š</u>- are distinct; that is, they do not represent morphophonemic alternants of the same prefix governed by such factors as the phonology or lexical class of the verb. Observe the following examples:

(64) a. yá.ys 'work'

b. s-yá.ys 'work, job', 'that accomplished by work'

c. š-yá.yʔəs 'tool'

(65) a. x̌íʔx̌eʔ 'be ashamed'

b. s-x̌íʔx̌eʔ-s 'his shame'
-3pos

c. š-x̌íʔx̌eʔ-s 'that which he is ashamed of', 'the cause of his shame'
-3pos

The (a) examples illustrate the verb. In the (b) examples, the verb is prefixed with s and the form expresses the 'product' or 'patient' of the verb. In the (c) examples, the verb is prefixed with š- and the form expresses the oblique nominal associated with the verb, e.g. instrument, locative, causal. Clearly, s- and š- have consistent semantic differences.

Thus, if 'patients' in 3-2 and Ben-2 advancement clauses were obliques, we would expect them to behave like obliques with respect to extraction. We have seen, however, that while obliques are extracted through nominalization with the prefix š-, 'patients' in 3-2 and Ben-2 advancement clauses are extracted through nominalization with the prefix s-.[6]

3.2.3 Two Alternatives: Chomage or Retreat

In the preceding sections, I have argued that 'patients' in 3-2 and Ben-2 advancement clauses are neither final objects nor final obliques. In this section, I propose two other alternatives: 'patients' in 3-2 and Ben-2 advancement clauses are chomeurs or they are indirect objects.[7] I discuss these alternatives with respect to nominal case marking and extraction.

Under the first alternative, the 3 or Ben in advancing to object places the initial object (i.e. the 'patient') en chómage, as represented in the following stratal diagram:

(66)

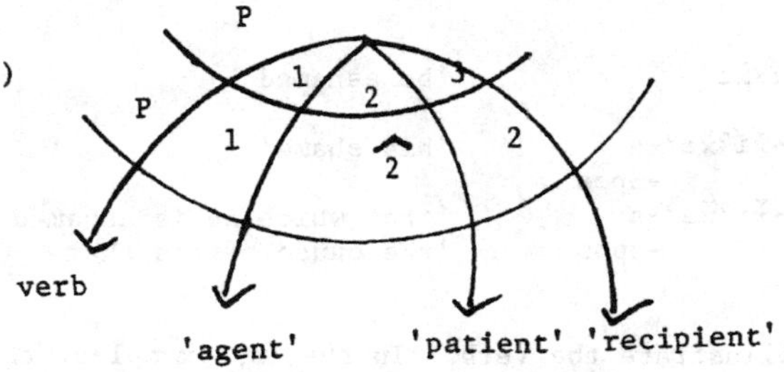

In order for this analysis to account for case marking and extraction, these rules must be modified. First, since the object chomeur is in the oblique case, a statement that oblique case is used for object chomeurs must be added to the case rule as follows:

(67) Nominal Case

a. Final nuclear terms are in the straight case.
b. Final obliques and final object-chomeurs are in the oblique case.

Apparently the relevant case distinction under such a formulation, is term/non-term; e.g.:

(68) Nominal Case

a. Final terms are in the straight case.
b. Final non-terms are in the oblique case.

Thus, the analysis in (66) together with the case rule in (68) accounts for the behaviour of 'patients' in 3-2 and Ben-2 advancement clauses with respect to case.

Second, it was pointed out above that 'patients' in 3-2 and Ben-2 advancement clauses are extracted through nominalization. Unlike obliques, which are extracted through nominalization with *š*-, 'patients' of 3-2 and Ben-2 advancement clauses are nominalized with s-. This information must be added to the rule of extraction as follows:

(69) a. Final subjects and final objects are directly extracted.
b. Final obliques and object chomeurs are extracted through nominalization.
i. extraction of obliques is indicated by š-.
ii. extraction of object-chomeurs is indicated by s-.

Again, the relevant distinction for extraction appears to be term/non-term: (69) can be restated as:

(70) a. Final terms are directly extracted.
b. Final non-terms are extracted through nominalization.

Thus, the analysis in (66) and the extraction rule in (70) account for the behaviour of the 'patient' nominal.

In summary, the analysis in (66), which posits that the 'patient' in 3-2 and Ben-2 advancement clauses is a final chomeur, allows for simple formulations of nominal case marking and extraction. Like obliques, objects chomeurs are final non-terms; thus, by referring to final non-terms in the rule for oblique case marking and by specifying that non-terms are extracted through nominalization, the similarity between obliques and object chomeurs can be captured. Under this analysis a simple account of the prefixes used in nominalization is possible; i.e., object chomeurs are nominalized with s-, while final obliques are nominalized with š-.

A second analysis is possible for 'patients' in 3-2 and Ben-2 advancement clauses; this analysis makes use of the concept of 'retreat'. A retreat (the opposite of an advancement) is a construction in which a nominal bearing a grammatical relation on one level bears a grammatical relation lower on the hierarchy in (71) at the next level.

(71) subject > object > indirect object

A retreat analysis, then, would posit that the 'patient', which is the initial object, is a final indirect object, as represented by the stratal diagram in (72):[8]

(72)

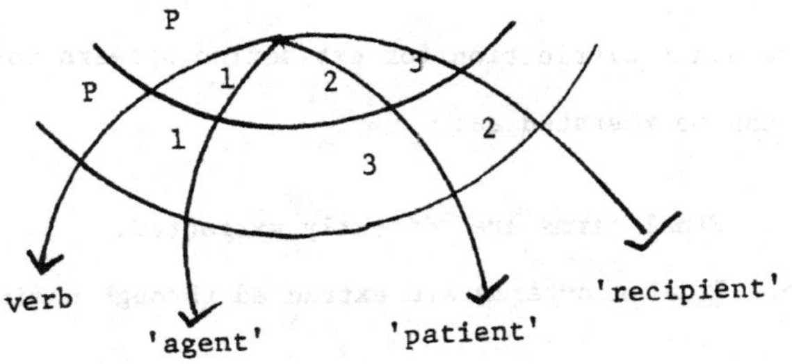

In order for this analysis to account for the behaviour of the 'patient' in 3-2 and Ben-2 advancement clauses with respect to Nominal Case and extraction, modifications in these rules must be made.

First, it should be noted that the rules for nominal case given previously make no reference to indirect object. As was pointed out in §3.1, initial indirect objects always advance to object. For this reason, no reference was made to final indirect object in the discussion of basic rules in Chapter 2.

However, under the analysis proposed in (72), 'patients' in 3-2 and Ben-2 advancement clauses are final indirect objects. Thus, Nominal Case must be modified as follows:

(73) a. Final subjects and final objects are in the straight case.
 b. Final indirect objects and final obliques are in the oblique case.

The relevant distinction for case marking is nuclear terms (i.e., subject and object)/other nominals, as stated in (74):

(74) Nominal Case

a. Final nuclear terms are in the straight case.

b. Other nominals are in the oblique case.

Thus, the retreat analysis together with the case rule given in (74) accounts for the behaviour of 'patients' in 3-2 and Ben-2 advancement clauses.

Likewise, the condition on extraction can be modified to accommodate a retreat analysis, as follows:

(75) a. Final subjects and final objects are directly extracted.

b. Final indirect objects and final obliques are extracted through nominalization.

i. Extraction of indirect objects in indicated by the nominalizer s.

ii. Extraction of obliques is indicated by the nominalizer š-.

Again the relevant distinction is nuclear terms/other nominals. Only nuclear terms can be directly extracted; other nominals cannot be. Thus, the rule of extraction in Halkomelem would be as follows:

(76) a. Final nuclear terms are directly extracted.

b. Other nominals are extracted through nominalization.

The retreat analysis together with the above rule for extraction accounts for the behaviour of 'patients' in 3-2 and Ben-2 advancement clauses.

In summary, the retreat analysis, like the chomage analysis, captures the similarities of 'patients' in 3-2 and Ben-2 advancement clauses and obliques. Both are <u>not</u> final nuclear terms. By referring to nominals which are not final nuclear terms in the rule for oblique case and by specifying that nominals which are not final nuclear terms are extracted through nominalization, final indirect objects and final obliques behave alike with respect to these rules. However, with respect to the prefix indicating nominalization, final indirect objects and final obliques behave differently: that is, final indirect objects are nominalized with s-, while final obliques are nominalized with š-.

In contrasting the chomage and the retreat analyses, both are able to account for nominal case and extraction. Each analysis is able to capture the similiarities and the differences between 'patients' in 3-2 and Ben-2 advancement clauses and obliques. Furthermore, I can present no evidence from Halkomelem that would distinguish these analyses. For this reason, I will refer to the final grammatical relation of 'patients' in 3-2 and Ben-2 advancement clauses by the cover term 3/2 chomeur. This is to be understood as representing either a final indirect object or an object chomeur. I will return to this problem in Chapter 4.

3.3 An Alternative to an Advancement Analysis

In the preceding sections, I have argued that there are clauses in Halkomelem involving 3-2 and Ben-2 advancement, e.g. (77) and (78) respectively:

(77) ni ʔám-əs-t-əs kʷθə sqʷəméyʔ ʔə kʷθə sθ'ámʔ
aux give-advA-tr-3erg det dog obl det bone
'He gave the dog the bone.'

(78) ni q'ʷə́l-əɬc-t-əs ɬə sɬéniʔ ʔə kʷθə səplíl
aux bake-advB-tr-3erg det woman obl det bread
'He baked the bread for the woman.'

I have shown that the initial indirect object or benefactive in such clauses are final objects. In addition, I have pointed out the initial object in such clauses is either an object chomeur or an indirect object at final level. Thus, (77) and (78) can be represented by the stratal diagrams in (79) and (80):

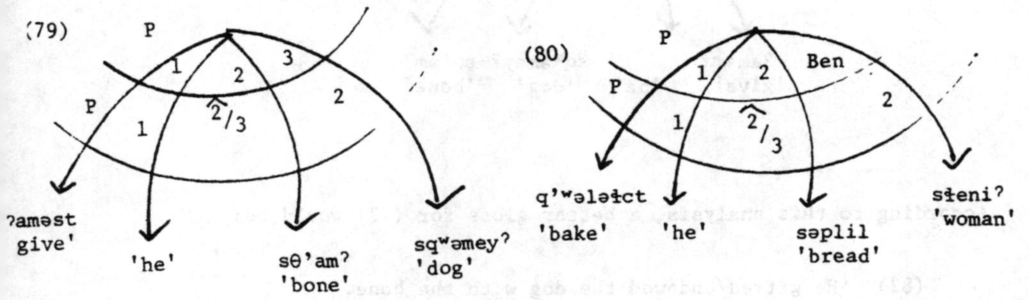

Under this analysis, which I will refer to as the advancement analysis, the assumption is maintained that initial grammatical relations correspond to the semantic role of the nominal: thus, the 'recipient' in (77) is an initial indirect object and the 'benefactive' in (78) is an initial Ben.

In this section, I contrast the advancement analysis with an alternate which I will refer to as the no-advancement analysis. Under this analysis different assumptions are made concerning the semantic roles of the nominals, and thus, different grammatical relations are assigned at initial level. Specifically, sqʷəméyʔ 'dog' in (77) is interpreted as playing the semantic role of 'patient' and thus bears the initial grammatical relation of object; sθ'ámʔ 'bone', on the other hand, is interpreted as having the semantic role of instrument (or some other oblique) and thus bears the initial grammatical relation of oblique. Under this analysis, (77) would be represented as:[9]

(81)

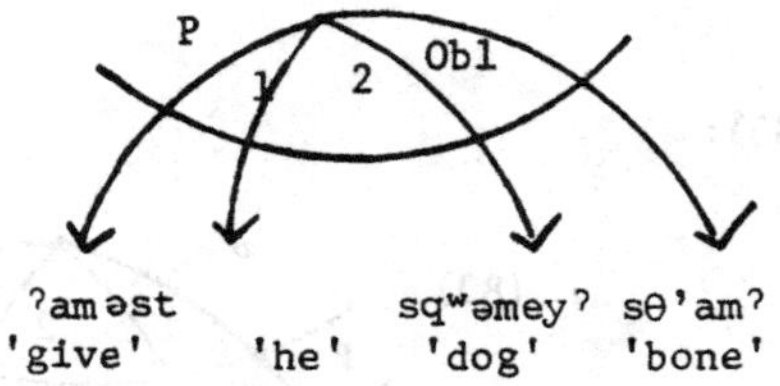

According to this analysis, a better gloss for (77) would be:

(82) 'He gifted/endowed the dog with the bone.'

Notice that under the no-advancement analysis, the structure of clauses like (77) can be represented in a single stratum: no advancement needs to be posited. Since both the no-advancement and the advancement analyses posit that sqʷəméyʔ 'dog' is the final object in (77), both equally well account for the behaviour of this nominal with respect to Nominal Case, Pronominal Case, etc. (cf. §3.1).

However, the no-advancement and advancement analyses differ in two important respects. First, the no-advancement analysis posits that nominals like sqʷəméyʔ 'dog' in (77) are initial objects while the advancement analysis posits that such nominals are initial indirect objects which advance to direct object. In §3.3.1 and 3.3.2 I present two arguments based on reflexives and control marking that such nominals are not initial objects. This evidence, then, favors the advancement analysis.

Second, the two analyses make different claims concerning the grammatical relations of nominals like sθ'ámʔ 'bone' in (77). Under the no-advancement analysis, such nominals are final obliques while under the advancement analysis, they are final 3s/2-chomeurs. In §3.3.3 I repeat the evidence involving extraction given in §3.2.2 that these nominals are not final obliques. Again, the evidence favors the advancement analysis.

3.3.1 Reflexives

The first argument that nominals like sqʷəméy̓ʔ 'dog' in (77) are not initial objects is based on the reflexive construction in Halkomelem. In §2.5.7, it was pointed out that clauses involving the coreference of the subject and the object are reflexives. In such clauses, only the subject is expressed: the reflexive marker, -θət, is suffixed to the verb, as seen in (83-84):

(83) ni cən ləx̌ʷ-əθət
aux 1sub blanket-self
'I covered myself with a blanket.'

(84) ni cən x̌íq'-əθət
aux 1sub scratch-self
'I scratched myself.'

However, when the subject is coreferent with the final object in 3-2 and Ben-2 advancement clauses, the reflexive construction is ungrammatical, as seen in (85-87):

(85) *ni cən ʔám-əs-θət
aux 1sub give-advA-self
(I gave it to myself.)

(86) *ni q'ʷə́l-əɬc-θət ʔə kʷθə səplíl
aux bake-advB-self obl det bread
(He baked the bread for himself.)

(87) *ni cən θə́y-əɬc-θət ʔə kʷθə snə́xʷəɬ
aux 1sub make-advB-self obl det canoe
(I made myself a canoe.)

Under the advancement analysis, the following condition on reflexives could be proposed to account for the difference between (83-84) and (85-87):

(88) In reflexives, the subject must be coreferential to the initial object.

In clauses like (83-84), the coreferent nominal is the 'patient' and therefore the initial object. Such clauses meet condition (88). In clauses like (85-86), the coreferent nominal is the 'recipient' or 'benefactive' and therefore the initial indirect object or Ben. Thus, 3-2 and Ben-2 advancement clauses do not meet condition (88) and reflexives are not possible.

Under a no-advancement analysis, a constraint like (88) is difficult to state; because all of the coreferent nominals in (83-87) are 'patients' according to this analysis, they are all initial objects. Therefore, any constraint making reference to initial object could not distinguish (83-84) from (85-87).

It could be suggested that coreference in clauses like (85-87) is semantically anomalous in Halkomelem, thus accounting for the ungrammaticality of these clauses. However, although coreference in clauses like (85-87) cannot be expressed via the reflexive, there is a second coreference construction in Halkomelem which can be used for such clauses; this construction is discussed in detail in §4.4.

Finally, it could be proposed that the verbs in clauses like (85-87) are somehow morphologically 'incompatible' with the reflexive suffix.[10] However, this is clearly not the case. In (89), (91), and (93) I have given examples of reflexives. In (90), (92), and (94) I have given examples of Ben-2 clauses with the same verbs:

(89) ni q'áy-θət
aux kill-self
'He killed himself.'

(90) ni q'ày-əɬc-θ-ám'ʔš-əs
aux kill-advB-tr-1obj-3erg
'He killed it for me.'

(91) ni cən θə́y-θət
aux 1sub fix-self
'I fixed myself up.'; 'I got well.'

(92) ni cən θə́y-əɬc-ət
aux 1sub fix-advB-tr
'I fixed it for him.'

(93) ni ɫə́x̌ʷ-əθət
aux blanket-self
'He covered himself with a blanket.'

(94) ni ɫə́x̌ʷ-əɬc-ət-əs
aux blanket-advB-tr-3erg
'He covered it with a blanket for him.'

Thus, a solution relying on the morphological 'incompatibility' of certain verb roots and the reflexive suffix is untenable.

Under the no-advancement analysis, then, no apparent account can be given of differences in clauses like (83-84) and (85-87). Under the advancement analysis, however, condition (88), limiting reflexives to clauses where the subject is co-referential with the initial object, accounts for this difference. Therefore, the advancement analysis is to be preferred.

3.3.2 Control Marking

The second argument that nominals like sqʷəméyʔ 'dog' in (77) are not initial objects is based on control marking in Halkomelem. In §1.4 and §2.3 above, it was pointed out that verbs in transitive clauses have transitive suffixes while verbs in intransitive clauses lack such suffixes. Also, I briefly discussed the semantic distinction between two transitive markers, -t, which is unmarked for control, and -nəxʷ, which marks limited control. This contrast can be seen in (95-96).

(95) a. ni q'ʷáqʷ-ət-əs ɬə sɬéniʔ ʔə kʷθə sq̓ə́məlʔ
aux club-tr-3erg det woman obl det paddle
'He clubbed the woman with the paddle. [on purpose]

b. ni q'ʷə́qʷ-nəxʷ-əs ɬə sɬéniʔ ʔə kʷθə sq̓ə́məlʔ
aux club-l.c.tr-3erg det woman obl det paddle
'He clubbed the woman with the paddle.' [accidentally]

(96) a. ni lém-ət-əs θə sɬéniʔ
aux see-tr-3erg det woman
'He looked at the woman.'

b. ni lə́m-nəxʷ-əs θə sɬéniʔ
aux see-l.c.tr-3erg det woman
'He saw the woman.'

However, in the case of 3-2 and Ben-2 advancement clauses, this contrast is not possible, as seen in (97-100):

(97) a. ni ʔám-əs-t-əs kʷθə sqʷəméyʔ ʔə kʷθə sθ'ámʔ
aux give-advA-tr-3erg det dog obl det bone
'He gave the dog the bone.'

b. *ni ʔám-əs-nəxʷ-əs kʷθə sqʷəméyʔ ʔə kʷθə sθ'ámʔ
aux give-advA-l.c.tr-3erg det dog obl det bone
(He managed to give the dog the bone.)

(98) a. ni yə́θ-əs-t-əs
aux tell-advA-tr-3erg
'He told her about it.'

b. *ni yə́θ-əs-nəxʷ-əs
aux tell-advA-l.c.tr-3erg
(He happened to tell her about it.)

(99) a. ni θə́y-əɬc-ət-əs kʷθə swə́yʔqeʔ ʔə kʷθə snə́xʷəɬ-s
aux fix-advB-tr-3erg det man obl det canoe-3pos
'He fixed the canoe for the man.'

b. *ni θə́y-əɬc-nəxʷ-əs kʷθə swə́yʔqeʔ ʔə kʷθə snə́xʷəɬ-s
aux fix-advB-l.c.tr-3erg det man obl det canoe-3pos
(He managed to fix the canoe for the man.)

(100) a. ni ʔíləq-əɬc-t-əs
aux buy-advB-tr-3erg
'He bought it for him.'

b. *ni ʔíləq-əɬc-nəxʷ-əs
aux buy-advB-l.c.tr-3erg
(He managed to buy it for him.)

Under the advancement analysis, the following condition can be placed on limited control marking to account for the difference between (95-97b) and (98-100b):

(101) Limited control marking is possible only if the final object is also the initial object of the clause.

Thus, in (95-97b), where the 'patient', i.e. the initial object, is the final object of the clause, limited control marking is possible. However, in (98-100b), the final object is a recipient or benefactive and therefore an initial indirect object or Ben; since condition (101) is not met, limited control marking is not possible.

In contrast, the no-advancement analysis can offer no obvious account for the difference between (95-97b) and (98-100). Under this analysis, the final objects in all the above examples are assumed to be 'patients' and therefore initial objects. Thus, a condition such as (101) is not statable under the no-advancement analysis.

Alternatively, it might be proposed that limited control marking is not possible in (98-100b) because the semantic concept of limited control is not compatible with the action expressed by the verbs in (98-100). However, although limited control cannot be marked by a transitive suffix in clauses like (98-100), the semantic concept of limited control can be expressed by periphrastic constructions, such as those in (102-103).

(102) ni x̌ə́l kʷθə John ʔu ʔíləq-əɬc-t-əs kʷθə ká.
aux hurt det lnk buy-advB-tr-3ssub det car
'John managed to buy him the car.'
literally: 'It hurt John when he bout him the car.'

(103) ʔi-əɬ tu ƛ̓ə́x̌ʷ k'ʷ s- ʔàm-əs-θ-ám̓ʔs-s kʷθə púkʷ
aux-pst just hard det nom-give-advV-tr-1obj-3pos det book
'He had a tough time giving me the book.'
literally: 'It was hard that he gave me the book.'

This proposal then is untenable.

Finally, it might be proposed that the verb roots in clauses like (98-100) are morphologically 'incompatible' with limited control marking. This is clearly not the case. In (104), (106) and (108), I have given examples of 3-2 and Ben-2 advancement clauses. In (105), (107), and (109) I have given examples of transitive clauses which are based on the same verb roots; the (b) examples are marked for limited control.

(104) a. ni kʷən-əɬc-θ-ámʔš-əs
aux take-advB-tr-1obj-3erg
'He got it for me.'

b. *ni kʷən-əɬc-n-ámʔš-əs
aux take-advB-l.c.tr-1obj-3erg
(He managed to get it for me.)

(105) a. ni kʷə́n-ət-əs
aux take-tr-3erg
'He took it.'

b. ni kʷə́n-nəxʷ-əs
aux take-l.c.tr-3erg
'He managed to take/catch/get.'

(106) a. ni lə́kʷ-ə́ɬc-t-əs tᶿə swíwʔləs ʔə kʷθə sc'ɛ̃́st
aux break-advB-tr-3erg det boy obl det stick
'She broke the stick for the boy.'

b. *ni ləkʷ-ə́ɬc-nəxʷ-əs tᶿə swíwʔləs ʔə kʷθə sc'ɛ̃́st
aux break-advB-l.c.tr-3erg det boy obl det stick
(She managed to break the stick for the boy.)

(107) a. ni ləkʷ-át-əs kʷθə sc'ɛ̃́st
aux break-tr-3erg det stick
'She broke the stick.'

b. ni lə́kʷ-nəxʷ-əs kʷθə sc'ɛ̃́st
aux break-l.c.tr-3erg det stick
'She managed to break the stick.'

(108) a. ni k'ʷə́ɬ-əɬc-t-əs ʔə kʷθə tí
aux pour-advB-tr-3erg obl det tea
'He poured her the tea.'

b. *ni k'ʷə́ɬ-əɬc-nəxʷ-əs ʔə kʷθə tí
aux pour-advB-l.c.tr-3erg obl det tea
(He managed to pour her the tea.'

(109) a. ni cən k'ʷɬé-t ní ʔə tᶿə ləṭém
aux 1sub pour-tr be obl det table
'I poured it on to the table.'

b. ni cən k'ʷəɬ-néxʷ ní ʔə tᶿə ləṭém
aux 1sub pour-l.c.tr be obl det table
'I spilled it on the table.'

Since (105b), (107b), and (109b) are possible, the proposal that clauses like (98-100b) are ungrammatical because of the 'incompatibility' of the limited control marking with certain verb roots is untenable.

The no-advancement analysis provides no apparent account of the difference between clauses like (95-97b) and (98-100b). In contrast, the advancement analysis, because it recognizes two levels of structure in 3-2 and Ben-2 advancement clauses, can differentiate final objects which are also objects at initial level and those which are not. By restricting limited control marking to the former type of object by means of condition (101), the advancement analysis can account for the difference between clauses like (95-96b) and (98-100b). Therefore, the advancement analysis is preferred over the no-advancement analysis.

3.3.3 Extraction

In this section, I briefly repeat the evidence involving the extraction of nominals like <u>sθ'ám?</u> 'bone' in (77). Under the no-advancement analysis, such nominals were assumed to be initial instruments (or obliques of some kind). Since there are no changes in grammatical relations, these nominals are also final obliques.

However, in §3.2 above, I presented an argument based on extraction that these nominals are not obliques. It was shown that while obliques were extracted through nominalization with the prefix <u>š-</u>, as seen in the example involving extraction of an instrument in (110), nominals like <u>sθ'ám?</u> 'bone' in (77) are extracted through nominalization with the prefix <u>s-</u> , as seen in (111).

(110) níɬ kʷθə ʔənʔ-šápəl-ʔəɬ ni nə-š-q'ʷáqʷ-ət
3emph det 2pos-shovel-pst aux 1pos-nom-club-tr
'It's your shovel that I clubbed it with.'

(111) níɬ kʷθə sθ'ám? ni s-ʔám-əs-t-s kʷθə sqʷəméy?
3emph det bone aux nom-give-advA-tr-3pos det dog
'It's a bone that he gave the dog.'

Thus, the no-advancement analysis, which posits that the extracted nominals in (110) and (111) are both obliques, has no apparent means of accounting for this difference.

In contrast, the difference between obliques and nominals like sθ'ám? 'bone' in (77) can be accounted for under the advancement analysis, which posits that the latter nominals are final 3s/2-chomeurs, as discussed in §3.2.3. In (112), I have stated the rule of the distribution of the nominalization prefixes.

(112) a. The extraction of final obliques is indicated by š-.
b. The extraction of final 3s/2-chômeurs is indicated by s-.

3.3.4 Conclusion

In this section, I have considered an alternative to an advancement analysis for clauses with 'recipients' and 'benefactives' in Halkomelem. Under this analysis, 'recipients' and 'benefactives' are initial objects; 'patients' in these clauses are initial obliques. Such an analysis need not posit advancement to account for the behaviour of 'recipients' and 'benefactives' as final objects.

However, there are three problems with the no-advancement analysis. First, it does not account for the fact that clauses with 'recipients' and 'benefactives' cannot be reflexive constructions. Second, it does not account for why such clauses cannot be marked for limited control. Finally, it predicts that 'patients' in such clauses should behave like obliques with respect to extraction, but this is not the case.

Thus, an alternative which avoids positing advancement for 3-2 and Ben-2 advancement clauses cannot be maintained.

3.4 Causal to Object Advancement

There is a third type of advancement--causal to object advancement. I am using causal to refer to the nominal that plays the semantic role of indirect clause.[11] This nominal differs from a <u>causer</u>, which is semantically, the direct cause. Causers are expressed by means of the causative construction which is discussed in §4.2.

Observe the following clauses, the causal is in the oblique case:

(113) ni cən c'ə́q' ʔə kʷθə scƛ̓ə́m-s
aux 1sub astonished obl det jump-3pos
'I was astonished at his jump.'

(114) ʔi cən sɬcíwʔs ʔə kʷθə ni ʔəɬ nə-syá.yʔs
aux 1sub tired obl det aux pst 1pos-work
'I am tired of working.'

(115) ni q'élʔ ʔə kʷθə š̌məθ'ənqínəm-s
aux believe obl det lie-3pos
'He believed his lies.'

In clauses like (113-115) the causal is expressed in the oblique case.

Several characteristics of clauses like (113-115) should be noted. First, there is no transitive marking suffixed to the verb. In fact, transitive marking is not possible in such clauses, as is seen in (116-117):

(116) *ni cən c'ə́q'-t ʔə kʷθə scƛ̓ə́m-s
aux 1sub astonished-tr obl det jump-3pos
(I was astonished at his jump.)

(117) *ni cən sɬcíwʔs-t ʔə kʷθə ni ʔəɬ nə-syá.yʔs
aux isub tired-tr obl det aux pst 1pos-work
(I am tired of working.)

As was discussed in §2.4, verbs in transitive clauses in Halkomelem are suffixed with a transitive marker while verbs in intransitive clauses lack such suffixes. Thus, clauses like (113-115) are intransitive clauses.

Furthermore, as was discussed in §2.5.2, in transitive clauses with 3rd person subjects, the verb is suffixed with the 3rd person agreement suffix -as. Note that this suffix is absent from (115). Furthermore, agreement is not possible:

(118) *ni q'élʔ-əs ʔə kʷθə šməθ'ənqínəm-s
aux believe-3erg obl det lie-3pos
(He believed his lies.)

Thus, 3rd person agreement provides a second argument that clauses like (113-115) are intransitive.

Finally, I should note that the causal in clauses like (113-115) bears an oblique relation. Evidence for this comes from the nominalizing prefix used in cases of extraction of causals. As stated in (112), the extraction of final obliques is indicated by the nominalizing prefix š-. As can be seen in (119-121), when the causal in clauses like (113-115) is extracted, the verb is prefixed with š-.

(119) scƛ'ə́m-s kʷθə ni nə-š-c'ə́q'
jump-3pos det aux 1pos-nom-astonished
'His jump is what astonished me.'

(120) stém k'ʷə ni nə-š-sɬcíwʔs
what det aux 1pos-nom-tired
'What am I tired from?'

(121) šməθ'ənqínəm-s kʷθə ni š-q'élʔ-s
lie-3pos det aux nom-believe-3pos
'His lies is what he believed.'

Thus, clauses like (113-115) are intransitive clauses with an oblique nominal. I assume that such clauses can be represented by stratal diagrams like that given in (122) for (113):[12]

(122)

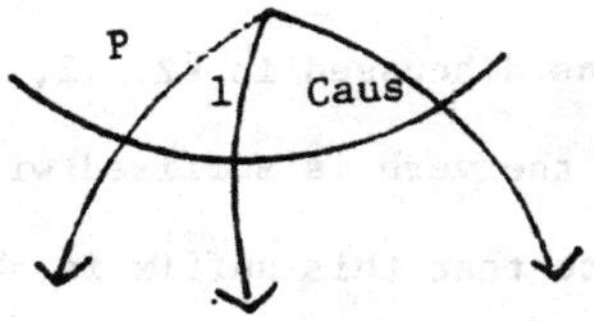

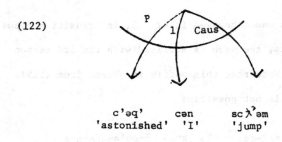

c'əq' cən scƛ̓əm
'astonished' 'I' 'jump'

Clauses like those in (113-115) contrast with clauses like the following:

(123) *ni* cən q'el?-mé?-t kʷθə ləplít
aux 1sub believe-advC-tr det priest
'I believed the priest.'

(124) ni cən wəɬ ɬcíws-mə-t tᶿə John
aux 1sub already tired-advC-tr det
'I'm already tired of John.'

(125) ni θ'ey?k'ʷ-mé?-t-əs kʷθə sqʷəméy?
aux startled-advC-tr-3erg det dog
'He was startled at the dog.'

In (123-125), the causal is <u>not</u> expressed in the oblique case. Furthermore, transitive marking is suffixed to the verbs, indicating that (123-125) are transitive clauses. Also, in (125), there is 3rd person agreement indicating that the 3rd person subject in (125) is the subject of a transitive clause. Finally, following the verb is the suffix <u>mé?-</u>, this suffix, which will be discussed in §3.8, was lacking in examples like (113-115).

To account for the semantic similarity between clauses like (113-115) and those like (123-125), I posit that both have the same initial stratum. I assume that the nominal playing the role of indirect cause is a causal (an oblique relation) at initial level. To account fot the differences between these types of clauses, I posit that in (123-125) the causal advances to object via causal to object advancement (Caus-2). Thus, clauses like (113-115), which do not involve Caus-2 advancement, are represented by stratal diagrams in (122) above, while clauses like (123-124) are represented by diagrams like the following for (123):

(126)

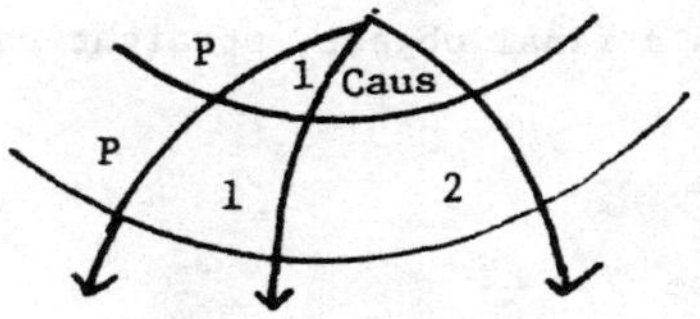

In this section, I give arguments based on nominal case, pronominal case, extraction, and quantifier extraction that the initial causal is advanced to object in clauses like (123-125), which I will refer to as Caus-2 advancement clauses.

3.4.1 Nominal Case

The first argument for Caus-2 advancement is based on Nominal Case (cf. §3.2.3):

(127) a. Final (nuclear) terms are in the straight case.
b. Other nominals are in the oblique case.

Since objects are nuclear terms, final objects are in the straight case. As seen in (123-125) above, the causal in these clauses is in the straight case. Furthermore, these nominals cannot be expressed in the oblique case, as is seen in (128-129):

(128) *ni cən q'elˀ-méˀ-t ˀə kʷθə ləplít
aux 1sub believe-advC-tr obl det priest
(I believed the priest.)

(129) *ni θ'əyˀk'ʷ-méˀ-t-əs ˀə kʷθə sqʷəméyˀ
aux startled-advC-tr-3erg obl det dog
(He was started at the dog.)

Straight case marking of the causals in clauses like (123-125) follows from an analysis positing Caus-2 advancement for these clauses. Since the initial causal is a final object, straight case is accounted for by (127a).

3.4.2 Pronominal Case

A second argument for Caus-2 advancement is based on Pronominal Case (discussed in §2.4.1 and 3.1.2):

(130) a. Final subjects are in the subjective case.
b. Final objects are in the objective case.
c. Final obliques are in the oblique case.

If the causal in clauses like (123-125) is the final object, then it should be in the objective case when it is a pronominal. This prediction is borne out, as is seen in (131-132):

(131) ni cən wəɬ ɬcìws-mə-θ-ámə
aux 1sub already tired-advC-tr-2obj
'I am already tired of you.'

(132) ni ˀə č q'èlˀ-meˀ-θ-ámˀš
aux int 2sub believe-advC-tr-1obj
'Did you believe me?'

Furthermore, the causal in such clauses cannot be expressed in the oblique case, as is seen in (133):

(133) *ni cən wəɬ ɬcíws-mə-t ʔə-ƛ̓ nə́wə
aux 1sub already tired-advC-tr obl-det 2emph
(I'm already tired of you.)

That the causal is in the objective case is accounted for in the analysis proposed here; the causal is a final object via Caus-2 advancement.

3.4.3 Extraction

Data involving extraction give a third argument for Caus-2 advancement. As discussed in §3.2.3, the rule for extraction is as follows:

(134) a. Final (nuclear) terms are directly extracted.
b. Other nominals are extracted through nominalization.

In (135-136) the causal in clauses like (123-125) is extracted; in each case the causal is directly extracted.

(135) níɬ t^{θ}ə John ni ɬcìws-meʔ-t-ʔé.nʔ
3emph det aux tired-advC-tr-1ssub
'It's John that I'm tired of.'

(136) níɬ kʷθə ləplít ni q'èlʔ-meʔ-t-ʔé.nʔ
3emph det priest aux believe-advC-tr-1ssub
'It's the priest who I believed.'

That causals can be directly extracted follows from an analysis positing Caus-2 advancement for such clauses. Since the causal is the final object, it can be directly extracted.

3.4.4 Quantifier Extraction

A final argument for Caus-2 advancement is based on the condition on quantifier extraction given in (43), which states that the quantifier <u>mə́k'ʷ</u> can only be extracted from final absolutives. If the causal in clauses like (123-125) is the final object, then it is the final absolutive, and an analysis involving Caus-2 advancement predicts that the quantifier can extract. This is the case, as is seen in (137-138):

(137) ni mə́k'ʷ ʔu ɬcíws-mə-t-əs tᶿə sɬənɬéniʔ
aux all lnk tired-advC-tr-3ssub det women
'He's tired of all the women.'

(138) ni mə́k'ʷ ʔu q'elʔ-méʔ-t-ət kʷθə xʷələnítəm
aux all lnk believe-advC-tr-lplssub det white men
'We believed all the white men.'

That the quantifier is extracted from the causal in such clauses follows from an analysis positing Caus-2 advancement for these clauses.

3.5 An Alternative to an Advancement Analysis

In the preceding section, I have shown that nominals playing the semantic role of indirect cause can be expressed in two types of constructions. First, the nominal can be an oblique and second an object. To account for the semantic similarities of these constructions, I have posited that the nominal is an initial causal in both constructions. In the second, the causal advances to object. I have given evidence from Nominal Case, Pronominal Case, extraction, and quantifier extraction that the causal is indeed the final object in such clauses.

However, an alternative analysis which also captures the semantic similiarities of the two constructions could be posited. Under such an analysis, nominals with the role of indirect cause would be assigned the initial grammatical relation of object, as represented in (139):

(139)

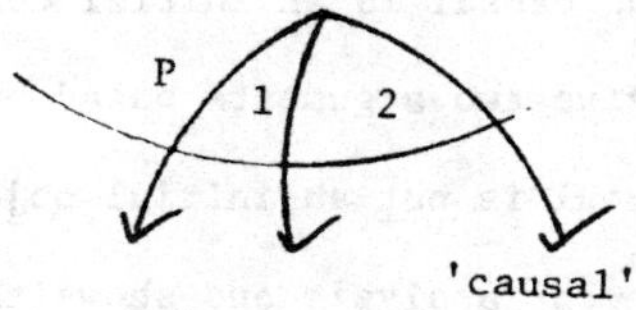

This analysis would account for the object properties of causals in clauses like (123-125) without needing to posit advancement for these clauses. Thus, the stratal diagram in (139) would represent that of clauses like (123-125) under this analysis.

However, such an analysis would require an explanation for clauses like (113-115); as we have seen above, these clauses are intransitive and the causal is a final oblique. To handle such clauses, this analysis could posit that the causal is an initial object which retreats to oblique, as represented in the stratal diagram in (140):[13]

(140)

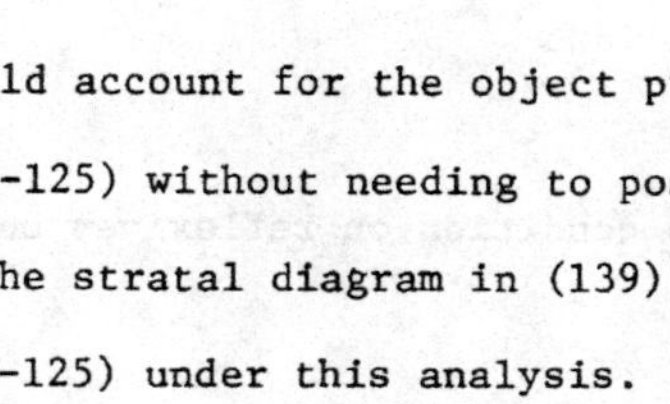

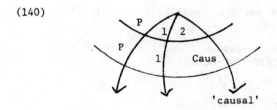

This analysis, while capturing the semantic similarities of clauses like (113-115) and (123-125), could also account for the behaviour of some causals as obliques; that is, some causals are final obliques via object to causal retreat.

The basic difference, then, between such an analysis, which I will call a retreat analysis, and one involving advancement, as posited in the previous section, is the initial grammatical relation of the causal. In the retreat analysis, the causal is an initial object; under the advancement analysis, the causal is an initial oblique.

In this section, I give two arguments based on reflexives and control marking that the causal is not an initial object. This evidence supports an advancement analysis and shows that a retreat analysis cannot be maintained.

3.5.1 Reflexives

In §3.3.1, I gave a condition on reflexives on Halkomelem as follows:

> (141) In reflexives, the subject must be coreferential to the initial object.

This condition accounted for the fact that reflexives were possible in clauses where an object was the initial object, but not possible in clauses where the object was initial indirect object or Ben.

In the case of clauses in which the causal is the final object, cf. (123-125), reflexives are not possible, as seen in (142-144):

(142) *ni cən ɬcíws-mə-θət
aux 1sub tired-advC-self
(I'm tired of myself.)

(143) *ni cən c'əq'-mí?-θət
aux 1sub astonished-advC-self
(I am astonished at myself.)

(144) *ni cən q'el-mé?-θət
aux 1sub believe-advC-self
(I believe myself.)

Under an advancement analysis, the ungrammaticality of (142-144) follows from condition (141); since the causal in these clauses is an initial causal which advances to object, condition (141) is not met.

Under the retreat analysis, however, there is no apparent account of the ungrammaticality of (142-143). Under this analysis, the causal in clauses like (142-144) is the initial as well as final object, as seen in the stratal diagram in (139). Thus, the retreat analysis predicts that condition (141) should be met.

3.5.2 Control Marking

In §3.3.2, I formulated a condition on limited control marking as follows:

(145) Limited control marking is possible only if the final object is also the initial object of the clause.

This condition accounts for the fact that 3-2 and Ben-2 advancement clauses can not be marked for limited control.

In clauses like (123-125), in which the causal is the final object, limited control marking is not possible, as seen in (146-148):

(146) *ni cən q'elˀ-méˀ-nəxʷ kʷθə ləplít
aux 1sub believe-advC-l.c.tr det priest
(I happened to believe the priest.)

(147) *ni θ'əyˀk'ʷ-méˀ-nəxʷ kʷθə sqʷəméyˀ
aux startled-advC-l.c.tr det dog
(I was accidentally startled at the dog.)

(148) *ni cən wəɬ ɬcíws-mə-nəxʷ tᶿə John
aux 1sub already tired-advC-l.c.tr det
(I already happen to be tired of John.)

The ungrammaticality of (146-148) follows from an advancement analysis. Although the causals in (146-148) are final objects, they are not initial objects, but rather initial causals. Therefore, condition (145) is not met and limited control marking is not possible.

In contrast, the retreat analysis predicts that limited control marking should be possible in clauses like (146-148). Under the retreat analysis, the causal is both the initial and final object, as seen in the stratal diagram in (139). Thus, condition (145) is met and limited control marking should be possible.

3.5.3 Conclusion

In §3.4 and 3.5, I have proposed an analysis involving Caus-2 advancement for clauses like (149-150):

(149) ni cən wəɬ ɬcíws-mə-t $t^{\theta}ə$ John
aux 1sub already tired-advC-tr det
'I am already tired of John.'

(150) ni cən q'əl?-mé?-t kʷθə ləplít
aux 1sub believe-advC-tr det priest
'I believed the priest.'

I have given evidence based on Nominal Case, Pronominal Case, extraction, and quantifier extraction that the nominal with the semantic role of indirect cause, i.e. the causal, is the final object.

Also, I have contrasted an analysis involving Caus-2 advancement, which posits that the causal is an initial causal (an oblique relation with one involving 2-Caus retreat, which posits that the causal is an initial object. I have argued that the advancement analysis is preferred, because the causal does not behave like an initial object with respect to constructions with reflexives and limited control marking. In §3.7, I discuss constraints on Caus-2 advancement. In §3.8, I discuss the morphology associated with Caus-2 advancement.

3.6 Directional to Object Advancement

In the preceding sections, I have discussed three types of advancements in Halkomelem: 3-2, Ben-2, and Caus-2 advancement. In this section, I briefly give evidence for a fourth type of advancement —directional to object advancement (Dir-2).

In the clauses with directionals discussed in Chapter 2, the directional was in the oblique case, as exemplified in (151-153):

(151) ni cám kʷθə níkʷ ʔə kʷθə smént
aux go up det uncle obl det mountain
'Uncle went up into the mountains.'

(152) ni ném? ɬə sɬéni? ʔə kʷθə stáʔluʔ
aux go det woman obl det river
'The woman went to the river.'

(153) ʔi yə-ʔewəʔ tθə John ʔə tθə nə-lélǝmʔ
aux ser-come det obl det 1pos-house
'John is coming to my house.'

Such directionals share a characteristic with other obliques; extraction of directionals is indicated by the nominalizer š-, as seen in (154-155):

(154) níɬ kʷθə stáʔluʔ ni š-némʔ-s ɬə sɬéniʔ
3emph det river aux nom-go-3pos det woman
'The river is where the woman went.'

(155) smént kʷθə ni nə-š-némʔ
mountain det aux 1pos-nom-go
'A mountain is where I went.'

The clauses in (151-153) are intransitive. This is evidenced by the lack of a transitive suffix on the verb. Also, although there are 3rd person subjects, there is no 3rd person agreement. Thus, the 3rd person subject is not the subject of a transitive clause. I am assuming for clauses like (151) the structure represented by the stratal diagram in (156); the directional is an initial and final oblique:

(156)

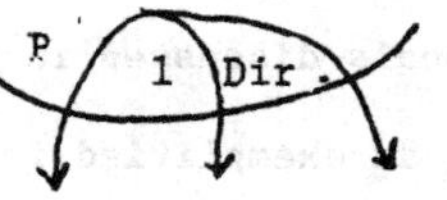

cam nikʷ sment
'go up' 'uncle' 'mountain'

There is a second way to express directionals in Halkomelem. For a limited class of verbs, clauses like the following are possible:

(157) ʔi č yə-ʔéʔwə-n-əs ɬə Mary
aux 2sub ser-come-advD-tr det
'You are coming toward/after Mary.'

(158) ni nəʔém-n-əs-əs kʷθə John
aux go-advD-tr-3erg det
'He went up to John.' /'He went to get John.'

(159) ʔi ʔəmí.-n- s-əs ɬə nə-stáʔləs
aux come-advD-tr-3erg det 1pos-spouse
'He came up to my wife.' / 'He came for my wife.'

In these clauses, the suffix -n, which I refer to as advancement marker D, is suffixed to the verb.

At first glance, these clauses appear to be intransitive because they lack the transitive suffix -t. However, in (158-159), where the subject is 3rd person, there is 3rd person agreement indicating that the 3rd person subject is the subject of a transitive clause. Thus, clauses like (158-159) are transitive. The problem of transitive marking in these clauses will be discussed briefly in §3.8.

I propose that clauses like (157-159) should be analyzed as involving directional to object advancement, as represented in the stratal diagram for (157) in (160):

(160)

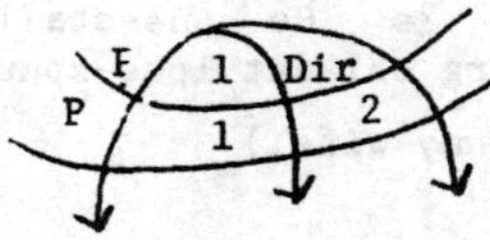

ʔeʔwə 'come'   č 'you'   Mary

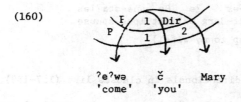

Under this analysis, the directional is an initial oblique which advances to final object of the clause. Since there is a final object, the clause is finally transitive, thus accounting for 3rd person agreement in (158-159).

In this section, I give evidence based on Nominal Case, Pronominal Case, and extraction that the directional in clauses like (157-159) is the final object.

3.6.1 Nominal Case

The first argument for Dir-2 advancement is based on Nominal Case (as discussed in §3.2.3):

(161) a. Final (nuclear) terms are in the straight case.
b. Other nominals are in the oblique case.

Directionals which are final obliques, as in (151-153) are in the oblique case. However, directionals which are final objects via Dir-2 advancement are final (nuclear) terms and, therefore, should be in the straight case. We have seen that this is the case in the clauses in (157-159). Furthermore, the directionals in these clauses cannot be expressed in the oblique case, as seen in (162-163):

(162) *ʔi č yə-éʔwə-n-əs ʔə-ƛ̓ Mary
aux 2sub ser-come-advD-tr obl-det
(You are coming toward/after Mary.)

(163) *ˀi ˀəmí.-n-əs-əs ˀə θə nə-stáˀləs
aux come-advD-tr-3erg obl det 1pos-spouse
(He was coming up to my wife.)

Straight case marking of the directionals in clauses like (157-159) follows from an analysis positing Loc-2 advancement for these clauses. Because the directional is the final object, straight case marking is accounted for by (161).

3.6.2 Pronominal Case

A second argument for Dir-2 advancement is based on Pronominal Case. We have seen above (cf. §2.5.1 and 3.1.2), that when the final object is pronominal, it is in the objective case. Thus, if the directional in clauses like (157-159) is the final object, it should be in the objective case when it is a pronominal. In (164-166), we see that this prediction is correct.

(164) ˀi yə-ˀèˀwə-n-əs-ámˀš-əs
aux ser-come-advD-tr-1obj-3erg
'He is coming toward/after me.'

(165) ni cən nəˀèmˀ-n-əs-ámə
aux 1sub go-advD-tr-2obj
'I went up to you :'/ 'I went for you.'

(166) ˀi ˀəmì.-n-əs-ámˀš-əs ɬə sɬéniˀ
aux come-advD-tr-1obj-3erg det woman
'The woman came up to me.' /'The woman came for me.'

Furthermore, other cases, e.g. oblique case, cannot be used for these pronominals.

(167) *ˀi ˀəmí.-n-əs-əs ˀə-ƛ̓ ˀé.nˀθə
aux come-advD-tr-3erg obl-det 1emph
(She came up to me.)

That the directional is in the objective case is accounted for under a Dir-2 advancement analysis; the directional is in the objective case because it is the final object.

3.6.3 Extraction

A final argument for Dir-2 advancement is based on extraction of the directional in clauses like (157-159). As discussed in §3.2.3, the rule for extraction is as follows:

(168) a. Final (nuclear) terms are directly extracted.
b. Other nominals are extracted through nominalization.

We have seen that directionals which are final obliques are extracted through nominalization, as seen in (154-155). In contrast, directionals in clauses like (157-159) are directly extracted, as seen in (169-170):

(169) níɬ ɬə Mary ʔi yə-ʔéʔwə-n-əs-əxʷ
3 emph det aux ser-come-advD-tr-2ssub
'It's Mary you are coming toward/ for.'

(170) níɬ kʷθə John ni nəʔə́m-n-əs-əs
3emph det aux go-advD-tr-3ssub
'It's John that he went up to/ for.'

That these directionals are directly extracted follows from an analysis positing Dir-2 advancement for these clauses. The directional is directly extracted because it is the final object of the clause.

3.6.4 Conclusion

In this section, I have posited an analysis involving Dir-2 advancement for clauses like the following:

(171) ni nə'ə́m-n-əs-əs kʷθə John
aux go-advD-tr-3erg det
'He went up to John.'

I have shown that the directional in such clauses behaves like a final object with respect to Nominal Case, Pronominal Case, and extraction. In the following section, I discuss a constraint on Dir-2 advancement in Halkomelem.

3.7 Conditions on Advancements

In the previous sections, I have given evidence for four types of advancement to object in Halkomelem: 3-2, Ben-2, Caus-2, and Dir-2 advancement. In this section, I contrast clauses with and without advancement and state a condition on advancement.

In the discussion of Caus-2 advancement in §3.4 above, I pointed out that causals could be expressed in two ways: first, in cases like (113-115), as a final oblique in an intransitive clause, as represented in the stratal diagram in (122), and second, in cases like (123-125), which involve causal as a final object in a finally transitive clause, as represented in the stratal diagram in (126). I maintain here that the distribution of these two clause types is regular and predictable.

Observe (172-174); the (b) examples are Caus-2 advancement clauses:

(172) a. ni cən c'ə́q' ʔə kʷθə sx̌t'ék'ʷ-s
aux 1sub astonished obl det carving-3pos
'I was astonished at his carving.'

b. ?*ni cən c'əq'-méʔ-t kʷθə sx̌t'ék'ʷ-s
aux 1sub astonished-advC-tr det carving-3pos
(I was astonished at his carving.)

(173) a. ni cən q'él? ?ə kʷθə sqʷáqʷəl?-s kʷθə ləplít
aux 1sub believe obl det words-3pos det priest

'I believed the words of the priest.'

b. ??ni cən q'el?-mé?-t kʷθə sqʷáqʷəl?-s kʷθə ləplít
aux 1sub believe-advC-tr det words-3pos det priest

'I believed the words of the priest.'

(174) a. ni cən sí?si? ?ə kʷθə tíntin
aux 1sub frighened obl det bell

'I was frightened at the bell/telephone.'

b. ?*ni cən sì?si?-mé?-t kʷθə tíntin
aux 1sub frightened-advC-tr det bell

(I was frightened at the bell/telephone.)

In the above examples, the (a) clauses, in which the causal is an oblique, are preferred. The (b) clauses, which involve Caus-2 advancement, are questionable.

In (175-177), the opposite pattern can be seen:

(175) a. ??ni cən c'ə́q' ?ə kʷθə sqʷəméy?
aux 1sub astonished obl det dog

'I was astonished at the dog.'

b. ni cən c'əq'-mí?-t kʷθə sqʷəméy? (MS)
aux 1sub astonished-advC-tr det dog

'I was astonished at the dog.'

(176) a. ??ni cən q'él? ?ə kʷθə ləplít
aux 1sub believe obl det priest

'I believed the priest.'

b. ni cən q'el?-mé?-t kʷθə ləplít
aux 1sub believe-advC-tr det priest

'I believed the priest.'

(177) a. ?? ni cən sí?si? ?ə kʷθə spəpəlqʷíθ'e?
aux 1sub frightened obl det screech owl

'I was frightened of the screech owl.'

b. ni cən sí?si?-me?-t kʷθə spəpəlqʷíθ'e?
aux 1sub frighten-advC-tr det screech owl

'I was frightened of the screech owl.'

In these examples, the Caus-2 advancement clauses are preferred over the clauses without advancement.

Note that the preference for clauses without advancement in (172-174) and with advancement in (175-177) is not a lexical property of the verb root; the same verb root can occur in each type of clause (cf. (172) vs. (175), etc.).

It appears that the difference between the two clause types lies in the animacy of the causal. In (172-174) the causal is inanimate and the clause without advancement is preferred; in contrast, in (175-177) the causal is animate and the clause with advancement is preferred. This distribution is captured by the following conditions on advancement:

(178) Causals which are animate advance to object.

(179) Causals which are inanimate do not advance to object.

In the case of clauses with directionals, a similar pattern is seen. As discussed in §3.6, directionals are either final obliques, e.g. (151-153), as represented in the stratal diagrams in (156) and (157), or final objects in Dir-2 clauses e.g. (157-159), as represented in (160). Observe the following; the (b) examples are Dir-2 advancement clauses:

(180) a. ʔi ʔéʔwə ʔə tθə nə-léləmʔ ɬə sɬéniʔ
aux come obl det 1pos-house det woman
'The woman comes to my house.'

b. *ʔi ʔéʔwə-n-əs-əs ɬə sɬéniʔ tθə nə-léləmʔ
aux come-advD-tr-3erg det woman det 1pos-house
(The woman comes to my house.)

(181) a. ni ném? ?ə kʷθə stá?lu?
aux go obl det river
'He went to the river.'

b. *ni nə?ám?-n-əs-əs kʷθə stá?lu?
aux go-advC-tr-3erg det river
(He went to the river.)

(182) a. ?i ?é?wə ?ə-ƛ̓ ?é.n?θə ɬə sɬéni?
aux come obl-det lemph det woman
'The woman comes to me.'

b. ?i ?e?wə-n-əs-ám?š-əs ɬə sɬéni?
aux come-advD-tr-1obj-3erg det woman
'The woman comes to me.'

(183) a. ni nem? ?ə-ƛ̓ John
aux go obl-det
'He went up to John.'

b. ni nə?ə́m?-n-əs-əs kʷθə John
aux go-advD-tr-3erg det
'He went up to John.'

In (180-181), the directional is inanimate; in these cases only clauses without advancement are possible. In (192-183), however, the directional is animate; in these cases clauses with or without advancement are possible. Either of the following conditions accounts for the distribution of Dir-2 advancement clauses in Halkomelem:

(184) Only directionals which are animate advance to object.

(185) Directionals which are inanimate do not advance to object.

As can be seen from the conditions on Caus-2 and Dir-2 advancement, obliques which are animate advance to object while obliques which are inanimate can not.

There is a similar condition on 3-2 and Ben-2 advancement clauses, discussed in §3.1. First note that unlike Caus-2 and Dir-2 clauses, 3-2 and Ben-2 clauses do not appear to have counterparts without advancement. That is, there are apparently no final indirect objects or final benefactives in Halkomelem. Thus, for 3-2 and Ben-2 advancement clauses like (186-187b), there are no clauses without advancement, as seen in (186-187a):

(186) a. *ni ʔám(-əs)-t-əs (ʔə) kʷθə sθʼám̓ ʔə kʷθə sqʷəméy̓
aux give-advA-tr-3erg obl det bone obl det dog
(He gave the bone to the dog.)

b. ni ʔám-əs-t-əs kʷθə sqʷəméy̓ ʔə kʷθə sθʼám̓
aux give-advA-tr-3erg det dog obl det bone
'He gave the dog the bone.'

(187) a. *ni qʼʷə́l(-əɬc)-t-əs (ʔə) kʷθə səplíl ʔə ɬə sɬéniʔ
aux bake-advB-tr-3erg obl det bread obl det woman
(He baked the bread for the woman.)

b. ni qʼʷə́l-əɬc-t-əs ɬə sɬéniʔ ʔə kʷθə səplíl
aux bake-advB-tr-3erg det woman obl det bread
'He baked the bread for the woman.'

The (a) sentences are ungrammatical regardless of the case of the 'patient' and regardless of the word order. Thus, it appears that 3-2 and Ben-2 advancement is obligatory in Halkomelem.

There is a second difference between 3-2 and Ben-2 advancement clauses and Caus-2 and Loc-2 clauses. I have not been able to elicit clauses in which the 'recipient' or the 'benefactive' is an inanimate. Perhaps this in part explains the obligatoriness of 3-2 and Ben-2 advancement. Since the tendency in Halkomelem is for animates to advance to object, and since initial direct objects and initial benefactives seem to always be animate, they will tend to advance to object.

The correlation of animacy and advancement is seen more clearly if we consider each type of advancement. As we have seen, indirect objects and benefactives seem always to be animate in Halkomelem and advancement of these nominals is obligatory. In contrast, directionals are most typically places, i.e. inanimate, rather than persons. We have seen in the case of directionals that animates can but need not advance. Finally, intermediate between these extremes are causals, which can be either animate or inanimate; apparently, these are equally prevalent. In the case of causals, Caus-2 advancement is preferred when the causal is animate.

As was pointed out in §2.1 instruments as obliques, are in the oblique case. I have not been able to elicit instances of instruments which are final direct objects; there appears to be no instrument to object advancement in Halkomelem. Furthermore, I have been unable to elicit examples where an instrument is an animate nominal.

I summarize this information in the chart in (188):

(188) Advancements to Object

initial relation	3/Ben	Caus	Dir	Instr
animate:	yes	yes	(yes)	xxx
inanimate:	xxx	no	no	no

A generalization can be made concerning these data, as stated in the following condition:

(189) Inanimate nominals cannot advance to object.

3.8 Verbal Morphology and Advancements

In the previous sections, I have discussed four types of advancement to object. In each example involving these constructions, there was a verbal suffix, which I refer to as advancement markers A, B, C, and D. (cf. §1.4.2) In this section, I briefly discuss the distribution of these four suffixes.

The most obvious account of their distribution, based on the examples given so far, is to associate the advancement markers with advancement constructions on the basis of the initial grammatical relation of the nominal which advances to object as follows:

(190)	Type of advancement	Advancement marker
	3-2	A
	Ben-2	B
	Caus-2	C
	Dir-2	D

I have found only two cases which do not fit this pattern. First, the initial grammatical relation is either indirect object or benefactive in (191), yet only advancement marker B is possible.

(191) ni x̌ə́lˀ-əɬc- t-əs kʷθə-enˀ mén ˀə kʷθə pípə-s
aux write-advB-tr-3erg det-2pos father obl det letter-3pos
'He wrote the letter <u>for</u> your father.'
/'He wrote the letter <u>to</u> your father.'

Second, the examples given above with advancement marker C <u>-méˀ</u> have all involved the advancement of a causal to object. In the following example, however, this is not the case; (192) is a Ben-2 advancement construction:

(192) ni kʷùkʷ-meˀ-θ-ámˀš̌-əs
aux cook-advC-tr-1obj-3erg
'He cooked for me.'

Therefore, while the distribution given in (190) is generally accurate, there are a few examples which do not fit this pattern. Certainly, this is a problem that deserves further research.

FOOTNOTES TO CHAPTER 3

[1]More precisely, advancements are defined in terms of neighboring strata and not in terms of final level; i.e. a nominal heading a 3-arc or an arc with an oblique R-ṡign in the c_i stratum heads a 2-arc in the c_{i+1} stratum.
In this chapter, the nominals advancing to object are always final objects, but, in Chapter 5, I give examples where this is not the case.

[2]Studies on various languages have included analyses involving 3-2 and Ben-2 advancements. Of note are Chung (1976a) and Aissen (to appear a).

[3]Many other cases of obligatory 3-2 and Ben-2 advancement have been noted. For a discussion of the most adequate statement to account for this, see Aissen (to appear a).

[4]Note that the analysis represented in (44) violates a law of RG--the Stratal Uniqueness Law. (Perlmutter and Postal (1977) to appear c). This law states, informally, that two different nominals cannot bear the same relation in the same stratum. In (43), since there are two objects in the final stratum, stratal uniqueness is violated. There have been cases cited which purport to violate this law, for example Seiter (1979).

[5]The analyses represented in (54) and (55) violate the Oblique Law, which, informally stated, specifies that any nominal bearing an oblique relation must do so in the initial stratum. (Perlmutter and Postal to appear c). Since the oblique in (54) or (55) is not an initial oblique, the oblique law is violated.

[6]I discuss another case of extraction through nominalization with the prefix <u>s</u>- in Chapter 4.

[7]Both of these analysis have been documented for other languages. For examples Chung (1976a) and Aissen (to appear a) posit analyses like (66) for Indonesian and Tzotzil and Perlmutter and Postal (to appear c) posit an analysis involving advancement to object with object retreat (as in (72)) for Kinyarwanda. The retreat analysis violates a law proposed earlier in RG but subsequently abandoned--the Chomeur Law. (cf. Perlmutter and Postal to appear c)

[8]See footnote 7.

[9]This analysis is frequently implied in studies on Salish languages. For example, see Leslie (1979) and Carlson (1980).

10 By morphologically incompatible I mean that there is a class of verb roots which are lexically marked for not having reflexive suffixes. This is a version of the approach taken by Leslie (1979) and Galloway (1977); they list the suffixes which can co-occur without trying to state general principles.

11 The term 'causal' as used here originates with the work of Eduardo Raposo on Portuguese causatives.

12 I point out in Chapter 5 that some clauses with causals are initially unaccusative, but, as this is irrelevant here, I represent all clauses with causals as in (122).

13 This violates the oblique law. (cf. f.n. 5). Postal (p.c.) has suggested an analysis involving antipassive for these clauses. (cf. Chapter 4). However, the causal does not behave like a 3/2 chomeur but rather like an oblique with respect to extraction.

Chapter 4

OBJECT RESIGNATIONS

4.0 Introduction

In the preceding chapter, I discussed constructions in Halkomelem which involve advancements to object. In this chapter, I discuss constructions in which an object at one level is neither the subject nor object at a subsequent level; these constructions I refer to as <u>object resignations</u>, which I define in (1):

(1) An object resignation contains the following sub-network:

(a) a nominal heading a 2-arc in the c_i stratum heads an X-arc in the c_{i+1} stratum, where $x \neq 1,2$.

and (b) no nominal heads a 2-arc in the c_{i+1} stratum.

I have represented object resignations in (2):

(2)

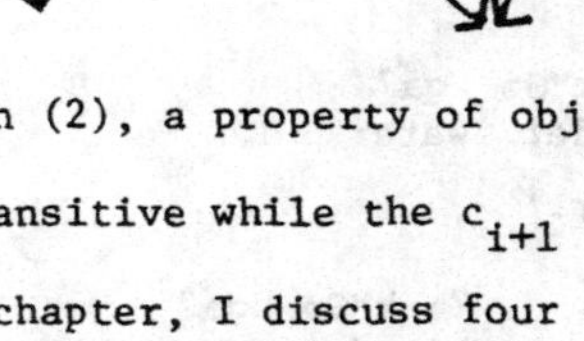

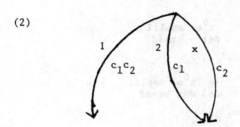

As can be seen in (2), a property of object resignations is that the c_i stratum is transitive while the c_{i+1} stratum is intransitive.

In this chapter, I discuss four object resignation constructions: antipassives, reflexives, reciprocals, and object cancellations. First, I give evidence based on Possessor extraction and quantifier extraction for the final intransitivity of antipassives and discuss causatives with respect to antipassives. Then, I argue that the final strata of reflexives, reciprocals, and object cancellations are intransitive. Finally, I discuss the final intransitivity of object resignations with respect to proposals made by Postal (1977) and Aissen (to appear b).

4.1 Antipassives

In Chapter 2, clauses involving an 'agent' and a 'patient' were discussed. Such clauses, as exemplified in (3-6a) below, were assumed to be both initially and finally transitive, as represented in the stratal diagram for (3a) given in (7). In this section, I discuss a second construction used to express the action of an 'agent' on a 'patient'. This construction, referred to as antipassive, is exemplified in (3-6b).[1]

(3) a. ni cən q'ʷə́l-ət tᶿə səplíl
aux 1sub bake-tr det bread
'I baked the bread.'

b. ni cən q'ʷə́l-əm ʔə tᶿə səplíl
aux 1sub bake-intr obl det bread
'I baked the bread.'

(4) a. ni cən k'ʷɬé-t kʷθə qáʔ
aux 1sub pour-tr det water
'I poured the water.'

b. ni cən k'ʷɬé-ls ʔə kʷθə qáʔ
aux 1sub pour-act obl det water
'I poured the water.'

(5) a. ni pə́n-ət-əs kʷθə swə́yʔqeʔ kʷθə sqéwθ
aux plant-tr-3erg det man det potato
'The man planted/buried potatoes.'

b. ni pə́n?-əm kʷθə swə́y?qe? ?ə kʷθə sqə́wθ
aux plant-intr det man obl det potato
'The man planted the potatoes.'

(6) a. ni qá?qa?-t-əs ɬə sɬéni? kʷθə qá?
aux drink-tr-3erg det woman det water
'The woman drank the water.'

b. ni qá?qa? ɬə sɬéni? ?ə kʷθə qá?
aux drink det woman obl det water
'The woman drank the water.'

(7)

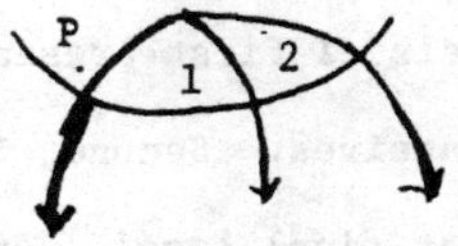

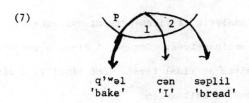

q'ʷəl cən səplil
'bake' 'I' 'bread'

If we maintain the assumption that semantic roles are encoded at the initial level of syntax, (cf. §0.3.1), we could posit the same initial stratum for the (a) and (b) clauses above. Specifically, the 'agent' is initial subject and the 'patient' is initial object as represented in the stratal diagram in (7).

I argue here that although the (a) and (b) clauses share the same initial stratum, the final strata of these clauses differ. In the (a) clauses, there is only one level, as represented in (7); these clauses are initially and finally transitive. In the (b) clauses, however, the initial object is not the final object but rather, I argue, a 3/2-chomeur at final level (cf. §3.2); this analysis is represented in the stratal diagram for (3b) given in (8):

(8')

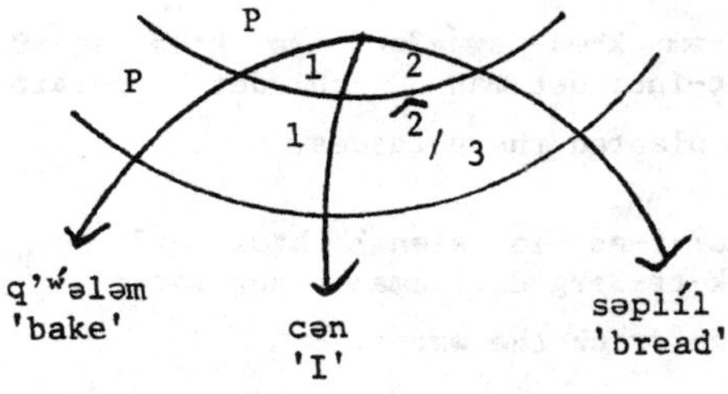

As seen in (8), antipassives are initially transitive but finally intransitive.

In arguing for this analysis, I first present evidence for the final intransitivity of antipassives. Second, I discuss the status of the 'patient' of antipassives at final level. And finally, I discuss two conditions on antipassives in Halkomelem.

4.1.1 Evidence for Final Intransitivity

In this section, I present arguments based on possessor extraction and quantifier extraction for the final intransitivity of antipassives. Also I discuss the proper formulation of Transitive Marking and 3rd Person Agreement with respect to antipassives.

The following condition on possessor extraction was formulated: (In §3.1.4 above)

(9) A possessor can be extracted only if the possessive phrase is a final absolutive.

When the subject of an antipassive is a possessive phrase, as in (10-12a), the possessor can be extracted, as seen in (10-12b).

(10) a. ni q'ʷə́l-əm kʷθə sqə́ʔəq-s ɬə sɬéniʔ ʔə kʷθə scé.ɬtən
aux bake-intr det y.b.-3pos det woman obl det salmon
'The woman's younger brother baked the salmon.'

b. státəl-stəxʷ cən ɬə sɬéniʔ ni q'ʷə́l-əm kʷθə sqéʔəq-s
know-cs lsub det woman aux bake-intr det y.b.-3pos
ʔə kʷθə scé.ɬtən
obl det salmon

'I know the woman whose younger brother baked the salmon.'

(11) a. ni qáʔqaʔ kʷθə sqéʔəq-s ɬə sɬéniʔ ʔə kʷθə qáʔ
aux drink det y.b.-3pos det woman obl det water

'The woman's younger brother drank the water.'

b. státəl-stəxʷ cən ɬə sɬéniʔ ni qáʔqaʔ kʷθə sqéʔəq-s
know-cs lsub det woman aux drink det y.b.-3pos
ʔə kʷθə qáʔ
obl det water

'I know the woman whose younger brother drank the water.'

(12) a. ni k'ʷɬé-ls kʷθə nə-sqéʔəq ʔə kʷθə tí
aux pour-act det lpos-y.b. obl det tea

'My younger brother poured the tea.'

b. ʔé.nʔθə ni k'ʷɬé-ls kʷθə nə-sqéʔəq ʔə kʷθə tí
lemph aux pour-act det lpos-y.b. obl det tea
'I'm the one whose younger brother poured the tea.'

That possessor extraction is possible in these cases follows from condition (9) and the analysis for antipassives represented in (8). Since antipassives are finally intransitive, the subject is the final absolutive; thus possessor extraction is possible.

As discussed in §3.1.5 above, the quantifier <u>mə́k'ʷ</u> can only be extracted from the <u>final absolutive</u> of the clause. In (13-15), the quanitifier <u>mə́k'ʷ</u> is extracted from an antipassive clause.

(13) ni mə́k'ʷ ʔu q'ʷə́l-əm tᶿə sƛ'əlʔíqəɬ ʔə kʷθə səplíl
aux all lnk . bake-intr det children obl det bread

'All the children baked the bread.'
*'The children baked all the bread.'

(14) ni mə́k'ʷ ʔu qáʔqaʔ kʷθə səwwə́yʔqeʔ ʔə kʷθə qáʔ
aux all lnk drink det men obl det water
'All the men drank the water.'
*'The men drank all the water.'

(15) ni mə́k'ʷ ʔu ʔə́ɬtən tᶿə sɬənɬéniʔ ʔə kʷθə scé.ɬtən
aux all lnk eat det women obl det salmon
'All the women ate the salmon.'
*'The women ate all the salmon.'

In these clauses, the quantifier is extracted from the final subject, thus providing evidence that the final subject in an antipassive is the final absolutive. That the subject is the final absolutive follows from an analysis which posits final intransitivity for antipassive clauses.

An analysis for antipassives positing final intransitivity provides an account of two other properties of antipassives. In §2.3 above, the following rule for Transitive Marking was formulated:

(16) Transitive marking is required in transitive clauses.

However, this rule, because it refers to the transitivity of a <u>clause</u>, is imprecise. Specifically, some constructions, e.g., antipassives or Caus-2 advancement clauses, involve both transitive and intransitive <u>strata</u>. In these cases, discussion of transitivity in terms of clauses is meaningless; reference must be made to strata.

In (3-6) above, a contrast in transitive marking can be observed; in the (a) clauses, represented in (7), there is transitive marking, but in the antipassives in (b) there is no transitive marking. Given the analysis for antipassives positing initial transitivity but final intransitivity (8), the absence of transitive marking in antipassives can be accounted for by limiting transitive marking to final level as follows:[2]

(17) Transitive marking is required in finally transitive clauses.

Since antipassives are finally intransitive, transitive marking is not required.

A second rule must be made more precise; 3rd Person Agreement was formulated in §3.4 as follows:

(18) Agreement is marked only for ergatives in main clauses.

According to the analysis of antipassives given in (8), subjects of antipassives are initial ergatives but final absolutives. As can be seen in (5-6b) above, there is no 3rd person agreement in antipassives. This can be accounted for by limiting 3rd Person Agreement to final level, as follows:

(19) Agreement is marked only for final ergatives in main clauses.

Since the subjects in antipassives are final absolutives, there is no 3rd person agreement.

4.1.2 The Initial Object in Antipassives

In this section, I present evidence from Nominal Case and extraction concerning the final grammatical relation of the initial object. In §3.2.3, Nominal Case was formulated as follows:

(20) a. Final nuclear terms and 3rd person common noun possessors are in the straight case.

b. Other nominals are in the oblique case.

As can be seen in (1-4b), initial objects in antipassives are in the oblique case; thus, these nominals are not final nuclear terms. This follows from the analysis of antipassives represented in (8) where the initial object is not final object. Extraction is formulated in §3.2.3 as follows:

(21) a. Final nuclear terms are directly extracted.
b. Other nominals are extracted through nominalization.
i. Extraction of final obliques is indicated by -<u>š</u>.
ii. Extraction of final 3s/2-chomeurs in indicated by <u>s</u>.

As is seen in (22-24b), it is possible to extract the initial object in antipassives:

(22) a. ni q'ʷə́l-əm ɬə sɬéniʔ ʔə kʷθə səplíl
aux bake-intr det woman obl det bread
'The woman baked the bread.'

b. səplíl kʷθə ni s-q'ʷə́l-əm-s ɬə sɬéniʔ
bread det aux nom-bake-intr-3pos det woman
'Bread is what the woman baked.'

(23) a. ni p'ə́nʔ-əm kʷθə swə́yʔqeʔ ʔə kʷθə sqéwθ
aux plant-intr det man obl det potato
'The man planted potatoes.'

b. sqéwθ kʷθə ni s-pə́nʔ-əm-s kʷθə swə́yʔqeʔ
potato det aux nom-plant-intr-3pos det man
'Potatoes is what the man planted.'

(24) a. ni cən k'ʷɬé-ls ʔə kʷθə tí
aux 1sub pour-act obl det tea
'I poured the tea.'

b. tí kʷθə ni nə-s-k'ʷɬé-ls
tea det aux 1-pos-nom-pour-act
'Tea is what I poured.'

In the above examples, the initial object of an antipassive, is extracted through nominalization; the nominalizer prefixed to the verb is s̲- . Since this prefix indicates the extraction of a final 3/2-chomeur, this supports the analysis of antipassives given in (8).

4.1.3 Conditions on Antipassives

In this section, I give examples of initially transitive clauses which do not have antipassive counterparts. I formulate two conditions on antipassives to account for these data.

In the examples of antipassives given above, the nominal which is the final 3/2-chomeur is also the initial object. In (25-27a), I have given examples of 3-2 and Ben-2 clauses; in these clauses the final object is not the initial object but rather an initial indirect object or benefactive. As seen in (25-27b), antipassive counterparts of these clauses are not possible.

(25) a. ni cən ˀám-əs-t kʷθə swə́yˀqeˀ ˀə kʷθə səplíl
aux 1sub give-advA-tr det man obl det bread
'I gave the man the bread.'

b. *ni cən ˀám-əs/ˀám-əs-əm/ˀám-əs-els ˀə kʷθə swə́yˀqeˀ
aux 1sub give-advA/give-advA-intr/give-advA-act obl det man
ˀə kʷθə səplíl
obl det bread
(I gave the man the bread.)

(26) a. ni cən q'ʷə́l-əɬc-t ɬə sɬéniˀ ˀə kʷθə səplíl
aux 1sub bake-advB-tr det woman obl det bread
'I baked bread for the woman.'

b. *ni cən q'ʷə́l-əɬc-əm ˀə ɬə sɬéniˀ ˀə kʷθə səplíl
aux 1sub bake-advB-intr obl det woman obl det bread
(I baked bread for the woman.)

(27) a. ni cən ʔíləq-əɬc-ət kʷθə nə-mə́nʔə
aux 1sub buy-advB-tr det 1pos-offspring
'I bought it for my son.'

b. *ni cən ʔíləq-əɬc-əm ʔə kʷθə nə-mə́nʔə
aux 1sub buy-advB-intr obl det 1pos-offspring
(I bought it for my son.)

I have represented (27b) in the stratal diagram in (28).

(28)

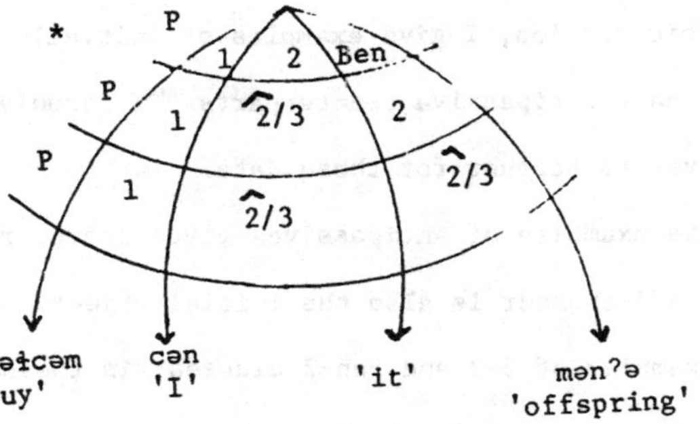

The contrast between clauses like (3-7b) and (25-27b) can be captured by placing the following condition on antipassives in Halkomelem:

(29) Only initial objects can be demoted in antipassives.

Since the object which is demoted in (25-27b) is not the initial object, as seen in (28), these clauses do not meet condition (29) and are therefore ungrammatical. Furthermore, because condition (29) makes use of the distinction initial/non-initial object (discussed in §3.3.1 and §3.3.2), it provides further evidence for that distinction.

A second condition on antipassives is required to account for the impossibility of clauses like (30-32b):

(30) a. ni cən pən-əθ-ámə
aux 1sub plant-tr-2obj
'I buried you.'

b. *ni cən pə́n'-əm ʔə-ƛ̓ nə́wə
aux 1sub plant-intr obl-det 2emph
(I buried you.)

(31) a. ni pən-əθ-ámʔš-əs
aux plant-tr-1obj-3erg
'He buried me.'

b. * ni pə́nʔ-əm ʔə-ƛ̓ ʔé.nʔθə
aux plant-intr obl-det 1emph
(He buried me.)

(32) a. ni səwʔq'-t-álʔxʷ-əs
aux seek-tr-1plobj-3erg
'He looked for us.'

b. *ni səwʔq' ʔə-ƛ̓ łníməł
aux seek obl-det 1plemph
(He looked for us.)

In each of the (b) clauses, the object which is demoted in the antipassive is 1st or 2nd person. In contrast, in the previous examples of antipassives (cf. 3-7b), the demoted object is always 3rd person. The following condition on antipassives in Halkomelem accounts for this contrast:

(33) 1st and 2nd persons cannot be demoted in antipassives.

4.2 Antipassives & Causatives

In this section, I discuss antipassives with respect to causatives in Halkomelem. In (34-36b), I have given causatives corresponding to the intransitive clauses in (34-36b):

(34) a. ni nə́mʔ kʷθə swíwʔləs
aux go det boy
'The boy went.'

b. ni cən nəʔə́m-əstəxʷ kʷθə swíwʔləs
aux 1sub go-cs det boy
'I made the boy go.'/'I took the boy there.'

(35) a. ʔi ʔəmʔí tᶿə swíwʔləs
aux come det boy
'The boy came.'

b. ʔi cən ʔəmʔí-stəxʷ tᶿə swíwʔləs
aux 1sub come-cs det boy
'I made the boy come.'/'I brought the boy.'

(36) a. ni ʔíməš ɬə sɬéniʔ
aux walk det woman
'The woman walked.'

b. ni cən ʔíməš-stəxʷ ɬə sɬéniʔ
aux 1sub walk-cs det woman
'I made/had/let the woman walk.'

I assume here that causatives like those in the (b) examples above involve causative clause union (CCU). That is, causatives consist of two clauses; the initial level of each clause can be represented by the stratal diagram for (34b) given in (37); -st 'cause' is the predicate of the upstairs clause, the 'causer' is the upstairs subject, and the corresponding non-causative clause (e.g. (34a)) is upstairs object.[3]

(37)

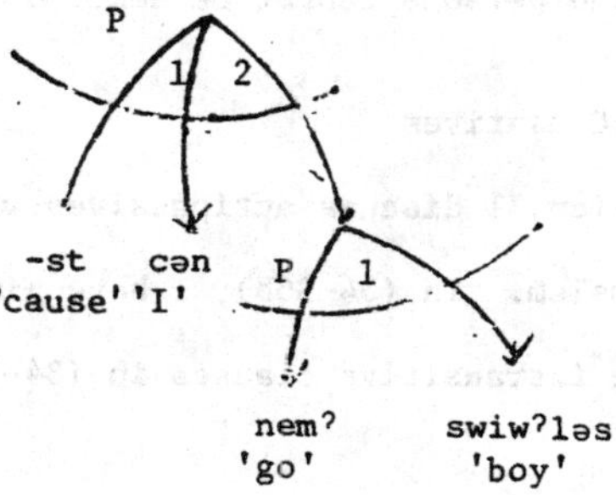

In CCU, the upstairs and downstairs clauses are merged; the downstairs elements are assigned grammatical relations in the upstairs clause. Perlmutter and Postal (1974) made the following universal prediction concerning the grammatical relations assigned to the downstairs elements in CCU:

(38) a. The downstairs predicate bears the union relation to the upstairs clause.

b. The downstairs final absolutive is upstairs object.

c. The downstairs final ergative is upstairs indirect object.

d. Other nominals bear the emeritus relation to the upstairs clause.

In the case of (34-36b), the final stratum of the downstairs clause is intransitive; the final subject is a final absolutive. In CCU, that nominal is upstairs object. I have represented the analysis for (34b) as predicted by (38) in the stratal diagram in (39):

(39)

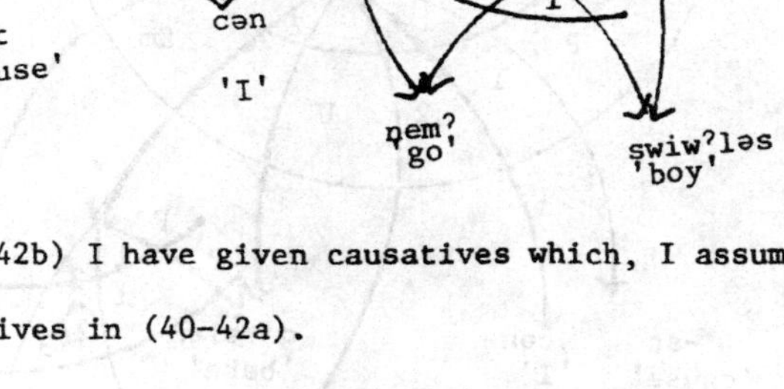

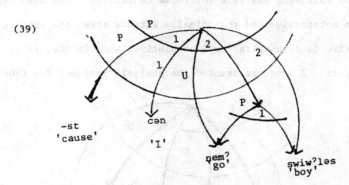

In (40-42b) I have given causatives which, I assume, correspond to the antipassives in (40-42a).

(40) a. ni q'ʷə́l-əm θə sɬéniʔ ʔə tᶿə səplíl
aux bake-intr det woman obl det bread
'The woman baked the bread.'

b. ni cən q'ʷə́l-əm-stəxʷ θə sɬéniʔ ʔə tᶿə səplíl
aux 1sub bake-intr-cs det woman obl det bread
'I made the woman bake the bread.'

(41) a. ni k'ʷɨ-éls ʔə kʷθə qáʔ
aux pour-act obl det water
'He poured the water.'

b. ni cən k'ʷɨ-éls-stəxʷ ʔə kʷθə qáʔ
aux 1sub pour-act-cs obl det water
'I made him spill the water.'

(42) a. ni qáʔqaʔ kʷθə sqʷəméyʔ ʔə kʷθə qáʔ
aux drink det dog obl det water
'The dog drank water.'

b. ni cən qáʔqaʔ-stəxʷ kʷθə sqʷəméyʔ ʔə kʷθə qáʔ
aux 1sub drink-cs det dog obl det water
'I gave the dog water to drink.'

I propose the following analysis for these causatives: the downstairs clause is an antipassive and thus finally intransitive; the subject of the antipassive is downstairs final absolutive, and, in CCU, it is upstairs object. I have represented the analysis proposed for (40b) in (43).

(43)

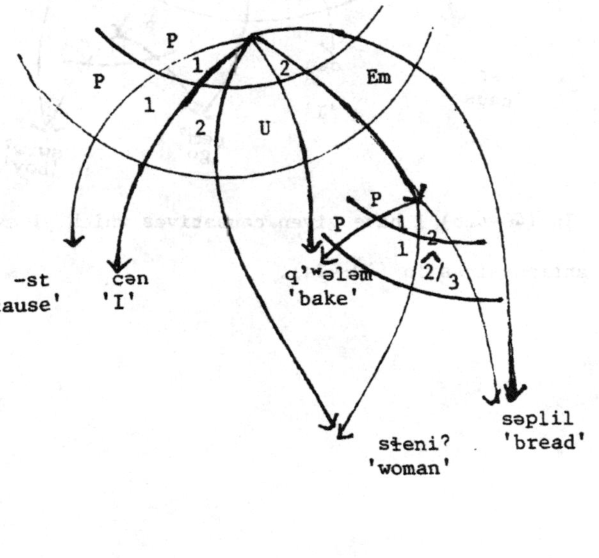

In this section, I give evidence to support the analysis represented in (43), which I refer to as the Antipassive-CCU analysis. First, I show that downstairs final absolutives are upstairs objects in causatives, as predicted in (38). Second, I discuss the grammatical relations of other downstairs nominals. In §4.2.3, I argue against an alternative to the Antipassive-CCU analysis. Finally, I formulate a condition on CCU in Halkomelem.

4.2.1 Evidence that the Downstairs Final Absolutive is Upstairs Object

I give two arguments, based on Pronominal Case and quantifier extraction, that the downstairs final absolutive is upstairs object in clauses involving CCU.

In §3.1.2 above, the rule for Pronominal Case was formulated as follows:

(44) a. Final subjects are in the subjective case.
b. Final objects are in the objective case.
c. Final obliques are in the oblique case.
d. Final possessors are in the possessive case.

In CCU, if a pronominal downstairs final absolutive is upstairs object, then it should be in the objective case. This prediction is borne out, as seen in the following examples; (45-46) are causatives in which the downstairs clause is initially (and finally) intransitive as represented in (39) and (47-48) are causatives in which the downstairs clause is antipassive as represented in (43):

(45) ni nə?em-əst-ám?š-əs
aux go-cs-lobj-3erg
'He made me go.'/ 'He took me there.'

(46) ni cən ?iməš-st-ámə
aux 1-sub walk-cs-2obj
'I made you walk.'

(47) ni q'ʷəl-əm-st-ám?š-əs ?ə tᶿə səplíl
aux bake-intr-cs-lobj-3erg obl det bread
'He made me bake the bread.'

(48) ni cən k'ʷɬ-els-st-ámə ?ə kʷθə qá?
aux 1sub pour-act-cs-2obj obl det water
'I had you pour the water.'

As discussed in §3.1.5 above, the quantifier <u>mək'ʷ</u> can only be extracted from final absolutives. In CCU, if the downstairs final absolutive is upstairs object, then it is the final absolutive of the upstairs clause, and quantifier extraction should be possible. This is the case, as is seen in the following examples; (49-50) are causatives as represented in (39) and (51-52) are causatives as represented in (43):

(49) ni mə́k'ʷ ?u nə?ém-əstəxʷ-əs kʷθə səwwə́y?qe? kʷθə sƛ̓əl?íqəɬ
aux all lnk go-cs-3erg det men det children
'The men made all the children go.'
*'All the men made the children go.'

(50) ni mə́k'ʷ ?u ?íməš-stəxʷ-əs kʷθə sɬənɬéni? kʷθə sqʷəmqʷəméy?
aux all lnk walk-cs-3erg det men det dog
'The women walked all the dogs.'
*'All the women walked the dogs.'

(51) ni mə́k'ʷ ʔu q'ʷəl-ə́m-stəxʷ-əs kʷθə słənłéni? ʔə kʷθə səplíl
aux all lnk bake-intr-cs-3erg det women obl det bread

'He had all the women bake the bread.'
*'They all had the women bake the bread.'
*'He had the women bake all the bread.'

(52) ni mə́k'ʷ ʔu pənʔ-ə́m-stəxʷ-əs kʷθə słənłéni? kʷθə səwwə́yʔqeʔ
aux all lnk plant-intr-cs-3erg det women det men

'The women had all of the men plant.'
*'All the women had the men plant.'

Thus, data involving Pronominal Case and quantifier extraction provide evidence that the downstairs final absolutive is upstairs object in clauses involving CCU.

4.2.2 The Status of Other Downstairs Nominals

In the previous section, I gave evidence that the downstairs final absolutive is upstairs object in constructions involving CCU in Halkomelem. Here, I discuss the status of other downstairs nominals. Drawing on data from nominal case and extraction, I discuss two alternative analyses for these nominals.

4.2.2.1 The Emeritus Relation

In (53-57b), I have given causatives corresponding to the clauses in (53-57a): (53-55a) involve a nominal bearing an oblique relation; the antipassive clauses in (55-57a) involve a nominal bearing the 3/2 chomeur relation. Note that these nominals are in the oblique case in both the (a) and (b) clauses.

(53) a. ni ʔíməš ɬə sɬéniʔ ʔə kʷθə stáʔluʔ
aux walk det woman obl det river
'The woman walked to the river.'

b. ni cən ʔíməš-stəxʷ ɬə sɬéniʔ ʔə kʷθə stáʔluʔ
aux 1sub walk-cs det woman obl det river
'I made the woman walk to the river.'

(54) a. ni némʔ kʷθə swíwʔləs ʔə kʷθə nə-léləmʔ
aux go det boy obl det 1pos-house
'The boy went to my house.'

b. ni cən nəʔə́m-əstəxʷ kʷθə swíwʔləs ʔə kʷθə nə-léləmʔ
aux 1sub go-cs det boy obl det 1pos-house
'I brought the boy to my house.'

(55) a. ni pə́nʔ-əm ʔə kʷθə sqéwθ ʔə kʷθə šə́ptən
aux plant-intr obl det potato obl det knife
'He planted potatoes with a knife.'

b. ni cən pə́nʔ-əm-stəxʷ ʔə kʷθə sqéwθ ʔə kʷθə šə́ptən
aux 1sub plant-intr-cs obl det potato obl det knife
'I had him plant potatoes with a knife.'

(56) a. ni q'ʷə́l-əm ɬə sɬéniʔ ʔə kʷθə səplíl
aux bake-intr det woman obl det bread
'The woman baked the bread.'

b. ni cən q'ʷə́l-əm-stəxʷ ɬə sɬéniʔ ʔə kʷθə səplíl
aux 1sub bake-intr-cs det woman obl det bread
'I had the woman bake the bread.'

(57) a. ni c'əkʷx̌-éls ʔə kʷθə scé.ɬten
aux fry-act obl det salmon
'He fried salmon.'

b. ni c'əkʷx̌-él-stəxʷ-əs ʔə kʷθə scé.ɬtən
aux fry-act-cs-3erg obl det salmon
'He had him fry salmon.'

In their universal predication concerning CCU (c.f. (38)), Perlmutter and Postal claim that all downstairs nominals other than the final absolutive and final ergative bear the emeritus relation to the upstairs clause. Under this analysis, causatives like (53b) and (57b) would be represented by the following stratal diagrams:

(58)

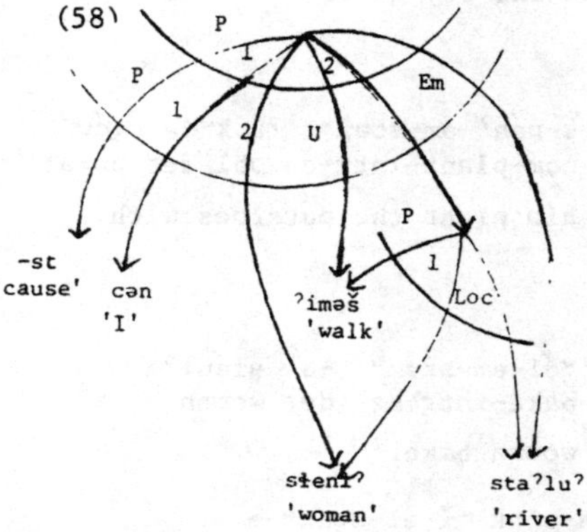

(59)

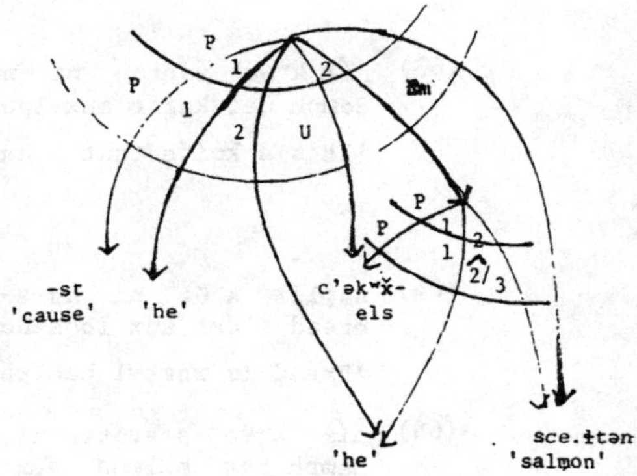

Under such an analysis, the oblique case of the emeritus nominals follows from the rule for nominal case, as given in (60):

(60) a. Final (nuclear) terms and 3rd person common nominal possessors are in the straight case.

b. Other nominals are in the oblique case.

Since the emeritus nominals are not final (nuclear) terms, they are in the oblique case.

Data involving extraction, however, poses a problem for an analysis positing the emeritus relation. As can be seen in (61-65) below, nominals which are downstairs final obliques or 3/2-chomeurs in causatives like (53-57b) can be extracted through nominalization.

(61) stáˀluˀ kʷθə ni nə-š-ˀíməš-stəxʷ ɬə sɬéniˀ
river det aux 1pos-nom-walk-cs det woman
'The river is where I made the woman walk.'

(62) níɬ kʷθə nə-lélǝm' ni nə-š-nə'ém-əstəxʷ kʷθə swíw'ləs
3emph det 1pos-house aux 1pos-nom-go-cs det boy
'It's my house that I made the boy go to.'

(63) níɬ kʷθə šə́ptən ni nə-š-pə́n'-əm-stəxʷ 'ə kʷθə sqéwθ
3emph det knife aux 1pos-nom-plant-intr-cs obl det potato
'It's a knife that I had him plant the potatoes with.'

(64) səplíl kʷθə ni nə-s-q'ʷə́l-əm-stəxʷ ɬə sɬéni'
bread det aux 1pos-nom-bake-intr-cs det woman
'Bread is what I had the woman bake.'

(65) níɬ kʷθə scé.ɬtən ni s-c'ək ʷx̌-él-stəxʷ-s
3emph det salmon aux nom-fry-act-cs-3pos
'It's the salmon that he had him fry.'

Although each of the extracted nominals is an emeritus under Perlmutter and Postal's proposal, these nominals do not behave alike with respect to the nominalizing prefix indicating extraction: extraction is indicated by <u>š-</u> in (61-63) and by <u>s-</u> in (64-65). We have seen elsewhere in Halkomelem that nominals bearing the same final grammatical relation are extracted in the same manner. Thus, an analysis which proposes that the extracted nominals above bear the same final grammatical relation, e.g. emeritus, makes the wrong prediction with respect to the behaviour of these nominals in extractions.

4.2.2.2 The Inheritance Principle

A second hypothesis concerning the grammatical relations of the downstairs nominals in CCU has been proposed by Gibson and Raposo (in preparation) and by Fauconnier (p.c.). This hypothesis, which Fauconnier has called the Inheritance Principle, proposes that in CCU all downstairs nominals other than final subject bear the same relation upstairs as they bear in the final stratum of the downstairs clause. Under this analysis, causatives like (53b) and (57b) would be represented by the following stratal diagrams:

(66)

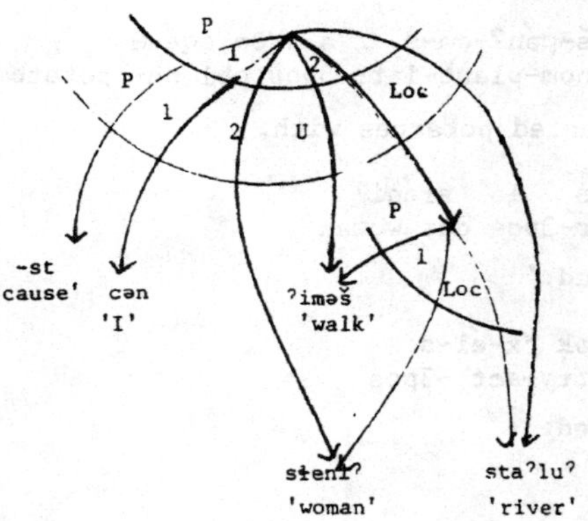

(67)

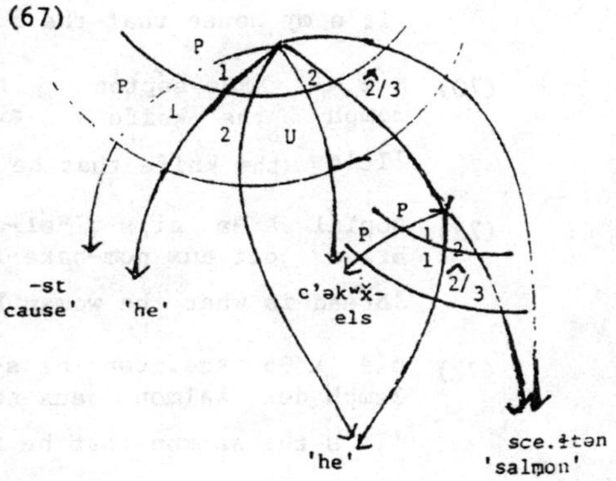

The Inheritance Principle together with the rule of nominal case given in (60) accounts for the case of nominals which are downstairs final obliques or 3s/2-chomeurs. Since these nominals bear the same relation in the upstairs clause, they are not final (nuclear) terms and are in the oblique case.

Furthermore, data involving extraction are accounted for under an analysis with the Inheritance Principle. The extraction of final obliques is indicated by <u>š</u>- (cf. 61-63) and the extraction of final 3s/2-chomeurs by <u>s</u>- (cf. 64-65). As predicted, nominals (other than the downstairs final subject) in causatives (e.g. (53-57b)) are extracted in the same manner as the corresponding nominal in the non-causative counterpart (e.g. (53-57a)), as seen in the following examples:

(68) stá?lu? kʷθə ni nem? š-?íməš-s ɬə sɬéni?
river det aux go nom-walk-3pos det woman
'The river is where the woman walked.'

(69) níɬ kʷθə nə-léləm? ni š-ném?-s kʷθə swíw?ləs
3emph det 1pos-house aux nom-go-3pos det boy
'It's my house that the boy went to.'

(70) níɬ kʷθə šə́ptən ni š-pə́n?-əm-s ?ə kʷθə sqéwθ
3emph the knife aux nom-plant-intr-3pos obl det potato
'It's the knife that he planted potatoes with.'

(71) səplíl kʷθə ni s-q'ʷə́l-əm-s ɬə sɬéni?
bread det aux nom-bake-intr-3pos det woman
'Bread is what the woman baked.'

(72) níɬ kʷθə scé.ɬtən ni s-c'ək ʷx̌-él-s
3emph det salmon aux nom-fry-act -3pos
'It's the salmon that he fried.'

Thus, an analysis of CCU involving the Inheritance Principle captures the similarity of nominals in causative and non-causative constructions.

4.2.3 An Alternative Analysis: CCU-3-2 Advancement

In the preceding section, I proposed that causatives like those in (40-42b) involve downstairs antipassive and CCU, as represented in the stratal diagram for (40b) given in (74):

(73) = (40b) ni cən q'ʷə́l-əm-stəxʷ θə sɬéni? ?ə kʷθə səplíl
aux 1sub bake-intr-cs det woman obl det bread
'I had the woman bake the bread.'

(74)

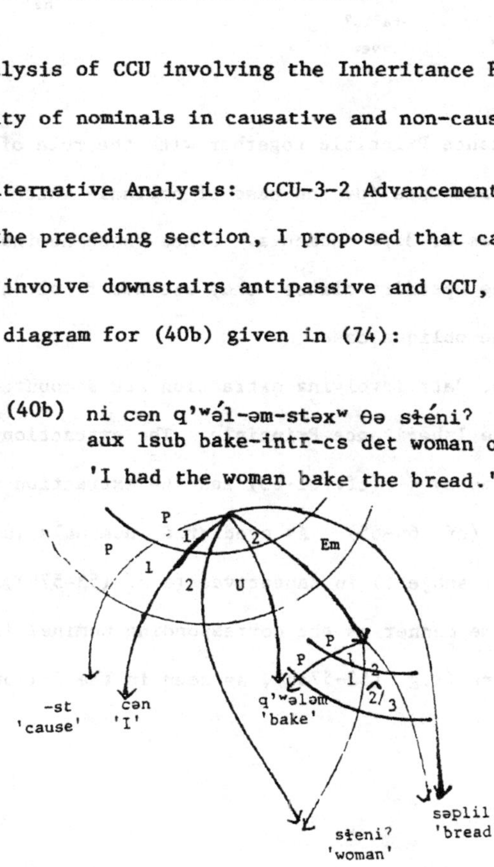

As predicted by Perlmutter and Postal's characterization of CCU (cf. (38)), the downstairs final absolutive is upstairs object. Also, as predicted by the Inheritance Principle, the downstairs final 3/2-chomeur is upstairs 3/2-chomeur. I gave evidence from Pronominal Case and quanitifer extraction that the downstairs final absolutive is upstairs object and from Nominal Case and extraction that the downstairs final 3/2-chomeur is upstairs 3/2-chomeur.

However, an alternative analysis would also account for these data. If we assume the final transitivity of the downstairs clause, the downstairs final absolutive is upstairs object and the downstairs final ergative is upstairs indirect object, as predicted in (38). To account for the behaviour of downstairs subject as upstairs object and downstairs object as a 3/2-chomeur, this analysis would propose that clauses like (73) involve 3-2 advancement in the upstairs clause, as represented in the stratal diagram in (75):

(75)

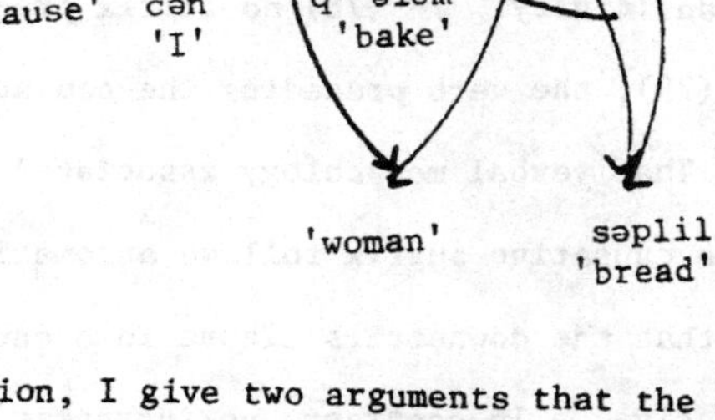

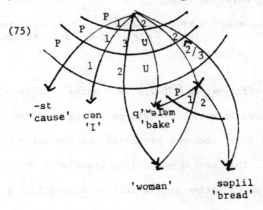

In this section, I give two arguments that the Antipassive-CCU analysis (cf. (74)) is to be preferred over the CCU-3-2 advancement analysis (cf. (75)).

In §1.4.2, I pointed out the verbal morphology associated with antipassives in Halkomelem. Verbs in antipassives are suffixed with -əm, -els, or occur without suffixes. In contrast, verbs in final transitive strata are suffixed with a transitive marker (cf. §2.4, 3.4). In addition, there is at least one case where the transitive and intransitive verbs do not resemble each other: ʔə́łtən 'eat' (intransitive); łəyx̌- 'eat' (transitive).

Observe the causatives in (76-79):

(76) ni cən q'ʷəl-ə́m-stəxʷ łə słéniʔ ʔə kʷθə səplíl
aux 1sub bake-intr-cs det woman obl det bread
'I had the woman bake the bread.'

(77) ni cən k'ʷł-els-stəxʷ ʔə kʷθə tí
aux 1sub pour-act-cs obl det tea
'I had him pour the tea.'

(78) ni cən qáʔqaʔ-stəxʷ kʷθə sqʷəméyʔ ʔə kʷθə qáʔ
aux 1sub drink-cs det dog obl det water
'I gave the dog water to drink.'

(79) ni cən ʔəłtə́n-əstəxʷ kʷθə sqʷəméyʔ ʔə kʷθə scé.łtən
aux 1sub eat-cs det dog obl det salmon
'I fed the dog the salmon.'

Preceding the causative suffix -st in (76-77) is a verbal suffix associated with final intransitivity. In (78) no suffix precedes the causative suffix. In (79), the verb preceding the causative suffix is the intransitive form. That verbal morphology associated with final intransitivity precedes the causative suffix follows automatically in an analysis that proposes that the downstairs clause in a causative is intransitive via antipassive.[4] In contrast, no intransitive stratum is proposed under the CCU-3-2 advancement analysis, and the intransitive verbal morphology remains a mystery.[5]

A second argument for preferring the Antipassive-CCU analysis over the CCU-3-2 advancement is based on conditions on antipassive (cf. §4.1.4).

In contrast to the examples of causatives given in the previous sections, the following are not possible:

(80) *ni ˀam-əs-əm-stəxʷ-əs ˀə ɬə sɬéniˀ ˀə kʷθə səplíl
aux give-advA-intr-cs-3erg obl det woman obl det bread
(He made him give the woman the bread.)

(81) *ni cən q'ʷəl-əɬc-əm-stəxʷ kʷθə swə́yˀqeˀ ˀə ɬə sɬéniˀ
aux 1sub bake-advB-intr-cs det man obl det woman
(I had the man bake it for the woman.)

(82) *ni pənˀ-əm-st-ámˀš-əs ˀə-ƛ̓ nə́wə
aux plant-intr-cs-3erg obl-det 2emph
(He made me bury you.)

(83) *ni pənˀ-əm-stəxʷ-əs ˀə-ƛ̓ ˀé.nˀθə
aux plant-intr-cs-3erg obl-det 1emph
(He had him bury me.)

Under the Antipassive-CCU analysis, the ungrammaticality of (80-83) could be accounted for by the conditions on antipassives formulated in §4.1.4 repeated here as (84) and (85).

(84) Only initial objects can be demoted in antipassives.

(85) Only 3rd persons can be demoted in antipassives.

In (80-81) the downstairs object is not an initial object and in (82-83) the downstairs object is not 3rd person; thus, antipassive is not possible in the downstairs clauses of these causatives.

Under the CCU-3-2 advancement analysis, causatives like (80-83) would not be accounted for unless conditions could be placed on causatives as follows:

(86) CCU is not possible if the downstairs final object is not the downstairs initial object.

(87) CCU is not possible if the downstairs final object is not 3rd person.

These conditions, however, duplicate those needed for antipassives. Thus, the CCU-3-2 advancement analysis misses a possible generalization.

4.2.4 A Condition on CCU

In the preceding section, I have argued on the basis of verbal morphology and conditions on antipassives for an Antipassive-CCU analysis of clauses like (88-89).

(88) ni cən q'ʷə́l-əm-stəxʷ ɬə sɬéniʔ ʔə kʷθə səplíl
aux 1sub bake-intr-cs det woman obl det bread
'I had the woman bake the bread.'

(89) ni cən pə́nʔ-em-stəxʷ ʔə kʷθə sqéwθ
aux 1sub plant-intr-cs obl det potato
'I had him plant the potatoes.'

Furthermore, causatives based on finally transitive clauses an in (90-92) are not possible.

(90) *ni cən q'ʷəl-ət-stəxʷ kʷθə səplíl ʔə ɬə sɬéniʔ
aux 1sub bake-tr-st det bread obl det woman
(I had the woman bake the bread.)

(91) *ni cən pən-ət-stəxʷ kʷθə sqéwθ
aux 1sub plant-tr-cs det potato
(I had him plant the potatoes.)

(92) *ni ɬəyx̌-t-stəxʷ-əs kʷθə sməýəθ ʔə kʷθə sqʷəméyʔ
aux eat-tr-cs-3erg det (deer)meat obl det dog
(He fed the deer meat to the dog.)

I have represented (90) in the stratal diagram in (93).

(93)

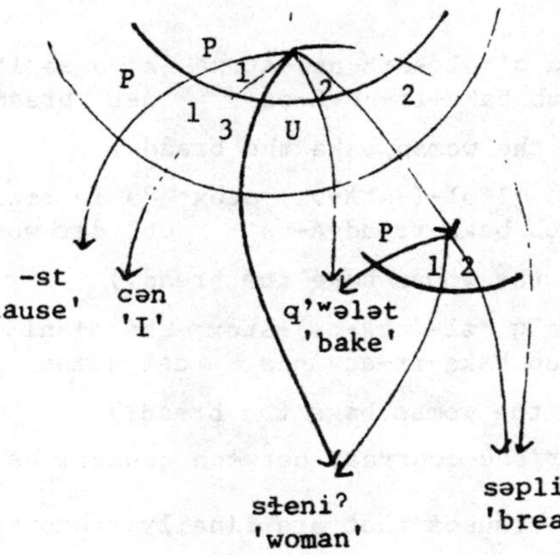

Although the causatives in (90-92) obey the universal prediction concerning CCU given in (38), they are not possible.

In §3.7, I pointed out that 3-2 advancement was obligatory in Halkomelem. If we assume this is also the case in causatives, then the ungrammaticality of (90-92) could be accounted for by the lack of 3-2 advancement in the upstairs clause. However, even if 3-2 advancement is proposed, as represented in (94), causatives are not possible.

(94)

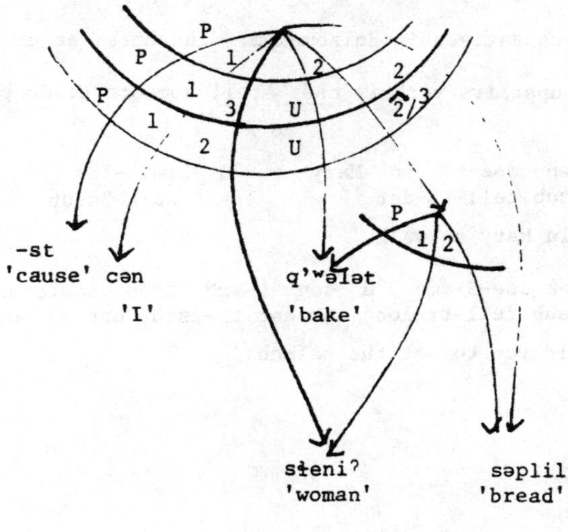

The causatives in (90-92) are ungrammatical regardless of the word order, the case of the nominals, or the presence of an advancement marker:

(95) a. * ni cən q'ʷəl(-ət)(-əs)-stəxʷ kʷθə səplíl (ʔə)ɬə sɬéniʔ
aux 1sub bake-tr-advA-cs det bread obl det woman
(I had the woman bake the bread.)

b. * ni cən q'ʷəl-(-ət)(-əs)-stəxʷ ʔə ɬə sɬéniʔ(ʔə) kʷθə səplíl
aux 1sub bake-tr-advA-cs obl det woman obl det bread
(I had the woman bake the bread.)

c. * ni cən q'ʷəl-(ət)(-əs)-stəxʷ ɬə sɬéniʔ kʷθə səplíl
aux 1sub bake-tr-advA-cs det woman det bread
(I had the woman bake the bread.)

To account for the contrast between causatives like (90-92), which have downstairs clauses that are finally transitive, and those like (88-89), which have downstairs clauses that are finally intransitive via antipassive, a condition on CCU in Halkomelem can be stated as follows:

(96) CCU is possible only if the downstairs clause is finally intransitive.

4.2.5 Periphrastic Causatives

Besides causatives involving CCU as discussed above, there are periphrastic causatives in Halkomelem. In these, as exemplified in (97-102), the upstairs verb is <u>csét</u> 'tell someone to do something.'

(97) ni cən csé-t ɬə Mary ʔu ʔíməš-ʔəs
aux 1sub tell-tr det lnk walk-3ssub
'I told Mary to walk.'

(98) ni cən cse-θ-ámə ʔu ɬəýx̌-t-əxʷ kʷθə scé.ɬtən
aux 1sub tell-tr-1obj lnk eat-tr-2ssub det salmon
'I told you to eat the salmon.'

(99) ni cse-θ-ám?š-əs ɬə sɬéni? ?u ?àm-əs-θ-àmə-?é.n?
aux tell-tr-1obj-3erg det woman lnk give-advA-tr-2obj-1ssub
?ə kʷθə scé.ɬtən
obl det salmon
'The woman told me to give you the salmon.'

(100) cse-t-álə cən ce? ?u q'ʷə̀l-əɬc-t-?ələp ?ə kʷθə səplíl
tell-tr-2plobj 1sub fut lnk bake-advB-tr-2plssub obl det bread
'I will tell you pl. to bake him some bread.'

(101) ni cən csé-t ?u q'ʷaqʷ-əθ-ám?š-əs
aux 1sub tell-tr lnk club-tr-1obj-3ssub
'I told him to club me.'

(102) cse-t-álə cən ce? ?u pən-əθ-ám?š-?ələp
tell-tr-2plobj 1sub fut lnk plant-tr-1obj-2plssub
'I will tell you to bury me.'

As seen above, csét is followed by an object and an embedded clause. Although I cannot motivate an analysis of periphrastic causatives here, I will point out that the object of csét must be coreferential to the subject of the embedded clause, as seen in (103-104).

(103) *ni cən csé-t ɬə Mary ?u ɬəyx̌-t-əxʷ kʷθə scé.ɬtən
aux 1sub tell-tr det lnk eat-tr-2ssub det salmon
(I told Mary for you to eat the salmon.)

(104) *csé-t-alə cən ce? ?u ?íməš-?əs ɬə Mary
tell-tr-2plobj 1sub fut lnk walk-3ssub det
(I tell you for Mary to walk.)

Unlike causatives involving CCU, which require the downstairs clause to be finally intransitive, periphrastic causatives allow any type of embedded clause. Thus, while the embedded clauses in (98-102) are transitive and would not meet condition (96), they are acceptable as embedded clauses in periphrastic causatives. Further, note that the embedded clauses in (99-102) cannot be finally intransitive via antipassive because of the conditions on antipassive given in (84) and

(85); in (99-100), the object is not the initial object, and in (101-102), the object is not a third person.

4.2.6 Double Causatives

Periphrastic causatives are used to form double causatives, i.e. causatives based on other causatives, as exemplified in (105-107):

(105) ni cən cséʹ-t ɬə Mary ʔu nəʔém-stəxʷ-əs kʷθə púkʷ-s
aux 1sub tell-tr det lnk go-cs-3ssub det boo-3pos
'I told Mary to bring her book there.'

(106) ni cən cse-t-álə ʔu ʔəɬtə́n-əstəxʷ-ʔələp kʷθə sqʷəméyʔ
aux 1sub tell-tr-2plobj lnk eat-cs-2plssub det dog
'I told you pl. to feed the dog.'

(107) cse-θ-ámə cən ceʔ ʔu q'ʷə́l-əm-stəxʷ-əxʷ ʔə kʷθə səplíl
tell-tr-2obj 1sub fut lnk bake-intr-cs-2ssub obl det bread
'I'm telling you to bake the bread.'

However, double causatives involving CCU in both causatives are not possible, as seen in (108-109):

(108) *ni cən nəʔem-stəxʷ-stəxʷ ɬə Mary (ʔə)kʷθə púkʷ-s
aux 1sub go-cs-cs det obl det book-3pos
(I had Mary take her book.)

(109) *ni cən ʔəɬtən-əstəxʷ-st-alə (ʔə) kʷθə sqʷəméyʔ
aux 1sub eat-cs-cs-2plobj obl det dog
(I told you pl. to feedthe dog.)

The ungrammaticality of (108-109) follows from aspects of the analysis presented above. First, I assumed that causatives with the suffix -st have bi-causal structures and involve CCU, as represented in (110):

(110)

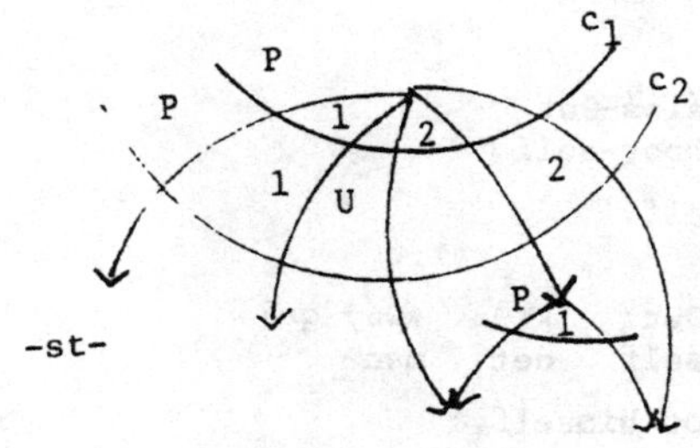

I gave evidence in §4.2.1 that the downstairs final absolutive is upstairs final object, and thus causatives with CCU are finally transitive. The final object, however, is not an initial object (that is, it is not an object in the stratum labelled c_1 in (110)), and, as stated in condition (84), only initial objects can be demoted in antipassives. This predicts that antipassives of causatives with CCU are not possible, and, as seen in (111-112), this is the case.

(111) *ni nəˀém-əst-əm ɬə Mary ˀə kʷθə púkʷ-s
aux go-cs-intr det obl det book-3pos

(Mary took her book.)

(112) *ni cé.p ˀə́ɬtən-əst-əm ˀə kʷθə sqʷəmé̓y̓ˀ
aux 2plsub eat-cs-intr obl det dog

(You pl. fed the dog.)

Since causatives with CCU cannot be finally intransitive via antipassive, causatives with embedded causatives cannot meet condition (96) and CCU is not possible.

4.3 Reflexives and Reciprocals

In §2.5 above, I discussed two constructions involving the coreference of the subject and object; reflexives, exemplified in (113-115), and reciprocals, exemplified in (116-118); verbs in reflexives are suffixed with <u>-θət</u> and those in reciprocals with <u>-təl</u>.

(113) ni cən kʷə́ləš-θət
aux 1sub shoot-self
'I shot myself.'

(114) ni kʷə́ləš-θət kʷθə swə́yʔqeʔ
aux shoot-self det man
'The man shot himself.'

(115) ni lə́x̌ʷ-əθət ɬə Mary
aux blanket-self det
'Mary covered herself with a blanket.'

(116) ni ct ləmáʔ-təl
aux 1plsub kick-rec
'We kicked each other.'

(117) ni θ̓íq'ʷ-ətəl kʷθə Bob ʔi George
aux punch-rec det cn
'Bob and George punched each other.'

(118) ni tíq'ʷ-təl
aux bump-rec
'They collided.'

In this section, I present evidence that reflexive and reciprocal clauses are finally intransitive in Halkomelem. I leave the discussion of analyses accounting for the final intransitivity of these clauses to §4.5 and §4.6 below.

4.3.1 3rd Person Agreement

In §4.1.1, the rule for 3rd Person Agreement was formulated as follows:

(119) Agreement is marked only for final ergatives in main clauses.

Thus, if the final stratum in reflexive and reciprocal clauses is transitive, then in examples with 3rd person subjects, there should be 3rd person agreement. As is seen in (114-115) and (117-118) above, this is not the case.

The lack of 3rd person agreement in reflexive and reciprocal clauses follows from an analysis which proposes final intransitivity for these constructions. If the final stratum is intransitive then the final subject is an absolutive, not an ergative, and 3rd Person Agreement is impossible.

4.3.2 Causatives

In §4.2.4, the following condition was formulated for CCU:

(120) CCU is possible only if the downstairs clause is finally intransitive.

In (121-123b), I have given causatives corresponding to the reflexives and reciprocals in (121-123a):

(121) a. ni k'ʷə́ləš-θət kʷθə swə́y̓ʔqeʔ
aux shoot-self det man
'The man shot himself.'

b. ni cən kʷə́ləš-θət-stəxʷ kʷθə swə́y̓ʔqeʔ
aux 1sub shoot-self-cs det man
'I made the man shoot himself.'

(122) a. ni cən lə̌x̌ʷ-əθət
aux 1sub blanket-self
'I covered myself with a blanket.'

b. ni lə̀x̌ʷ-əθət-st-ə́mʔš-əs kʷθə Bob
aux blanket-self-cs-1obj-3erg det
'Bob had me cover myself with a blanket.'

(123) a. ni tíq'ʷ-təl kʷθə səwwə́y?qe?
aux bump-rec det men
'The men collided.'

b. ni cən tíq'ʷ-təl-stəxʷ kʷθə səwwə́y?qe?
aux 1sub bump-rec-cs det men
'I made the men collide.'

Since CCU is possible only if the downstairs clause is finally intransitive and CCU is possible in the examples above where a reflexive or reciprocal clause is the downstairs clause in a causative, reflexive and reciprocal clauses must be finally intransitive.

4.4 Object Cancellation

In this section, I discuss an additional construction used to express coreference of subjects and objects in Halkomelem. This construction, which I refer to as object cancellation following Aissen (to appear b), is exemplified in the main clauses in (124-125) and the embedded clauses of the periphrastic causatives in (126-127). Notice that the advancement marker in (124-127) is followed by the intransitive suffix.[6,7]

(124) @ni cən q'ʷə́l-əɬc-əm ?ə kʷθə səplíl
aux 1sub bake-advB-intr obl det bread
'I baked myself some bread.'

(125) @ni cən θə́y-əɬc-əm ?ə kʷθə snə́xʷəɬ
aux 1sub make-advB-intr obl det canoe
'I made myself a canoe.'

(126) cse-t-álə cən ce? ?u q'ʷə́l-əɬc-əm-?ələp ?ə kʷθə səplíl
tell-tr-2plobj 1sub fut lnk bake-advB-intr-2plssub obl det bread
'I'm telling you pl. to bake bread for me.' (unambiguous)

(127) cse-θ-ámə cən ceʔ ʔu k'ʷəɬ-ə́ɬc-əm-əxʷ ʔə k'ʷ tí
tell-tr-2obj 1sub fut lnk pour-advB-intr-2ssub obl det tea
'I will tell you to pour me some tea.' (unambiguous)

In §4.4.1, I present evidence that object cancellation clauses, like reflexive clauses, are finally intransitive; in §4.4.2, I give evidence that the cancelled nominal in this construction is an object; and in §4.4.3, I discuss conditions on object cancellation.

4.4.1 Evidence for Final Intransitivity

The first evidence for the final intransitivity of object cancellation clauses comes from transitive marking. As formulated in §4.1.1, Transitive Marking is:

(128) Transitive marking is required in finally transitive clauses.

However, as can be seen in (124-127) above, object cancellation constructions lack transitive marking. Instead, they are suffixed with -əm, which we have seen in §4.1.3 indicates final intransitivity.

As formulated in §4.1.1, the rule for 3rd Person Agreement is:

(129) Agreement is marked only for final ergatives in main clauses.

In the object cancellation clauses given in (130-131), the subjects are 3rd person, yet there is no 3rd person agreement.

(130) @ni q'ʷə́l-əɬc-əm ˀə kʷθə səplíl
aux bake-advB-intr obl det bread
'He baked bread for himself.'

(131) @ni θə́y-əɬc-əm
aux make-advB-intr
'He made it for himself.'

Thus, subjects in clauses like (130) and (131) are final absolutives rather than final ergatives. This follows from an analysis positing final intransitivity for these clauses.

4.4.2 Evidence for the Cancellation of the Object

For the object cancellation clauses above, I am assuming an initial structure as represented in (132):

(132)

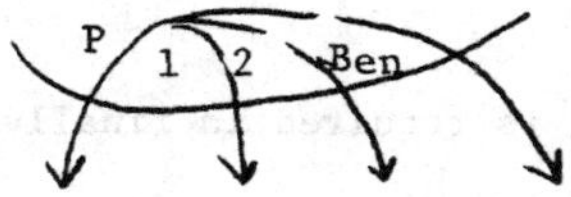

I consider two analyses which could account for the final intransitivity of these clauses. First, the initial object could be demoted to a 3/2-chomeur via antipassive and the initial benefactive, which is coreferent to some subject, is cancelled, represented by a blank in the following stratal diagram:

(133)

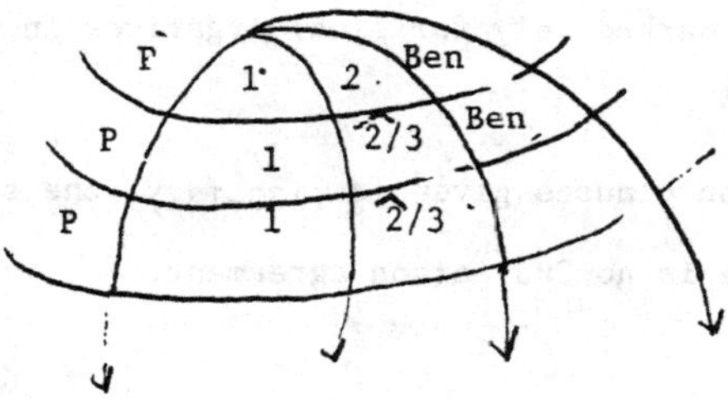

Second, the object cancellation clause could involve advancement to object, as represented in (134); in this case it is a non-initial object, which is coreferent to some subject, that is cancelled.

(134)

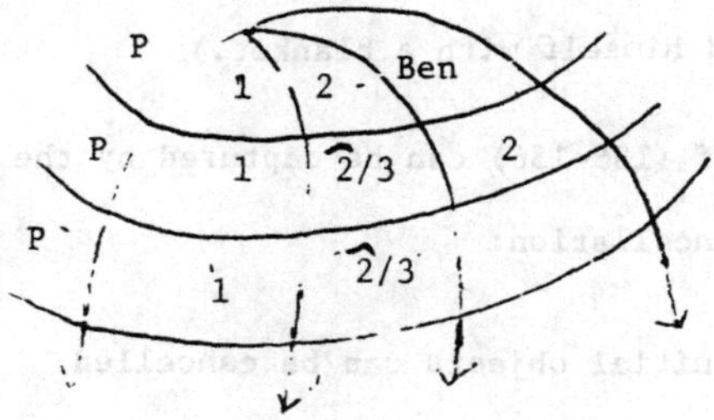

Under both analyses, the initial object is a final 3/2-chomeur which accounts for its being in the oblique case.

There is one argument, based on advancement marking, that the analysis represented in (134) is preferred. In §3.8, I discussed the verbal morphology correlated with advancements to object. In the object cancellation constructions above, such as advancement marker is present. This is automatically accounted for under an analysis which posits advancements to object for these clauses, like that represented in (134). Since no advancement to object is posited in (133), it does not account for the presence of the advancement marker. Thus, I take (134) to be the preferred analysis.

4.4.3 Conditions on Object Cancellations

In this section, I formulate two conditions on object cancellations. In the above examples, the cancelled objects were non-initial objects. In fact, object cancellation constructions are not possible if the cancelled object is an initial object, as seen in (135-136):

(135) *ni k'ʷə́ləš-əm
aux shoot-intr
(He shot himself.)

(136) *ni lə̂x̌ʷ-əm
aux blanket-intr
(He covered himself with a blanket.)

The ungrammaticality of (135-136) can be captured by the following condition on object cancellation:

(137) Only non-initial objects can be cancelled.

In the above examples, two types of object cancellations are exemplified. In the first, exemplified in (124-125), the cancelled object and the subject it is coreferent to are in the same clause; in the second, exemplified in (126-127), the cancelled object, in the embedded clause, is coreferent to the matrix subject. Thus, it is not a requirement in object cancellation constructions that the cancelled object be a clause-mate of the subject it is coreferent to.

However, when the cancelled object is not a clause-mate of the coreferent subject, only 1st and 2nd person objects can be cancelled, (cf. (126-127)); 3rd person objects cannot be, as seen in (138-139):

(138) *cse-θ-ámʔš-əs ceʔ ʔu q'ʷə̀l-əɬc-əm-ʔé.nʔ ʔə kʷθə səplíl
tell-tr-1obj-3erg fut lnk bake-advB-intr-1ssub obl det bread
(He's telling me to bake the bread for him.)

(139) *cse-θ-ámʔš-əs ceʔ ʔu k'ʷəɬ-əɬc-əm-ʔé.nʔ ʔə k'ʷ tí
tell-tr-1obj-3erg fut lnk pour-advB-intr-1ssub obl det tea
(He's telling me to pour the tea for him.)

This is not the case when the coreferential subject and object are clause-mates; (124-125) and (130-131) are equally acceptable regardless of the person of the cancelled object. This distinction can be captured by the following condition on object cancellations:[8]

(140) A 3rd person object can be cancelled only if it is coreferent to the subject of its clause.

In the following sections, I discuss conditions on object cancellation further, contrasting them to conditions on other object resignations.

4.5 Postal's Analysis of 'Detransitivization'

In the preceding sections, I have presented evidence for constructions involving object resignation: antipassives, reflexives, reciprocals, and object cancellations. Here, I discuss these with respect to the analysis of detransitivization proposed by Postal (1977).

In §4.1 above, I argued for the final intransitivity of antipassives in Halkomelem; specifically, the initial object is either a final 3 or a chomeur, as represented in (141) and (142):

(141)

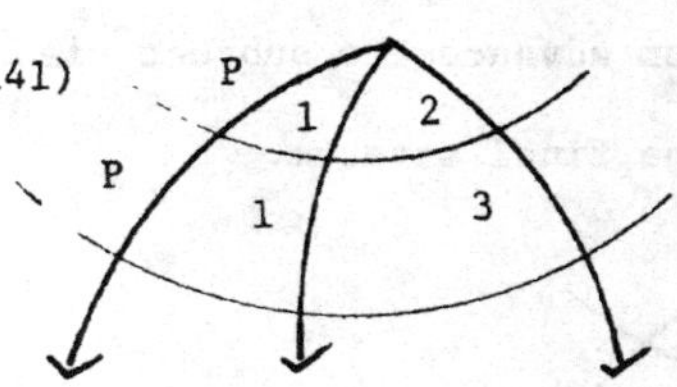

(142)

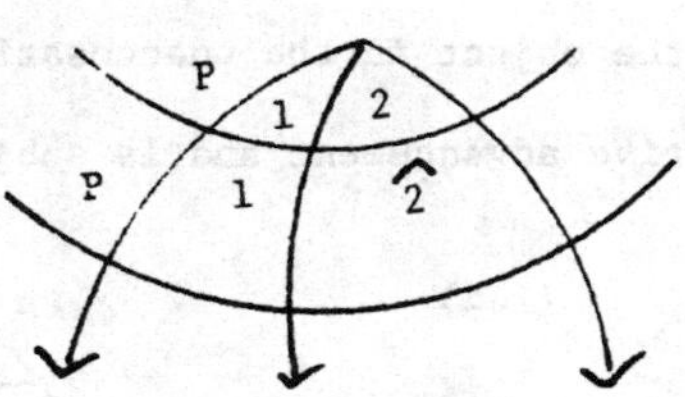

An analysis involving 2-3 retreat (130) does not violate any laws currently maintained in Relational Grammar; however, an analysis such as (142) violates the Motivated Chomage Law, given in (143):

(143) An RN containing an arc of the form [Cho (a,b) < $c_i c_w$ >] also contains distinct arcs of the form [$Term_x$ (a,b) < $c_u c_{i-1}$ >] and [$Term_x$ (c,b) < $c_i c_z$ >].

(Perlmutter and Postal, to appear c)

Informally stated, the Motivated Chomage Law rules out constructions where a nominal is a $term_x$ in the c_i stratum and a chomeur in the c_{i+1} stratum where no nominal assumes the $term_x$ relation in the c_{i+1} stratum. It also rules out the possibility of having initial chomeurs.

In the analysis of (142), since the initial object is a chomeur yet no nominal assumes the object relation, the conditions of the Motivated Chomage Law are not met.

Discussing data from several languages, Postal (1977) proposes an analysis of antipassive clauses which does not violate the Motivated Chomage Law. In this analysis, represented in (144), the initial subject retreats to object, placing the initial object en chomage, and thus satisfying the Motivated Chomage Law. The (b) stratum, with an object but no subject, is an unaccusative stratum (cf. §5.6.2); the object in the unaccusative stratum advances to subject via unaccusative advancement and is subject in the final stratum.

(144)

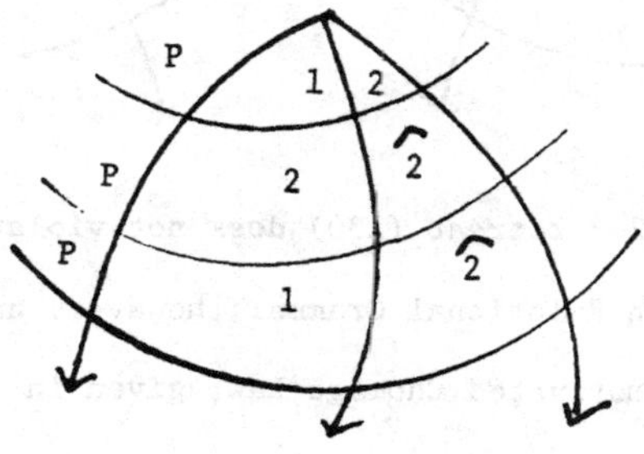

In the case of Halkomelem antipassives, as Hukari (1979b) has pointed out, there is no evidence either for or against the analysis represented in (144). In the following discussion, I assume that this analysis is tenable for Halkomelem.

In addition, Postal makes the claim that all cases involving a clause which is transitive at one level and intransitive at a subsequent level due to the apparent demotion or deletion of the object should be accounted for by one of two analyses: <u>2-3 retreat</u> or <u>antipassive</u>.

Specifically, he discusses cases from various languages where reflexives and reciprocals are finally intransitive. These, he claims, are finally intransitive via antipassive.

Under Postal's proposal, then, all of the object resignation constructions discussed in this chapter would be antipassives. In this section, I examine the adequacy of this analysis, which I refer to as mega-antipassive, with respect to the conditions on object resignations. I argue that the various object resignations are too diverse to be considered as a single construction.

I have discussed conditions on object resignations above; these are of two types, referring to the person and the level of the object (i.e., initial or non-initial). In addition, the constructions vary according to clause-boundedness and obligatoriness. I have summarized these conditions and requirements on object resignations in the chart in (145).

(145)

	Persons	Type of Object	Clause-bounded	Obligatory
1) Antipassive	3rd	initial	yes	(no)
2) Reflexive	all	initial	yes	yes
3) Reciprocal	all	initial	yes	yes
4) Object cancellation	a) all	non-initial	yes	yes
	b) 1st/2nd	non-initial	no	no

If object resignations were reduced to a single construction, mega-antipassive, it would be possible to state conditions on it, but each condition would have to include characteristics of the constructions it refers to; for example, the condition on type of object is stated in (146) and the condition on person is stated in (147):

(146) Condition on Mega-antipassive:

Only initial objects which are nominals or unspecified or which are coreferent to the subject of the clause and non-initial objects which are coreferent to some subject can be placed en chomage in mega-antipassive.

(147) Condition on Mega-antipassive:

All persons can be placed en chomage in mega-antipassive, unless the object placed en chomage is the initial object which is not coreferent to the subject of the clause, in which case, only 3rd persons can be placed en chomage, or, unless the object placed en chomage is a non-initial object of an embedded clause which is coreferent to the subject of the matrix clause, in which case, only 1st and 2nd persons can be placed en chomage.

Because each condition would require a repetition of the characteristics of the constructions, conditions in the mega-antipassive analysis are needlessly complicated. Apparently, the only thing gained by the mega-antipassive analysis is a unified account of final intransitivity.

4.6 Aissen's Proposal: Coreference and Cancellation

Because of the complications required under a mega-antipassive analysis, it is not a satisfying account of object resignations in Halkomelem. Although antipassive may account for some object resignations, it cannot elegantly account for all of them. If the mega-antipassive analysis is rejected, some alternative analyses accounting for the final intransitivity of object resignations, must be proposed. In this section, an alternative concerning coreference and intransitivity proposed by Aissen (to appear b) is discussed.

Giving evidence from several languages, Aissen (to appear b) discusses the problem of the final intransitivity of reflexive constructions. She argues that, contrary to the claims of Postal, antipassive is not an adequate means of accounting for the intransitivity of reflexive constructions and concludes that some languages may require cancellation of nominals (cf. §4.4.2) under the condition of coreference.

Her evidence for this claim comes from cases in Tzotzil and Gerogian where an <u>indirect object</u> which is coreferent to the subject is cancelled.[9] In Tzotzil, as in Halkomelem, there are no final indirect objects; these advance to object and 3-2 advancement is marked by the verbal suffix -<u>be</u>, as seen in (148):

(148) (Tzotzil)

7i -s-meltzan-be	jun	falta
cp -E3-MAKE-be	ONE	SKIRT

'She made her a skirt.'

The above clause can only mean that the subject made a skirt for someone else. To express the meaning of the subject making a skirt for herself, the following clause is used:

(149) (Tzotzil)
7i -s-meltzan jun falta
cp -E3-MAKE ONE SKIRT

For the clause in (149), Aissen posits the following analysis:

(150)

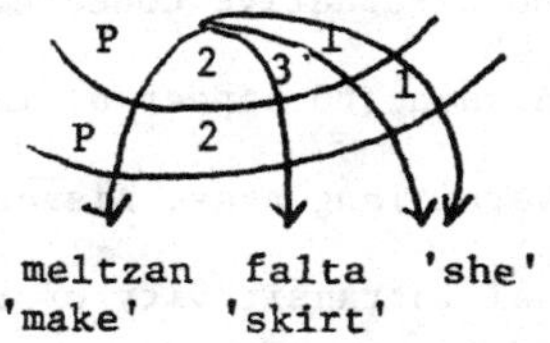

Unlike the case of object cancellation in Halkomelem presented in §4.4 above, which involves the advancement of the benefactive to object (as marked by the advB suffix), the Tzotzil clause in (149) does not contain the suffix -be, which marks 3-2 advancement. Thus, Aissen proposes that the indirect object does not advance to object in the stratum before cancellation. Since the initial object is not placed en chomage by 3-2 advancement, the clause is finally transitive, as is evidenced by ergative agreement.

After giving evidence for a similar example in Georgian, Aissen points out that cancellation in these cases can not be the result of antipassive, which as defined by Postal (cf. 144)) involves the retreat of subject to object, not to indirect object or oblique. Thus, the cancellation of indirect objects cannot be accounted for by proposing that they are chomeurs via antipassive. Aissen concludes that another construction, i.e. cancellation, accounts for the disappearance of the indirect object. Note that in this analysis there are no chomeurs posited, and thus violation of the Motivated Chomage Law is not an issue.

Extending this analysis to examples of reflexives which are finally intransitive, like those cited by Postal, Aissen concludes that cancellation may account for these as well. Under this analysis, reflexives in Halkomelem would be represented as in (151); the object in the initial stratum is cancelled in the next.

(151)

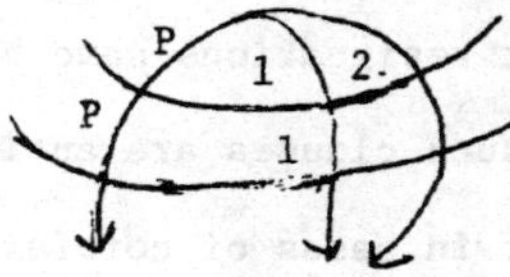

However, the Halkomelem data present a difficulty for such an analysis.

There are two constructions in Halkomelem involving coreference and intransitivity--object cancellations and reflexives. As discussed previously, these constructions are associated with different conditions. While reflexives are limited to cases where the <u>initial</u> object is coreferent to the subject, object cancellations are limited to cases where a <u>non-initial</u> object is coreferent to the subject, and, when 1st or 2nd person embedded objects are coreferent to the matrix subject, object cancellations, but not reflexives are possible. Because of these differences, it would be difficult to analyze object cancellations and reflexives in Halkomelem as a single construction, i.e. cancellation. Thus, Aissen's analysis, which may account for some cases of the disappearance of a nominal under coreference , does not account for all such cases.

4.7 Conclusion

In this chapter, I have presented evidence for four object resignation constructions in Halkomelem--antipassives, reflexives, reciprocals, and object cancellations. In each of these constructions a nominal which is object in one stratum does not bear any nuclear term relation in the subsequent stratum, and, since no other nominal assumes the object relation, the clause is finally intransitive.

Two analyses proposed within Relational Grammar to account for the final intransitivity of object resignations have been discussed. First, Postal (1977) claims that such clauses are antipassives. Second, Aissen (to appear b) suggests that in cases of coreference, the constructions involve cancellation. I argued that because of the differences in the conditions associated with the various object resignation constructions in Halkomelem, it is futile to try to reduce all of them to a single construction.

Thus, the analyses currently available within Relational Grammar cannot adequately account for object resignations in Halkomelem. Furthermore, the data from Halkomelem alone is insufficient to motivate explicit analyses that could account for the final intransitivity of these constructions. However, I conclude that a proper account of object resignations would need to accommodate the individual properties of each construction.

Footnotes to Chapter 4

[1] Several scholars, including Davis, Kuipers, Mattina, and Thompson and Thompson, working on other Salish languages have discussed antipassives calling this construction by various names including pseudo-transitive, pseudo-intransitive, and middle.

Hukari (1979) has also discussed antipassives. He points out the similarities of 3s/2-chomeurs in antipassives and advancement to object constructions.

Frantz (1977) has pointed out similar data concerning antipassives and causatives.

[2] Transitive Marking is discussed further in Chapter 5.

[3] Arguments for the bi-clausal initial structure of Halkomelem causatives could be given based on the data presented in the following discussions. I show that antipassives, reflexives, and reciprocals can be bases for causatives. Assuming that these constructions are syntactic, then causatives, since they can be based on these constructions, are also syntactic.

[4] Moreover, this analysis allows for a statement of a general principle of Halkomelem (and maybe universal) morphology which I call the Satellite Principle. Basically, affixes are ordered from the root outward (i.e. suffixes are order from left to right and prefixes from right to left) according to the order of the syntactic strata, as follows: initial to final strata, and downstairs clauses to upstairs clauses. Thus, since antipassives are downstairs constructions, the verbal suffix associated with them precedes the causative suffix. This will be discussed further in Chapter 5.

[5] Postal (p.c.) has suggested that perhaps the -əm suffix could be marking the presence of a 2-chomeur; thus it would be present in causatives under the CCU-3-2 advancement analysis to mark the presence of an upstairs 2-chomeur. However, since other morphology signals antipassive as well as -əm, this analysis is not tenable.

[6] Although all the speakers I have worked with accept object cancellation constructions like (126-127), only some of them accept cancellation in cases like (124-125), involving a single clause. However, all speakers agree that in (126-127) the cancelled object is coreferent to the matrix subject and not the subject of the embedded clause.

[7] I discuss object resignations with respect to constructions involving lexical suffixes in Gerdts (1981b, c).

[8] Timberlake (1979, 1980) points out cases in Russian where reflexives involving 1st and 2nd persons and those involving 3rd persons differ in acceptability.

[9] Actually, the Georgian case parallels the Halkomelem case of object cancellation. Only indirect objects that are such via inversion, advancement, or ascension (i.e., in my terminology, non-initial objects) can cancel.

Chapter 5

PASSIVES

5.0 Introduction

This chapter discusses a Halkomelem construction referred to as passive.[1] In (1-5b) I give passives which correspond to the finally transitive clauses in (1-5a):[2]

(1) a. ni lə́m-ət-əs θə sɬéniʔ t^{θ}ə xʷənítəm
aux look-tr-3erg det woman det white man
'The woman looked at the white man.'

b. ni lə́m-ət-əm ʔə θə sɬéniʔ t^{θ}ə xʷənítəm
aux look-tr-intr obl det woman white man
'The white man was looked at by the woman.'

(2) a. @ni q'ʷə́l-ət-əs θə Jane t^{θ}ə scé.ɬtən[3]
aux bake-tr-3erg det det salmon
'Jane baked the salmon.'

b. ni q'ʷə́l-ət-əm ʔə-[illegible] Jane t^{θ}ə scé.ɬtən
aux bake-tr-intr obl-det det salmon
'The salmon was baked by Jane.'

(3) a. ni pə́n-ət-əs kʷθə sqéwθ
aux plant-tr-3erg det potato
'He planted potatoes.'

b. ni pə́n-ət-əm kʷθə sqéwθ
aux plant-tr-intr det potato
'The potatoes were planted.'

(4) a. ni c'éw-ət-əs θə sɬéniʔ t^{θ}ə swə́yʔqeʔ
aux help-tr-3erg det woman det man
'The woman helped the man.'

b. ni c'éw-ət-əm t^{θ}ə swə́yʔqeʔ ʔə θə sɬéniʔ
aux help-tr-intr det man obl det woman
'The man was helped by the woman.'

(5) a. @ni q'ʷə́qʷ-nəxʷ-əs t^{θ}ə John t^{θ}ə Bob
aux club-l.c.tr-3erg det det

'John accidentally clubbed Bob.'

b. ni q'ʷə́qʷ-n-əm ʔə-ƛ̓ John t^{θ}ə Bob
aux club-l.c.tr-intr obl-det det

'Bob was accidentally clubbed by John.'

Halkomelem passives have several features which distinguish them from finally transitive clauses. First, while the (a) clauses have transitive marking, the (b) clauses have transitive marking followed by an intransitive suffix, in these examples <u>-əm</u>.[4,5] Second, while finally transitive clauses with 3rd person subjects have 3rd person agreement, there is no agreement in passives. Finally, while subjects in transitive clauses are in the straight case, the corresponding nominal in passives are in the oblique case.

In the following sections, I consider these and other properties of passives with respect to several alternative analyses available in Relational Grammar.[6] At first glance, Halkomelem passives seem parallel to passive constructions posited for other languages. However, a careful treatment reveals that Halkomelem passives have contradictory properties which make it difficult to present evidence for an analysis of this construction.

First, I give evidence that the nominal which corresponds to the final subject in finally transitive clauses is not the final subject in passives. Then, I contrast analyses available for the nominal in passives which corresponds to the final object in finally transitive clauses. In discussing this complicated topic, I deal first with 3rd person nominals then with 1st and 2nd persons. Finally, I discuss passives of advancement clauses, showing that passives of some clauses involving Caus-2 advancement violate a law proposed as a universal in Relational Grammar.

5.1 The Departure Subject

In the following discussion, I assume that the finally transitive clauses in (1-5a) and the passives in (1-5b) partially share stratal diagrams; e.g. the structure for (1a) represented in (6).

(6)

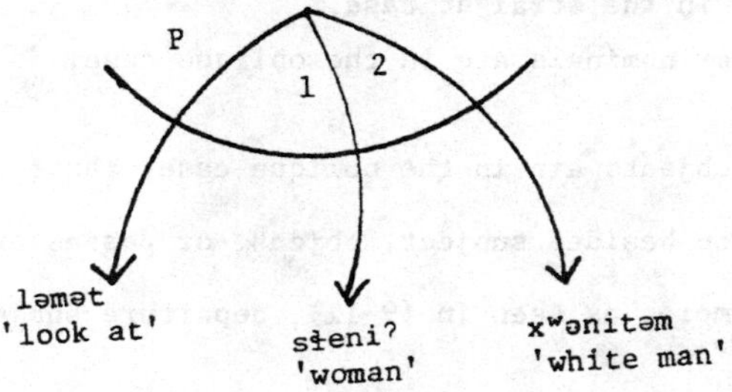

However, in passives like (1b), as I argue below, the nominal corresponding to the final subject in (1a) is not the final subject in (1b) but rather a chomeur, as represented in (7); the status of the object at final level, represented by ?, is discussed in §5.2-5.4.

(7)

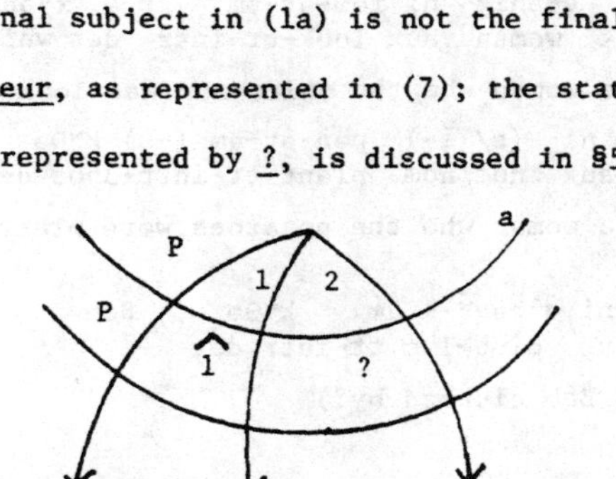

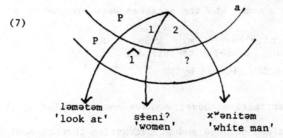

I refer to the last stratum shared by finally transitive clauses and passives as the departure stratum, labelled a in (7); the subject and object in this stratum are referred to as departure subject and object.[7,8]

In this section, I present evidence based on Nominal Case and extraction concerning the status of the departure subject at final level. Also, I discuss a condition on Halkomelem passives.

5.1.1 Arguments Concerning the Final GR of the Departure Subject

As pointed out above, departure subjects in passives are in the oblique rather than the straight case. Nominal Case (cf. §3.2.2) is formulated as follows:

(8) a. Final nuclear terms and 3rd person common noun possessors are in the straight case.

b. Other nominals are in the oblique case.

Since departure subjects are in the oblique case, these nominals must bear some other relation besides subject, object, or possessor at final level.

Furthermore, as seen in (9-11), departure subjects cannot be extracted:[9]

(9) *ní̵ł θə sə̵łéniʔ ni lə́m-ət-əm t$^{\theta}$ə xʷənítəm
3emph det woman aux look-tr-intr det white man
(It's the woman who the white man was looked at by.)

(10) *słéniʔ ni (s/ š-) pən-ət-əm (-s) kʷθə sqéwθ
woman aux nom/nom plant-tr-intr-3pos det potato
(It was a woman who the potatoes were planted by.)

(11) *łwet ni q'ʷəqʷ-n-ám kʷθə Bob
who aux club-l.c.tr-intr det
(Who was Bob clubbed by?)

In the discussion of extraction above, we have seen examples of the direct extraction of subjects and objects and of extraction through nominalization of obliques and 3s/2-chomeurs. As seen in (9-11), neither of these is possible for departure subjects. That departure subjects cannot be extracted indicates that they are not final subjects, objects, obliques, or 3s/2-chomeurs. Thus, I propose that departure subjects are final 1-chomeurs, as represented in (7) above.[10]

5.1.2 A Condition on Passives

In the above discussion, I have given examples of passives and the corresponding finally transitive clauses. In this section, I discuss cases where passives are not possible.

In the above examples, the 1-chomeurs were either 3rd person nominals or unspecified. As can be seen in (12-14b), the 1-chomeur cannot be 1st or 2nd person.

(12) a. ni cən lə́m-ət tᶿə spéˀəθ
aux 1sub look-tr det bear
'I looked at the bear.'

b. *ni lə́m-ət-əm ˀə-ƛ̓ ˀé.nˀθə tᶿə spéˀəθ
aux look-tr-intr obl-det 1emph det bear
(The bear was looked at by me.)

(13) a. ni ct q'ʷə́l-ət kʷθ̀ə scé.ɬtən
aux 1plsub bake-tr det salmon
'We baked the salmon.'

b. *ni q'ʷə́l-ət-əm ˀə-ƛ̓ ɬníməɬ kʷθə scé.ɬtən
aux bake-tr-intr obl-det 1plemph det salmon
(The salmon was baked by us.)

(14) a. ni ˀə č ˀu q'ʷə́qʷ-nəxʷ ˀalˀ kʷθə Bob
aux int 2sub just club-l.c.tr just det
'Did you accidentally club Bob?'

b. *ni ˀə q'ʷəqʷ-n-ám ˀə-ƛ̓ nə́wə kʷθə Bob
aux intr club-l.c.tr-intr obl det 2emph det
(Was Bob clubbed by you accidentally?)

To account for this, the following condition on passives can be formulated:[11]

(15) 1st and 2nd person pronominals cannot be placed en chomage in Passives.

5.2 3rd Person Departure Objects: Personal Passive vs. Unmotivated Chomage

In this section, I contrast two analyses of Halkomelem passives in which the departure object is 3rd person. As discussed in §0.3.2, according to Perlmutter and Postal (1977) passives are universally characterized in terms of the following subnetwork:

(16)

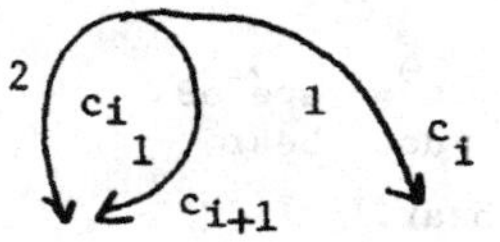

That is, a nominal bearing the object relation in the c_i stratum, in which there is also a nominal bearing the subject relation, bears the subject relation in the c_{i+1} stratum. In cases where the nominal which I have referred to above as the departure object advances to subject, the passive construction is a <u>personal</u> passive. Under a personal passive analysis, a Halkomelem passive such as (1b) would be represented as follows:

(17)

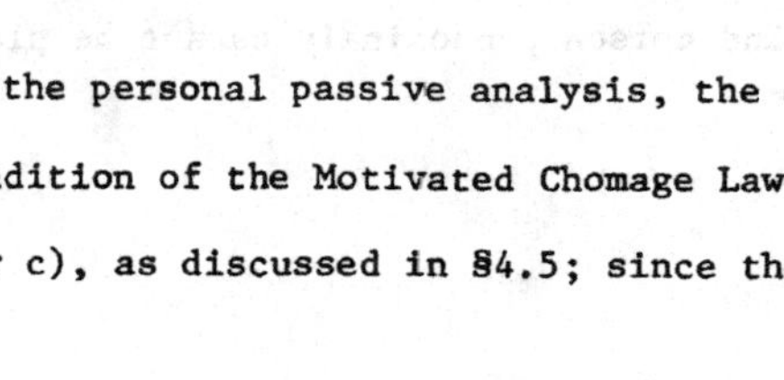

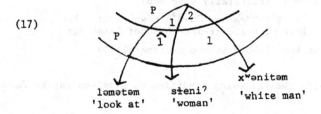

Note that, under the personal passive analysis, the structure in (17) satisfies the condition of the Motivated Chomage Law (Perlmutter and Postal, to appear c), as discussed in §4.5; since the departure object assumes the subject relation in the final stratum, the Motivated Chomage Law is not violated. Thus, the analysis posited in (17) accounts for the behaviour of the departure subject as a final 1-chomeur.

Recently, there has been some debate over the validity of the Motivated Chomage Law. Specifically, Comrie (1977) proposes that constructions are possible in which the departure subject is a final chomeur but no nominal advances to final subject.[12] Under this analysis, referred to as the unmotivated chomage analysis, a Halkomelem passive such as (1b) would be represented as follows:

(18)

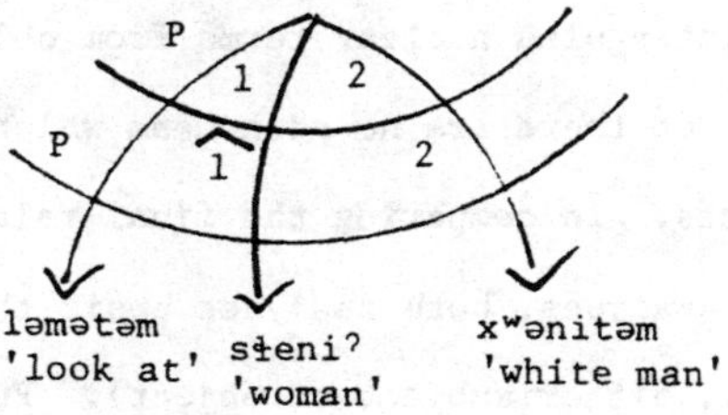

In the structure represented in (18), since the departure subject is a final chomeur but no nominal bears the subject relation at final level, the Motivated Chomage Law is violated. In addition, the analysis in (18) violates the Final 1 Law (Perlmutter and Postal, to appear c), which, stated informally, requires every final stratum to have a subject. Since there is no final subject in (18), the Final 1 Law is violated.

In fact, Hukari (1980) suggests that Halkomelem passives may be cases of unmotivated chomage and, thus, constitute a counterexample to the universal characterization of passive proposed by Perlmutter and Postal (1977) and to the Motivated Chomage Law and Final 1 Law (Perlmutter and Postal, to appear c). In this section and the following one, I discuss the evidence pertaining to the proper characterization of passives in Halkomelem. First, phenomena which can be handled by either a personal passive or an unmotivated chomage analysis are discussed. Second, I discuss constructions involving raising, concluding that a personal passive analysis is to be preferred over one involving unmotivated chomage.

5.2.1 Phenomena Handled by Either Analysis

In the case of passives as exemplified above, in which the departure object is a 3rd person nominal, none of the phenomena discussed in Chapter 2 can serve to distinguish a personal passive from an unmotivated chomage analysis. As pointed out in §2.8, there are phenomena which distinguish nuclear terms from obliques and ergatives from absolutives, but there are no phenomena which distinguish nominal subjects and objects. In comparing the final relation of the departure object in the two analyses, both analyses posit that it is a final nuclear term (i.e., either subject or object). Furthermore, assuming the definition of absolutive given in §0.3.4, the departure object, since it heads a final nuclear-term arc in an intransitive stratum in both (17) and (18), is the final absolutive.

In this section, I show that as predicted by both analyses the departure object is a final nuclear term and a final absolutive.

First, according to Nominal Case as given in (8) above, final nuclear terms are in the straight case. As is seen in (1-5b), the departure object is in the straight case; this follows from either the personal passive or the unmotivated chomage analyses, which posit that the departure object is a final nuclear term.

Second, departure objects, like other final nuclear terms, can be directly extracted (cf. §3.2), as seen in (19-21).

(19) xʷənítəm ni lə́m-ət-əm ʔə ɬə sɬéniʔ
white man aux look-tr-intr obl det woman

'A white man was what was looked at by the woman.'

(20) níɬ kʷθə scé.ɬtən ni q'ʷə́l-ət-əm ʔə-ƛ̓ John
3emph det salmon aux bake-tr-intr obl-det

'It's the salmon that was baked by John.'

(21) ɬwét k'ʷ ni q'ʷə́qʷ-n-əm ʔə-ƛ̓ Bob
who det aux club-l.c.tr-intr obl-det

'Who was accidentally clubbed by Bob?'

This follows from either analysis, since both posit that the departure object is a final nuclear term.

In addition, when the departure object is a possessive phrase, the possessor can be extracted, as seen in (22-24).

(22) státəl-stəxʷ ʔə č kʷθə xʷənítəm ni q'á.y-t-əm kʷθə šxʷʔáq'ʷa-s
know-cs int 2sub det white man aux kill-tr-intr det brother-3pos

'Do you know the white man whose brother was killed.'

(23) níɬ kʷθə John ni q'ʷə́l-ət-əm kʷθə scé.ɬtən-s ʔə-ƛ̓ Bob
3emph det aux bake-tr-intr det salmon-3pos obl-det

'It was John whose salmon was cooked by Bob.'

(24) ʔé.nʔθə kʷθə ni q'á.y-t-əm kʷθə nə-šə́yəɬ ʔə kʷθə qíqəq'əʔls
1emph det aux kill-tr-intr det 1pos-o.b. obl det police

'I'm the one whose older brother was killed by the police.'

Since possessor extraction is limited to cases where the possessive phrase is the final absolutive (cf. §3.1.4), it provides evidence that the departure object is the final absolutive.

Finally, when the departure object is a quantifier phrase with the quantifier <u>mə́k'ʷ</u> 'all', the quantifier can be extracted, as seen in (25-27):

(25) ni mə́k'ʷ ʔu q'ʷə́l-ət-əm t^θə sθə́qiʔ ʔə t^θə słənłéniʔ
aux all lnk bake-tr-intr det sockeye obl det women

'All the sockeye(salmon) were baked by the women.'
*'All the women baked the sockeye.'

(26) ni mə́k'ʷ ʔu pə́n-ət-əm kʷθə sqéwθ
aux all lnk plant-tr-intr det potato

'All the potatoes were planted.'

(27) ni mək'ʷ ʔu q'á.y-t-əm kʷθə səwwə́yʔqeʔ ʔə kʷθə qíqəq'əʔls
aux all lnk kill-tr-intr det men obl det police

'All the men were killed by the police.'

Quantifier extraction, as discussed in §3.1.5, is limited to cases where the quantifier phrase is the final absolutive. Thus, quantifier extraction provides evidence that the departure object is a final absolutive.

5.2.2 Raising

Although the phenomena previously discussed do not distinguish nominal subjects and objects, there is one construction involving raising which does. This construction was first pointed out for Central Salish by Davis (1980), who gives one argument for personal passive in Sliammon based on raising.

Sliammon has finally transitive clauses and passives similar to Halkomelem, as seen in (28a-b):[13]

(28) (Sliammon)

a. qə́qəy-t-əs Joe Jim
beat-trans-(s)he

'Joe beats Jim up.'

b. qə́qəy-t-əm ʔə Joe Jim
beat-trans-intr obl

'Jim is being beaten up by Joe.'

These clauses can be embedded under the verb <u>pápkʷa-</u>'watch' as seen in (29-30a); in addition, constructions are possible where a nominal of the embedded clause is apparently the object of the matrix clause, as seen in (29-30b).

(29) (Sliammon)

a. pápkʷa-t č [s qə́qəy-t-s Joe Jim]
watch-trans I that bear-trans-(s)he
'I watch Joe beat up Jim.'

b. pápkʷa-t č <u>Joe</u> [s qə́qəy-t-s Jim]
watch-trans I that beat-trans-(s)he
'I watch Joe beat up Jim.'

c. pápkʷa-t č <u>Jim</u> [s qə́qəy-t-s <u>Joe</u>]
watch-trans I that beat-trans-(s)he
'I watch Jim beat up Joe.'
*'I watch Joe beat up Jim.'

(30) (Sliammon)

a. pápkʷa-t č [s qə́qəy-t-it ˀə Joe Jim]
watch-trans I that beat-trans-intr obl
'I watch Jim being beaten up by Joe.'

b. pápkʷa-t č <u>Jim</u> [s qə́qəy-t-it ˀə <u>Joe</u>]
watch-tr I that beat-trans-intr obl
'I watch Jim being beaten up by Joe.'

c.* pápkʷa-t č (ˀə) <u>Joe</u> [s qə́qəy-t-it Jim]
watch-tr I obl that beat-trans-intr

Davis assumes that the (b) and (c) sentences involve raising and that the downstairs nominal in ascending to upstairs object leaves a pronominal copy, i.e. the verbal suffix <u>-s</u> labelled <u>(s)he</u> in (29b-c). As seen in (29b) and (30b), final subjects of transitives and the departure object of passives can raise. Furthermore, as seen in (29c) and (30c), objects of transitives and departure subjects in passives cannot raise.

These data would follow from an analysis which (1) posited advancement to subject by departure objects and (2) limited raising to final subjects.

In Halkomelem, as first noted by Hukari (1980), there is a similar construction involving x̌ec- 'figure out'/'check out'/'notice'/'wonder'; in (31-34a) x̌ec- is followed by a subordinate clause which is bracketed while in (31-34b) the subject of the subordinate clause is apparently the object of the matrix clause. I have underlined this nominal in (31-34b).[15]

(31) a. ʔi cən x̌éc-t [ʔu ni-ʔəs ceʔ ʔu
aux 1sub wonder-tr lnk aux-3ssub fut lnk
c'ew-ət-álʔxʷ-əs tᶿə swə́yʔqeʔ]
help-tr-1plobj-3ssub det man
'I'm checking out the man if he will help us.'

b. ʔi cən x̌éc-t tᶿə swə́yʔqeʔ [ʔu ni-ʔəs ceʔ
aux 1sub wonder-tr det man lnk aux-3ssub fut
ʔu c'ew-ət-álʔxʷ-əs]
lnk help-tr-1plobj-3ssub
'I'm checking out the man if he will help us.'

(32) a. ʔi cən x̌éc-t [kʷ s-ʔi -s-əɬ yəxʷ
aux 1sub wonder-tr det nom-aux-3ssub-pst sup
lèʔləmʔ-ə t-álʔxʷ-əs kʷθə xʷənítəm]
look(cont)-tr-1plobj-3ssub det white man
'I am figuring out that the white man must have been looking at us.'

b. ʔi cən x̌éc-t kʷθə xʷənítəm [kʷ s-ʔi -s-əɬ
aux 1sub wonder-tr det white man det nom-aux-3ssub-pst
yəxʷ leʔləmʔ-ə t-álʔxʷ-əs]
sup look(cont)-tr-1plobj-3ssub
'I am figuring out the wite man that he must have been looking at us.'

(33) a. ʔi cə x̌eʔx̌cí-t [ʔu nemʔ-əs xʷčə́θət
aux 1sub wonder(cont)-tr lnk aux-3ssub go where
kʷθə sqʷəméyʔ]
det dog
'I'm wondering where the dog is going to go.'

b. ʔi cə x̌eʔx̌cí-t kʷθə sqʷəméyʔ [ʔu nemʔ-əs
aux 1sub wonder(cont)-tr det dog lnk aux-3ssub
xʷčə́θət]
go where
'I'm wondering where the dog is going to go.'

(34) a. ʔi cən x̌éc-t [ʔu ʔiʔ-əs cəlkʷstáʔmət
aux 1sub wonder-tr lnk aux-3ssub do
tᶿə xʷələnítəm]
det white men
'I wonder what the white men are doing.'

b. ʔi cən x̌éc-t tᶿə xʷələnítəm [ʔu ʔiʔ-əs
aux 1sub wonder-tr det white men lnk aux-3ssub
cəlkʷstaʔmət]
do
'I wonder what the white men are doing.'

In the following discussion, I assume, following Hukari (1980), that examples like (31-34b) involve raising. Furthermore, I assume that the subordinate clauses are the initial objects in the above examples. Thus, an example not involving raising. e.g. (31a), can be represented as in (35), and one involving raising, e.g. (31b), can be represented in (36).[16]

(35)
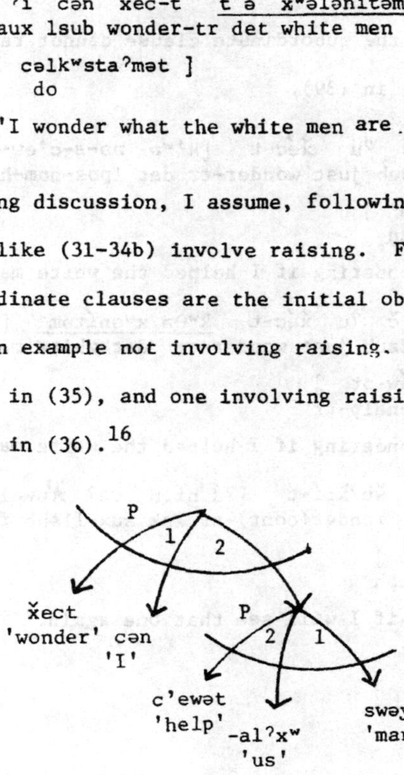

(36)

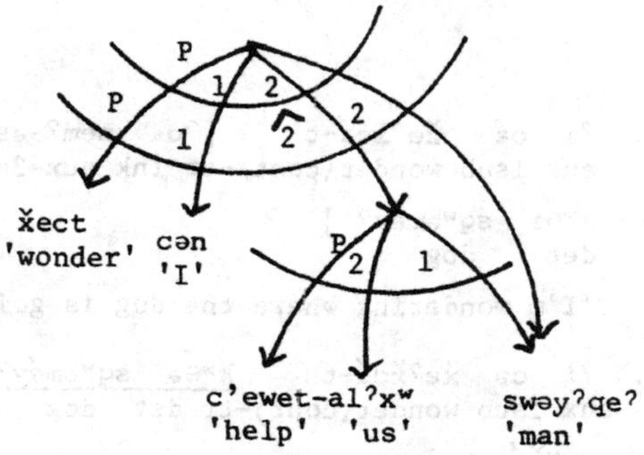

As in Sliammon, the downstairs nominal in ascending to object leaves a pronominal copy. I do not indicate the pronominal copy in the stratal diagram.

In (31-32b), we have seen examples where the subordinate clause is finally transitive and the subject raises. As seen in (37-38b), the object of the subordinate clause cannot raise; I have represented (37b) in (39).

(37) a. ʔi ʔə č ʔu x̌éc-t [k'ʷə nə-s-c'ew-ət kʷθə
aux int 2sub just wonder-tr det 1pos-nom-help-tr det
xʷənítəm]
white man
'Are you wondering if I helped the white man.'

b. *ʔi ʔə č ʔu x̌éc-t <u>kʷθə xʷənítəm</u> [k'ʷə
aux int 2sub just wonder-tr det white man det
nə-s-c'éw-ət]
1pos-nom-help-tr
(Are you wondering if I helped the white man.)

(38) a. ʔi cən x̌eʔx̌cí-t [ʔu ni.n ceʔ ƛ̓əwəɬ lə́m-nəxʷ
aux 1sub wonder(cont)-tr lnk aux-1lsub fut again see-l.c.tr
kʷθu níɬ]
det 3emph
'I wonder if I will see that one again.'

b. *ˀi cən x̌eˀx̌cí-t kʷθu níɬ [ˀu ni.n ceˀ ƛ̓əwəɬ lə́m-nəxʷ]
aux 1sub wonder-tr det 3emph lnk aux-1ssub fut again see-l.c.tr
(I wonder if I will see that one again.)

(39)

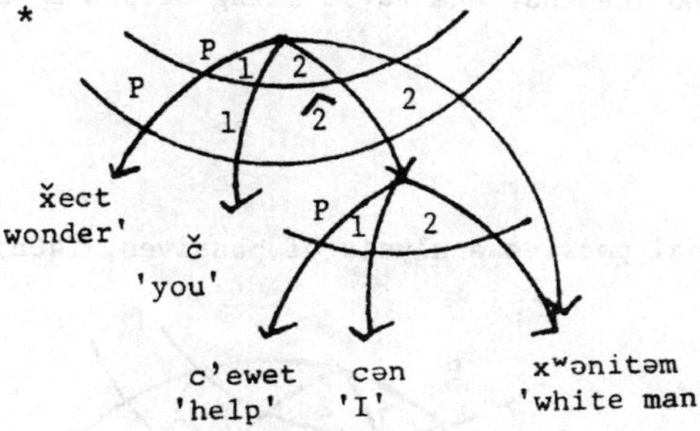

As in Sliammon, when the subordinate clause is passive, the departure object can raise, as seen in (40-41b).[17]

(40) a. ˀi cən x̌eˀx̌cí-t [ˀu ˀiˀ-əs lə́ˀləm-ˀət-əmˀ
aux 1sub wonder-tr lnk aux-3ssub look(cont)-tr-intr
ˀə-ƛ̓ John kʷθə Bob]
obl-det det
'I'm wondering if Bob is being watched by John.'

b. ˀi cən x̌eˀx̌cí-t kʷθə Bob [ˀu ˀiˀ-əs lə́ˀləm-ˀət-əmˀ
aux 1sub wonder-tr det lnk aux-3ssub look-tr-intr
ˀə-ƛ̓ John]
obl-det
'I'm wondering if Bob is being watched by John.'

(41) a. ˀi cən x̌éc-t [ˀu ˀiˀ-əs c'ewˀ-ət-əmˀ kʷθu níɬ
aux 1sub wonder-tr lnk aux-3ssub help-tr-intr det 3emph
ˀə-ƛ̓ John]
obl-det
'I notice that that one is being helped by John.'

(41) b. ʔi cən x̌éc-t kʷθu níɬ [ʔu ʔiʔ-əs c'éwʔ-ət-əmʔ
aux 1sub wonder-tr det 3emph lnk aux-3ssub help-tr-intr
ʔə-ƛ̓ John]
obl-det

'I notice that one to be being helped by John.'

Under the personal passive analysis of passives, (40b) can be represented in (42).

(42)

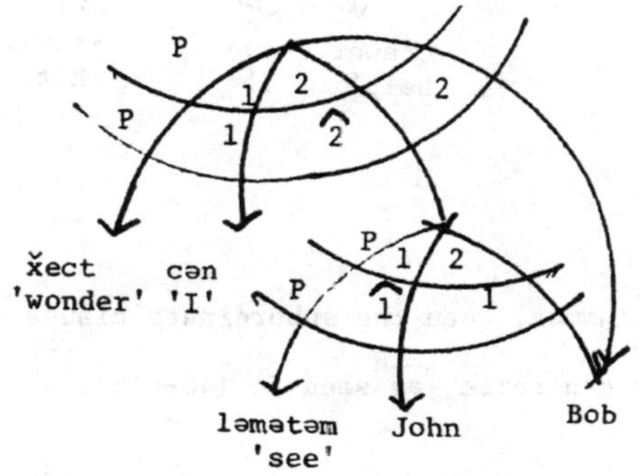

In contrasting (36) and (42) with (39), a generalization concerning raising is possible under the personal passive analysis: final subjects can raise while final objects cannot.

In contrast, (40b) would be represented as (43) under the unmotivated chomage analysis.

(43)

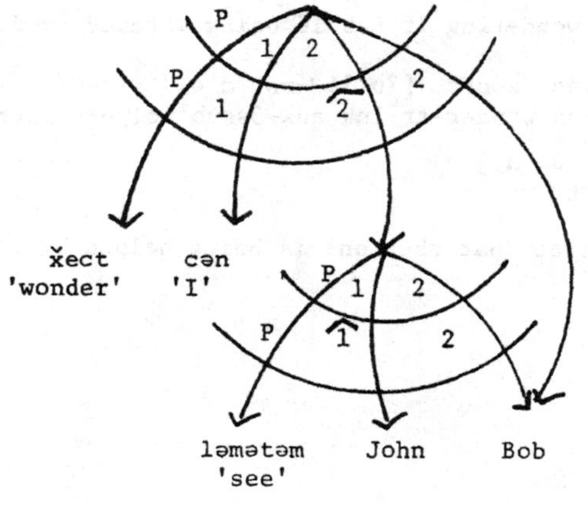

Since the unmotivated chomage analysis posits that the departure object is a final object, departure objects and objects of finally transitive clauses should behave alike with respect to raising. In contrasting (39) and (43), however, we see that this is not the case; while departure objects can raise, objects in finally transitive clauses cannot. Thus, a generalization concerning raising is not possible under the unmotivated chomage analysis.

In addition, as Hukari (1980) notes, departure subjects can raise, as seen in (44-45b).[18]

(44) a. (same as (40a))

b. ʔi cən x̌eʔx̌cí-t kʷθə John [ʔu ʔiʔ-əs
aux 1sub wonder-tr det lnk aux-3ssub

léʔləmʔ-ət-əmʔ kʷθə Bob]
look-tr-intr det

'I'm wondering if Bob is being watched by John.'
(literally: 'I'm wondering John if Bob is being helped (by him.)')

(45) a. (same as (41a))

b. ʔi cən x̌éc-t kʷθə John [ʔu ʔiʔ-əs c'éwʔ-ət-əmʔ
aux 1sub wonder-tr det lnk aux-3ssub help-tr-intr

kʷθu níɬ]
det 3emph

'I notice that that one is being helped by John.'
(literally: 'I notice John that that one is being helped (by him).')

Under the personal passive analysis, (44b) can be represented as in (46).

(46)

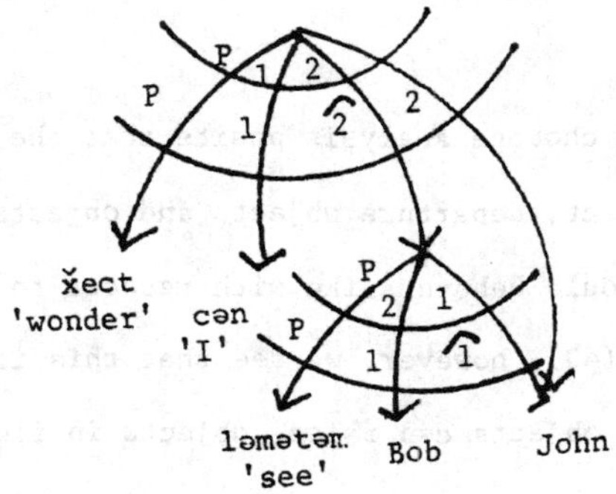

Under this analysis, the class of nominals which can raise includes: 1) final subjects and 2) 1-chomeurs. Such a class of nominals has been referred to as acting 1s. (cf. Perlmutter and Postal, to appear d; Perlmutter, to appear) The notion of an acting term is defined as follows:

(47) Acting Term_x:

A nominal node is an acting term_x of clause b if and only if:

i) it heads a term_x arc, A, with tail b whose last coordinate is c_i, and

ii) it does not head an arc B with tail b and with a term R-sign distinct from term_x and with coordinate c_j, where $j > i$.

(Perlmutter, to appear, p. 39)

According to this definition, final subjects and also final 1-chomeurs, since they do not bear a term relation at the final level, are grouped together as acting 1s. Under the personal passive analysis, the condition on raising can be stated in terms of this notion as follows:[19]

(48) Only acting 1s can raise.

In contrast, under the unmotivated chomage analysis, such a generalization is not possible. The class of nominals which raise are:

1) final subjects, 2) 1-chomeurs, and 3) departure objects in passives. Since objects of finally transitive clauses do not raise, there is no apparent generalization with which to state the condition on raising.

In summary, the data involving raising in Halkomelem provides one argument that the personal passive analysis is to be preferred over one involving unmotivated chomage. Under the personal passive analysis, the condition on raising refers to acting 1s. Under the unmotivated chomage analysis, however, objects of passives raise while objects of finally transitive clauses do not, and no apparent generalization is possible.

5.3 1st and 2nd Person Departure Objects: Unmotivated Chomage vs. Impersonal Passive

In the preceding section, I presented two analyses of passives with 3rd person departure objects. Although the two analyses could both account for data involving Nominal Case, extraction, possessor extraction, and quantifier extraction, data involving raising gave one argument that the personal passive analysis is preferred over the unmotivated chomage analysis.

In this section, passives with 1st and 2nd person departure objects are discussed. I contrast two analyses of these constructions: unmotivated chomage, as discussed above, and impersonal passive (cf. Perlmutter, 1978, and Perlmutter and Postal, to appear c,d). Perlmutter and Postal have characterized impersonal passives as the advancement of a dummy (D), which is inserted as an object, to subject. In (49), I have represented an impersonal passive in which the departure stratum is transitive; note that (49) meets the universal definition of passive, as discussed above, since the object in a transitive stratum advances to subject.

(49)

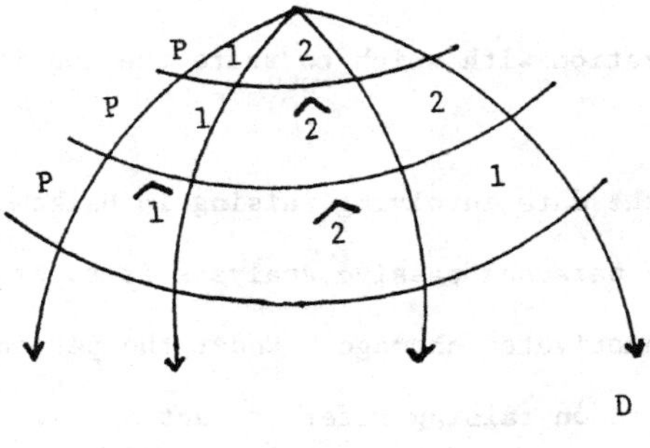

Under the impersonal passive analysis, the insertion of the dummy (D) places the departure object en chomage; thus, at final level, the departure object is a chomeur.

In the following discussion, I first present phenomena that can be handled by either the unmotivated chomage or the impersonal passive analysis. Second, data involving a phenomenon referred to as doubling is presented. I argue that while an analysis involving impersonal passive can account for this phenomenon, one positing unmotivated chomage cannot. Finally, I discuss raising pointing out the difficulties of stating a condition on raising for both analyses.

5.3.1 Phenomena Handled by Either Analysis

In (50-54b) below, I have given examples of passives with 1st and 2nd person departure objects; the corresponding finally transitive clauses are given in (a):

(50) a. ni ləm-əθ-ámˀš̌-əs ɬə sɬéniˀ
aux look-tr-1obj-3erg det woman
'The woman looked at me.'

b. ni ləm-əθ-él-əm ˀə ɬə sɬéniˀ
aux look-tr-1pas-intr obl det woman
'I was looked at by the woman.'

(51) a. ni c'ew-ət-ál?xʷ-əs ɬə sɬéni?
aux help-tr-1plobj-3erg det woman
'The woman helped us.'

b. ni c'ew-ət-álə-m ?ə ɬə sɬéni?
aux help-tr-1plpas-intr obl det woman
'We **were** helped by the woman.'

(52) a.* ni ləm-əθ-ámə-s ɬə sɬéni?
aux look-tr-2obj-3erg det woman
(The woman looked at you.)

b. ni ləm-əθ- á.-m ?ə ɬə sɬéni?
aux look-tr-2pas-intr obl det woman
'You were looked at by the woman.'

(53) a. @ni q'ʷaqʷ-n-ám?š-əs kʷθə Bob
aux club-l.c.tr-1obj det
'Bob accidentally clubbed me.'

b. ni q'ʷəqʷ-n-él-əm ?ə-ƛ' Bob
aux club-l.c.tr-1pas-intr obl-det
'I was accidentally clubbed by Bob.'

(54) a. *ni ləm-n-ámə-s
aux look-l.c.tr-2obj-3erg
(He saw you.)

b. ni ləm-n-á.-m
aux look-l.c.tr-2pas-intr
'You were seen.'

These passives are characterized by several features: first, the verb is suffixed with a transitive marker, then, there is a suffix marking the person of the departure object, and finally, there is an intransitive suffix, in the above examples, -<u>əm</u> . Furthermore, the 1-chomeur, if it is specified, is a third person nominal in the oblique case, as discussed in §5.1.

I have listed the pronominal suffixes for the departure object in passives in (55).

(55) Passive person suffixes:

	sg.	pl.
1st	-el	-alə
2nd	-amə	-alə

Note that the transitive marker -t, when it precedes the passive person suffixes, has the form -θ, as it does before the object suffixes. Comparing these suffixes with those of the other pronominal cases given in §1.4.5, we see that the passive personal suffixes bear no resemblance to the subject pronominal clitics or suffixes. They do, however, bear a resemblance to the objective pronominal markers, which I have repeated here as (56):

(56) Objective pronominal suffixes:

	sg.	pl.
1st	-amʔš̌	-alʔxʷ
2nd	-amə	-alə

Notably, the 2nd person forms are the same in each set.[20] Apparently, the 2nd plural passive suffix is also used for 1st person. Because of the difference in the 1st person suffixes, the two sets of suffixes are kept distinct, at least synchronically. The diachronic evidence, however, points to the existence of two object sets in Central Salish; the passive person suffixes are reconstructable as object suffixes.[21] Perhaps it is because of this that Hukari (1980) says that Halkomelem 'maintains object inflection on passive verbs.' In the following discussion, I assume that it is possible to propose an analysis in which the passive person suffixes and objective suffixes are both object suffixes. Under such an analysis, some morphological feature or rule would determine the choice of objective suffixes; perhaps a rule could make reference to the presence of an intransitive suffix following the objective suffixes in the case of passives.

In Halkomelem passives, then, 1st and 2nd person pronominal departure objects are in the objective case. In the rule for pronominal case discussed in §3.1.2, final subjects are in the subjective case, while final objects are in the objective case. Under the unmotivated chomage analysis, since the departure object is the final object, its pronominal case follows from the rule discussed above.

Under the impersonal passive analysis, the departure object is a 2-chomeur. Since pronominal 2-chomeurs have not been posited elsewhere, it is possible to propose that they are in the objective case. Specifically, the class of pronominals in the objective case are final objects and 2-chomeurs; according to the definition of acting term given in (47), these are <u>acting 2s</u>. Thus, Pronominal Case should be modified as follows:

(57) Acting 2s are in the objective case.

The impersonal passive analysis and Pronominal Case as stated in (57) account for the objective case of 1st and 2nd person pronominal departure objects.

Data involving extraction can also be handled by either analysis. As seen in (58-60), 1st or 2nd person departure objects can be extracted.

(58) ʔé.nʔθə ni q'ʷəqʷ-n-é l-əm ʔə-ƛ̓ Bob
lemph aux club-l.c.tr-lpas-intr obl-det
'I'm the one who was accidentally clubbed by Bob.'

(59) nə́wə ni ləm-əθ-á.-m
2emph aux look-tr-2pas-intr
'You are the one who was looked out.'

(60) ɬníməɬ ni c'ew-ət-á l-əm
lplemph aux help-tr-lplpas-intr
'We're the ones who were helped.'

In (58-60), the departure object is directly extracted. In addition, the extracted departure object leaves a pronominal copy. As pointed out in §2.6.3, while both subjects and objects are directly extracted, objects leave a pronominal copy while subjects do not. According to Hukari (1980), this provides evidence that departure objects are final objects, thus supporting the unmotivated chomage analysis.

However, an account of pronominal copy in extractions is also possible under the impersonal passive analysis. Final objects and departure objects, if the latter are 2-chomeurs, are acting 2s, and the statement concerning pronominal copies in extractions can refer to this notion. Thus, while extracted acting 2s leave pronominal copies, extracted subjects do not.

In the above discussion, I gave evidence that 1st and 2nd person departure objects behave like final objects in two respects: they are in the objective pronominal case, and, when they are extracted, they leave pronominal copies. This follows from the unmotivated chomage analysis, which posits that departure objects are final objects. However, the notion of acting 2, which groups final objects and 2-chomeurs, can also be used to make generalizations concerning the above phenomena.

Thus, the impersonal passive analysis, which posits that 1st and 2nd person departure objects are chomeurs, also accounts for these data.

5.3.2 Doubling

In (50-54b) above, I have given examples of passives where the 1st and 2nd person departure object is a passive person suffix. Although this is the predominant form for passives, a second pattern of person marking, which I refer to as doubling, is possible for some speakers.[22] In doubling, in addition to the passive person suffix, there is a pronominal subjective clitic, in (63-64), there is a subordinate subjective suffix, (cf. §1.4.5) and in (65-66), which have nominalized subordinate clauses, there is a possessive affix.[23]

(61) @ni cən c'ə q'ʷaq̇ʷ-əθ-él-əm
aux 1sub evid club-tr-1pas-intr
'Evidentally, I was hit.'

(62) @ ni ct ʔu ləm-n-álə-m ʔalʔ
aux 1plsub just look-l.c.tr-1plpas-intr just
'We were seen, alright.'

(63) @ ʔi cən x̌éc-t ʔu ni-ʔət ceʔ ʔu c'ew-ət-álə-m
aux 1sub wonder-tr lnk aux-1plssub fut lnk help-tr-1plpas-intr
'I wonder if we will be helped.'

(64) @ ʔi cən x̌éc-t ʔu ni-ʔələp ceʔ ʔu c'ew-ət-ál-əm
aux 1sub wonder-tr lnk aux-2plssub fut lnk help-tr-2plpas-intr
'I wonder if you pl. will be helped.'

(65) @ ʔə́wə k'ʷ nə-s-c'ew-əθ-é.l-t
neg det 1pos-nom-help-tr-1pas-st
'I was not helped.'

(66) @ sk'ʷéy k'ʷə nə-s-kʷən-n-é.l-t
impossible det 1pos-nom-catch-l.c.tr-1pas-st
'It's impossible for me to get caught.'

Assuming that the pronominal morphology in the above examples gives evidence for a final subject, doubling presents a problem in the unmotivated chomage analysis. Since this analysis claims that passives do not have a subject at final level, the above examples cannot be accounted for.

In contrast, the impersonal passive analysis posits that there is a final subject, i.e. the dummy, which is inserted as an object, placing the departure object en chomage, and advances to subject, placing the departure subject en chomage. Thus, the appearance of subjective morphology in the above examples can be accounted for by assuming that the dummy, which is the final subject, is in the subjective case, like other final subjects. However, such an analysis must account for the variation in person of the subjective forms since passives occur with and without doubling. This variation is seen most clearly in cases where the passive is in a subordinate clause. In (67-68a) the subjective form in the passive is 3rd person, while in (67-69b) there is doubling and the person and number of the subjective form agree with the departure object.

(67) a. ʔi cən x̌éc-t [ʔu niʔ-əs ceʔ ʔu c'ew-ət-álə-m]
aux 1sub wonder-tr lnk aux-3ssub fut lnk help-tr-1plpas-intr /2plpas
'I'm wondering if we will be helped.'

b. @ʔi cən x̌éc-t [ʔu ni-ʔət ceʔ ʔu c'ew-ət-álə-m]
aux 1sub wonder-tr lnk aux-1plssub fut lnk help-tr-1plpas-intr
'I'm wondering if we will be helped.'

(68) a. (same as (67a))

b. @ʔi cən x̌éc-t [ʔu ni-ʔələp ceʔ ʔu c'ew-ət-álə-m]
aux 1sub wonder-tr lnk aux-2plssub fut lnk help-tr-2plpas-intr
'I'm wondering if you pl. will be helped.'

(69) a. ʔi cən x̌ex̌cí-t [ʔu ʔiʔ-əs lèʔləmʔ-əθ-á.-mʔ]
aux 1sub wonder-tr lnk aux-3ssub look-tr-2pas-intr
'I'm checking out to see if you're being watched.'

b. @ʔi cən x̌əx̌cí-t [ʔu ʔi-əxʷ lèʔləmʔ-əθ-á.-mʔ]
aux 1sub wonder-tr lnk aux-2ssub look-tr-2pas-intr
'I'm checking out to see if you are being watched.'

I propose that under the impersonal passive analysis this variation in person can be accounted for by means of the <u>brother-in-law</u> relation posited by Perlmutter and Postal (1974). As they define it, the brother-in-law relation holds between a dummy and the first nominal it places en chomage. In (70), I give the representation of (67) under the impersonal passive analysis; since the departure object is the first nominal placed en chomage by the dummy, the brother-in-law relation (which I have indicated with =) holds between the departure object and the dummy.

(70)

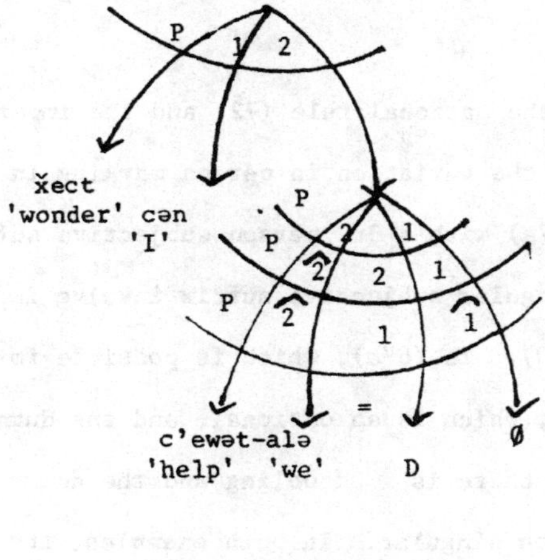

In the analyses of various languages, Perlmutter and Postal have made use of the brother-in-law relation to account for various agreement and case phenomena. They claim that many languages, including English, have brother-in-law agreement, as stated in (71):[24]

(71) Brother-in-law agreement:

Where the nominal referenced by an agreement rule is a dummy, agreement is determined by the dummy's brother-in-law instead.

For Halkomelem, I propose that cases of doubling be treated similarly, as a brother-in-law phenomenon. The rule for doubling is given in (72):

(72) Doubling: (for some speakers)

When the final subject is a dummy, it assumes the person and number of its brother-in-law.

Furthermore, I posit that (72) is an optional rule. When doubling does not occur, the dummy, like dummies in many languages, is 3rd person singular.

In summary, the optional rule (72) and the impersonal passive analysis account for the variation in person marking in (67-69) above. For example, both (67a) with a 3rd person subjective suffix and (67b) with a 1st person singular subjective suffix involve impersonal passive, as represented in (70). In (67a), which is possible for all speakers, there is no doubling, which is an optional, and the dummy is 3rd person singular. In (67b), there is doubling and the dummy assumes the features of 1st person singular. In both examples, the dummy is the final subject and is therefore in the subjective case.

By making reference to the brother-in-law relation, an analysis for doubling consistent with the impersonal passive analysis is possible. In contrast, no analysis for doubling is possible under the unmotivated chomage analysis, since under this analysis there is no final subject and therefore no account for subjective morphology. The data involving doubling, then, provide evidence that the impersonal passive analysis is to be preferred over the unmotivated chomage analysis for passives with 1st and 2nd person departure objects.

5.3.3 Raising

In §5.2.2 above, I discussed constructions with raising in Halkomelem, showing under the personal passive analysis raising is limited to acting 1s. In this section, I discuss raising constructions involving 1st and 2nd person pronominals.

As seen in (73-75b), pronominal subjects of clauses embedded under the verb x̌ec- can be raised to matrix object.

(73) a. ʔi cən tu x̌éc-t [ʔu ni-əxʷ ceʔ ʔu c'éw-ət]
aux 1sub just wondet-tr lnk aux-2ssub fut lnk help-tr
'I am just wondering if you are going to help him.'

b. ʔi cən tu x̌ec-θ-ámə [ʔu ni-əxʷ ceʔ ʔu c'éw-ət]
aux 1sub just wonder-tr-2obj lnk aux-2ssub fut lnk help-tr
'I am just wondering if you are going to help him.'

(74) a. ʔi ʔə č x̌éc-t [ʔu ni.n ceʔ ʔu c'éw-ət]
aux int 2sub wonder-tr lnk aux-1ssub fut lnk help-tr
'Are you figuring out if I will help him?'

b. ʔi ʔə č x̌ec-θ-ámʔš [ʔu ni.n ceʔ ʔu c'éw-ət]
aux int 2sub wonder-tr-1obj lnk aux-1ssub fut lnk help-tr
'Are you figuring out if I will help him?'

(75) a. ʔi ʔə č x̌éc-t [k'ʷə nə-s-ni q'ə́l-nəxʷ]
aux int 2sub wonder-tr det 1pos-nom-aux mad-l.c.tr
'Did you notice that I got mad at him?'

b. ʔi ʔə č x̌ec-θ-ámʔš [k'ʷə nə-s-ni q'ə́l-nəxʷ]
aux int 2sub wonder-tr-1obj det 1pos-nom-aux mad-l.c.tr
'Did you notice that I got mad at him?'

Furthermore, as seen in (76-78b), pronominal objects cannot raise.

(76) a. ʔi ʔə č ʔu x̌éc-t [ʔu niʔ-əs ceʔ c'ewə-t-álʔxʷ-əs]
aux intr 2sub just w.-tr lnk aux-3ssub fut help-tr-1plobj-3ssub
'Are you checking if he will help us?'

b. *ʔi ʔə č x̌ec-t-álʔxʷ ["]
aux int 2sub w.tr-1plobj
(Are you checking if he will help us.)

(77) a. ʔi ʔə č x̌éc-t [ʔuʔi-əs ceʔ c'ew-əθ-amʔš -əs]
aux int2sub w-tr lnk aux-3ssub fut help-tr-1obj-3ssub
'Are you figuring out if he is helping me.'

b. *ʔiʔə č x̌ec-θ-ámʔš ["]
aux int 2sub w.-tr-1obj
(Are you figuring out if he is helping me.)

(78) a. ʔi x̌éc-t-əs [ʔu ni-ʔəxʷ yəx ləm-n-ámʔš]
aux w.-tr-3erg lnk aux-2ssub sup see-l.c.tr-1obj
'He's figuring out that you must have seen me.'

b. *ʔi x̌ec-θ-ámʔš-əs ["]
aux w.-tr-1obj-3erg
(He's figuring out that you must have seen me.)

This follows from the condition on raising formulated in §5.2.2:

(79) Only acting 1s can raise.

However, as can be seen in (80-82b), 1st and 2nd person departure objects can also raise.

(80) a. ni ʔə č ʔu x̌éc-t [kʷ s-ʔi-s-əɬ c'ew-əθ-él-əm
aux int 2sub just w.-tr det nom-aux-3ssub-pst help-tr-
ʔə kʷθə xʷənítəm] 1pas-intr
obl det white man

'Did you figure that I was helped by the white man?'

b. ʔi ʔə č ʔu x̌ec-θ-amʔš ["]
aux intr 2sub just w.-tr-1obj

'Are you figuring that I was helped by the white man?'

(81) a. ʔi cən x̌əx̌cí-t [ʔu ʔi-ʔəs lèʔləmʔ-əθ-á.-mʔ]
aux 1sub w.-tr lnk aux-3ssub look-tr-2pas-intr

'I'm checking out to see if you're being watched.'

b. ʔi cən x̌əx̌ci-θ-áʔmə ["]
aux 1sub w.-tr-2obj

'I'm checking you out to see if you are being watched.'

(82) a. ʔi cən x̌éc-t [ʔu ni-ʔələp ceʔ ʔu c'ew-ət-álə-m]
aux 1sub w.-tr lnk aux-2plssub fut lnk help-tr-2plpas-intr

'I'm wondering if you pl. will be helped.'

b. ʔi cən x̌ec-t-álə ["]
aux 1sub w.-tr-2plobj

'I'm wondering if you pl. will be helped.'

This presents a problem for both unmotivated chomage and the impersonal passive analyses of passives with 1st and 2nd person departure objects.

First, the unmotivated chomage analysis can offer no account of the contrast between (80-82b), in which the departure object is raised, and (76-78b), in which the final objects do not raise. Since departure objects are final objects under this analysis, no generalization concerning raising is possible.

Under the impersonal passive analysis, which posits that departure objects are 2-chomeurs, the contrast between (80-82b) and (76-78b) is not a problem; while 2-chomeurs can raise, final objects cannot. However, there is a problem in stating a generalization concerning the condition on raising. The class of nominals which raise are:

(83) a. Final subjects.
b. 1-chomeurs.
c. 2-chomeurs.

Apparently, there is no non-disjunctive means of stating the condition on raising. That a statement referring to (83) is necessary calls into question the adequacy of the impersonal passive analysis.

Perhaps an account of raising making reference to the brother-in-law relation is possible. One alternative would be to claim that it is not the 2-chomeur that is raised in cases like (80-82b) but rather the dummy which is the final subject; under this analysis, (79) could be maintained. Such an analysis would posit that the person and number of the raised dummy would follow from Doubling, as formulated in (72). In fact, one speaker has the following pattern of constructions; for him, raising is possible only if doubling has also occurred, as in (85b).

(84) a. ʔi cən x̌eʔx̌cí-t [ʔu ʔi-ʔəs leʔləmʔ-əθ-á.mʔ ʔə t^θə swə́yʔqeʔ]
aux 1sub-w.-tr lnk aux-3ssub look-tr-2pas-intr obl det man
'I'm taking notice if you're being watched by the man.'

b. *ʔi cən x̌eʔx̌ci-θ-ámə ["]
aux 1sub w.-tr-2obj
(I'm taking notice if you're being watched by the man.)

(85) a. ʔi cən x̌eʔx̌cí-t [ʔu ʔiʔ-əxʷ leʔləmʔ-əθ-á.-mʔ
aux 1sub w.-tr lnk aux-2ssub look-tr-2pas-intr
ʔə tθə swə́yʔqeʔ]
obl det man
'I'm taking notice if you're being watched by the man.'

b. ʔi cən x̌eʔx̌ci-θ-ámə ["]
aux 1sub w.-tr-2obj
'I'm taking notice if you're being watched by the man.'

Other evidence contradicts this proposal, however. Raising in Halkomelem, as noted above, leaves a copy. Note that in (86-87), where a non-3rd person nominal is the matrix object corresponding to the departure object, the subordinate subject is 3rd person, since doubling has not occurred.

(86) ʔi ʔə č ʔu x̌ec-θ-ámʔš [kʷ s-ʔi-s-əɬ c'ew-əθ-él-əm]
aux intr 2sub just w.-tr-1obj det nom-aux-3ssub-pst help-tr-1pas-intr
'Are you figuring that I was helped?'

(87) ʔi cən x̌əx̌ci-θ-áʔmə [ʔu ʔiʔ-əs lèʔləmʔ-əθ-á.-mʔ]
aux 1sub w.-tr-2obj lnk aux-3ssub look-tr-2pas-intr
'I'm checking you to see if you are being watched.'

Examples like (86-87) are possible for some speakers, even if they allow doubling. Furthermore, there are speakers for whom doubling is not possible but who nevertheless accept raising constructions like (84b), and (86-87). (For these speakers (85a) and (85b), are not grammatical.) Thus, an alternative which posits that the dummy is raised but not the 2-chomeur and that 1st and 2nd person marking of the raised nominal is accounted for by doubling does not adequately account for the raising data.

A second alternative using the brother-in-law relation would posit that 2-chomeurs in impersonal passives can be raised because they are brothers-in-law of the final subjects. Under this analysis, the condition on raising would be stated as follows:

(88) Only acting 1s or their brothers-in-law can raise.

Although this statement is possible, it involves an extension of the use of the brother-in-law relation, since Perlmutter and Postal have employed this notion only to account for phenomena like agreement and case. Such an extension would require sufficient motivation; certainly the evidence available from Halkomelem is inadequate.

In summary, data involving the raising of 1st and 2nd person departure objects poses problems for the unmotivated chomage and the impersonal passive analyses. Under the former, departure objects are final objects yet final objects of transitives do not raise. Under the impersonal passive analysis, a generalization concerning the nominals which raise is possible but the class of nominals referred to in it is a strange one: final subjects, 1-chomeurs, and 2-chomeurs. In addition, an analysis of raising making reference to the brother-in-law relation would need further justification.

5.4 Summary

In the preceding sections, I have discussed passives in Halkomelem. I gave evidence based on Nominal Case and extraction that the departure subject is not the final subject but a 1-chomeur. I contrasted an analysis involving unmotivated chomage, as posited for Halkomelem by Hukari (1980), with analyses involving advancement of an object in a transitive stratum to subject. I gave two arguments, based on raising and doubling, that an analysis involving advancement is preferred over one involving unmotivated chomage; thus Halkomelem passives can not be considered to be a counterexample to the universal characterization of passive (Perlmutter and Postal, 1977).

Halkomelem passives with 1st and 2nd person departure objects have presented some difficulty in analysis. I have posited that these constructions involve impersonal passive. Giving evidence from pronominal morphology and copy extractions, I show two ways in which 1st and 2nd person departure objects behave like objects, concluding that this similarity be captured by means of the notion acting 2. Furthermore, I showed that in one construction, raising, departure objects and final objects do not behave alike, thus supporting the claim that departure objects are not final objects. Finally, I discussed doubling, showing that under the impersonal passive analysis this phenomenon can be accounted for by reference to the brother-in-law relation.

Data involving raising does present a problem for the impersonal passive analysis, since under this analysis the class of nominals which can raise are final subjects, 1-chomeurs, and 2-chomeurs, a class which does not lend itself to an elegant statement.

Certainly, Halkomelem passives, because their departure objects have conflicting properties, deserve a more thorough treatment.

In the following discussion, since evidence to the contrary is lacking, I assume that Halkomelem passives involve advancement to subject.

5.5 Passives and Transitive Marking

Under the analyses of passives that I have presented above, there is a problem concerning the rule of transitive marking which was formulated in §4.1.1 as follows:

(89) Transitive marking is required in finally transitive clauses.

This accounts for the presence of transitive marking in mono-stratal transitive clauses like (90), as represented in (91), and in clauses involving advancement to object like (92), represented in (93).

(90) ni cən q'ʷáqʷ-ət kʷθə spéʔəθ
aux 1sub club-tr det bear
'I clubbed the bear.'

(91)

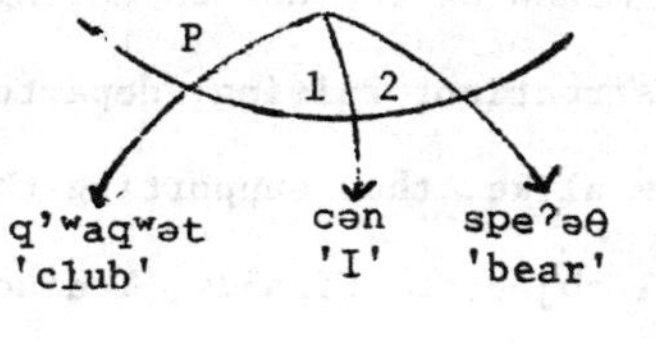

(92) ni cən wəɬ ɬcíws-mə-t tθə John
aux 1sub already tired-advC-tr det
'I'm already tired of John.'

(93)

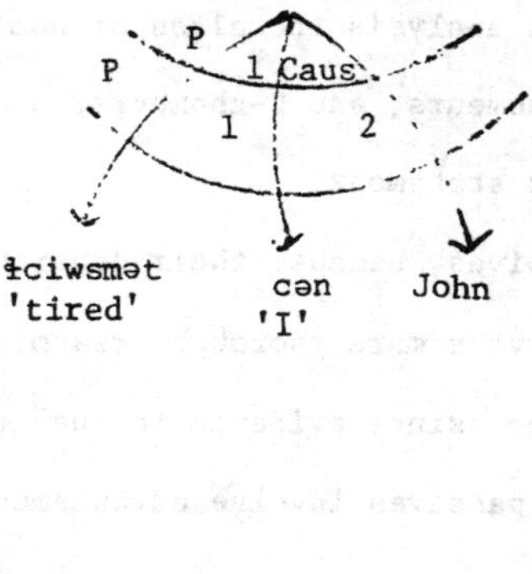

Furthermore, (89) accounts for the absence of transitive marking in antipassives like (94) as represented in (95).

(94) ni cən pə́n?-əm ?ə kʷθə sqéwθ
aux 1sub plant-intr obl det potato
'I planted the potatoes.'

(95)

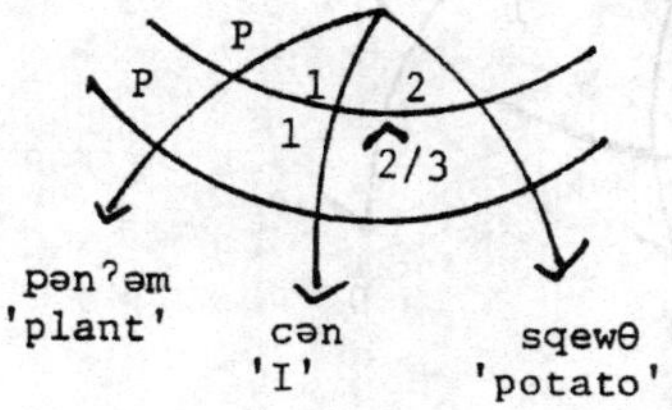

However, (89) would incorrectly predict that passives such as (96), represented in (97), and (98), represented in (99), would not have transitive marking.

(96) ni q'ʷáqʷ-ət-əm ɬə sɬéni?
aux club-tr-intr det woman
'The woman was clubbed.'

(97)

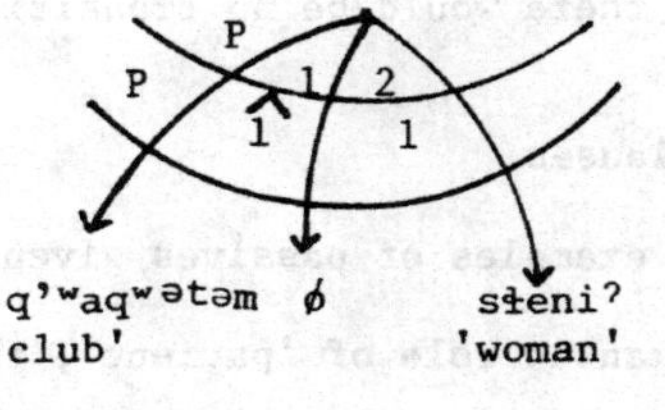

(98) ni q'ʷàqʷ-θ-él-əm
aux club-tr-1pas-intr
'I was clubbed.'

(99)

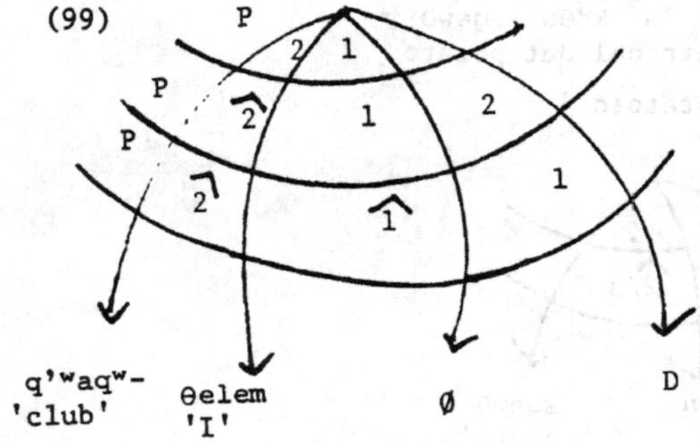

To handle all the cases involving transitive marking, I reformulate the rule of transitive marking as follows:

(100) **Transitive marking is required if there is a nominal which is both an object and a final nuclear term.**

Thus, in passives, since there is a nominal which is an object at one level and a subject at the final level, transitive marking would be required. In contrast, in antipassives, since the nominal which is object is a final 3/2-chomeur, there would be no transitive marking.

5.6 Passives of Advancement Clauses

For the most part, the examples of passives given above involve a departure object with the semantic role of 'patient'; the departure stratum in these passives is the initial stratum. Passives are also possible when the departure object is a non-initial object, as in the following examples; (101-105) involve advancements to object, (106-107) involve causatives, and (108-109) involve raising.

(101) ʔi ʔámʔ-əs-t-əm tᶿə John ʔə-ƛ̓ Mary ʔə kʷθə šckí.ks
aux give-advA-tr-intr det obl-det obl det vanilla extract
'John is being given vanilla extract by Mary.'

(102) ni θə́y-əɬc-t-əm kʷθə swə́yʔqeʔ ʔə-ƛ̓ Bob ʔə kʷθə snə́xʷəɬ
aux make-advB-tr-intr det man obl-det obl det canoe
'Bob fixed the canoe for the man.'

(103) ni x̌ə́lʔ-əɬc-ət-əm kʷθənʔ mén ʔə kʷθə pípə-s
aux write-advB-tr-intr det-2pos father obl det paper-3pos
'He wrote the letters for your father.'

(104) ni θ'eyʔk'ʷ-méʔ-t-əm kʷθə sqʷəméyʔ
aux startle-advC-tr-intr det dog
'He was startled at the dog.'

(105) ʔi yə-ʔéʔwə-nəsəm ɬə sɬéniʔ
aux ser-come-advD-tr-intr det woman
'He went towards the woman.'

(106) ni ʔíməš-st-él-əm
aux walk-cs-1pas-intr
'I was made to walk.'

(107) ni q'ʷə́l-əm-st-əm ɬə sɬéniʔ ʔə kʷθə səplíl
aux bake-intr-cs-intr det woman obl det bread
'The woman was made to bake the bread.'

(108) ni x̌íc-t-əm kʷθə John ʔu ʔiʔ-əs c'éw-ət-əm
aux wonder-tr-intr det lnk aux-3ssub help-tr-intr
'John was being checked out to see if he was helped.'

(109) ʔi x̌əx̌ci-θ-él-əm ʔu ʔi.nʔ léʔləmʔ-ət
aux wonder-tr-1pas-intr lnk aux-1ssub look-tr
'He's wondering if I have been looking at it.'

In this section, I discuss a sub-set of these passives, namely those involving 3-2 and Ben-2 advancements, as exemplified in (101-103). I contrast two analyses for these constructions. The first, as represented in (110) posits that the initial indirect object or benefactive, in advancing to subject goes through an intermediate level where it is the direct object via 3-2 or Ben-2 advancement.

(110) a. b.

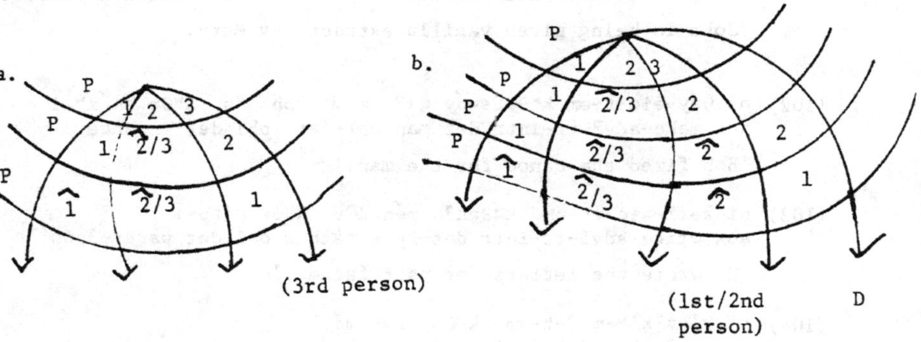

The second posits that the initial indirect object or benefactive advances directly to subject without an intermediate level where it is the direct object, as represented in (111).

(111)

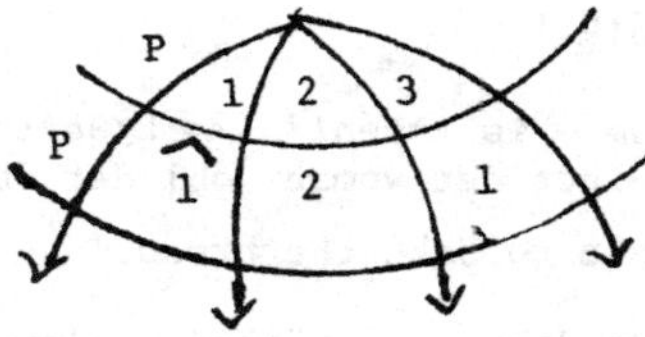

Note that these analyses make different claims with respect to the initial object. In (110), the initial object is a final 3/2-chomeur, like other initial objects in advancement clauses. In (111), however, since there is no advancement to object, the initial object is final object. The analyses in (110) and (111) also make different claims with respect to final transitivity. In (110), the final stratum is intransitive and the subject of that stratum is the final absolutive. However, in (111), since the initial object is the final object, the final stratum is transitive and the subject of that stratum is a final ergative.

In the following discussion, I give two types of arguments that the analysis in (110) is correct. First, I give evidence that the initial object is a final 3/2-chomeur. Second, I argue that the final subject in these clauses is a final absolutive.

5.6.1 Arguments that the Initial Object is a Final 3/2-Chomeur

There are two arguments based on Nominal Case and extraction that the initial object in clauses like (101-103) is a final 3/2-chomeur and not the final object.

Nominal Case is formulated in §3.2.2 as follows:

(112) a. Final nuclear terms and 3rd person common noun possessors are in the straight case.
b. Other nominals are in the oblique case.

As can be seen in (101-103) the initial objects are in the oblique case. This follows from the analysis in (110), which posits that these nominals are final 3/2-chomeurs. Furthermore, the analysis in (111), which posits that these nominals are final objects, makes the wrong prediction since they are not in the straight case.

As discussed in §3.2.2 and 4.1.2, final 3/2-chomeurs are extracted through nominalization. In these nominalizations, the extraction is indicated by the nominalizer s-. As seen in (113-115) below, the nominals corresponding to the initial objects in (101-103) are extracted in this manner:

(113) šəptən kʷθə ni s-ʔám-əs t-éw-ət tθə swíwʔləs
knife det aux nom-give-advA-tr-3pas-st det boy
'It's a knife that the boy was given.'

(114) sc'ə̌št kʷθə ni s-lə́kʷ-əɬc-t-əw-ət ʔə-ƛ̓ Bob
stick det aux nom-break-advB-tr-3pas-st obl-det
'A stick is what Bob broke for him.'

(115) stém k'ʷə ni s-θə́y-əɬc-t-əw-ət kʷθə Bob
what det aux nom-make-advB-tr-3pas-st det
'What was made for Bob?'

This follows from the analysis in (110) which posits that these nominals are final 3s/2-chomeurs. Since final objects are directly extracted and cannot be extracted through nominalization, the analysis in (111) makes the wrong prediction.

5.6.2 Arguments that the Final Subject is the Final Absolutive

Three arguments, based on 3rd Person Agreement, possessor extraction, and quantifier extraction, give evidence that the final subjects in clauses like (101-103) are final absolutives.

First, as discussed in §4.1.1, in clauses with final 3rd person ergatives, there is 3rd person agreement, i.e. the suffix -əs. However, as seen in (101-103) above, there is no 3rd person agreement. This is accounted for under the analysis in (110), which posits that the final subject is an absolutive; (111), in contrast, predicts incorrectly that 3rd person agreement should occur in (101-103).

Second, as discussed in §3.1.4, a possessor can be extracted only if the possessive phrase is a final absolutive. In (116-118), I give examples where the final subject in clauses like (101-103) is a possessive phrase; possessors in these examples can be extracted, as seen in (116-118).

(116) státəl-stəxʷ cən ɬə sɬéniʔ ni ʔám-əs-t -əm
know-cs 1sub det woman aux give-advA-tr-intr
kʷθə sqéʔəq-s ʔə kʷθə swé.tə
det y. brother-3pos obl det sweater

'I know the woman whose younger brother was given the sweater.'

(117) ʔé.n̤ʔθə ni x̌élʔ-əɬc-t-əm kʷθə nə-mén ʔə-ƛ̓ Trudeau
lemph aux write-advB-tr-intr det 1pos-father obl-det

'I'm the one whose father was written to by Trudeau.'

(118) níɬ kʷθə xʷənítəm ni θéy-əɬc-t-əm kʷθə sqéʔəq-s
3emph det white man aux make-advB-tr-intr det y.brother-3pos
ʔə-ƛ̓ Bob ʔə kʷθə snéxʷəɬ
obl-det obl det canoe

'It's the white man's younger brother that Bob made the canoe for.'

This follows from the analysis in (110); since the possessive phrase is the final absolutive, possessor extraction is possible. Again, (111) makes the wrong prediction.

Finally, as discussed in §3.1.5, quantifier extraction is possible only if the quantifier phrase is the final absolutive. In (119-121), examples of quantifier extraction for the final subject in clauses like (101-103) are given:

(119) ni mə́k'ʷ ʔu q'ʷél-əɬc-t-əm kʷθə sɬənɬéniʔ ʔə-ƛ̓ Bob
aux all lnk oake-advB-tr-intr det women obl-det

'All the women were cooked for by Bob.'

(120) ni mək'ʷ ʔu ʔám-əs-t-əm kʷθə sƛ̓əlʔíqəɬ ʔə kʷθə púkʷ
aux all lnk give-advA-tr-intr det children obl det book

'All the children were given books.'

(121) ni mə́k'ʷ ʔu x̌ə́lʔ-əɬc-t-əm ʔə-x̌ Trudeau kʷθə sɬənɬéniʔ
aux all lnk write-advB-tr-intr obl-det det women
'All the women were written to by Trudeau.'

That quantifier extraction is possible indicates that the final subject is the final absolutive, as predicted in (110). Since (111) predicts that it is the final ergative, (111) cannot be maintained for Halkomelem.

In summary, the above evidence shows that clauses like (101-103) involve both 3-2 or Ben-2 advancement and passive. An analysis positing that the indirect object or benefactive advances directly to subject cannot be maintained.

5.7 Passives of Caus-2 Advancement Clauses

In this section, I discuss passives of Caus-2 advancement clauses, as exemplified in (122-126) below:

(122) a. ni x̌iʔx̌eʔ-méʔ-t-əs tᶿə swə́yʔqeʔ θə sɬéniʔ
aux ashamed-advC-tr-3erg det man det woman
'The man was ashamed in front of the lady.'

b. ni x̌iʔx̌eʔ-méʔ-t-əm θə sɬéniʔ ʔə tᶿə swə́yʔqeʔ
aux ashame-advC-tr-intr det woman obl det man
literally: 'The woman was gotten ashamed in front of by the man.'

(123) a. ni ɬcíws-mə-t-əs kʷθə swíwʔləs kʷθə sqʷəméyʔ
aux tired-advC-tr-3erg det boy det dog
'The boy is tired of the dog.'

b. ni ɬcíws-mə-t-əm kʷθə sqʷəméyʔ ʔə kʷθə swíwʔləs
aux tired-advC-tr-intr det dog obl det boy
literally: 'The dog was gotten tired of by the boy.'

(124) a. ni siˀsiˀ-méˀ-t-əs kʷθə · spéˀəθ
aux frightened-advC-tr-3erg det bear
'He was frightened of the bear.'

b. ni siˀsiˀ-méˀ-t-əm kʷθə spéˀəθ
aux frightened-advC-tr-intr det bear
literally: 'The bear was frightened of by him.'

(125) a. @ni c'ìwəlˀ-meˀ-θ-ámˀš-əs kʷθə John
aux annoyed-advC-tr-1obj-3erg det
'John was annoyed at me.'

b. ni c'ìwəlˀ-meˀ-θ-él-əm ˀə-ƛ̓ John
aux annoyed-advC-tr-1pas-intr obl-det
literally: 'I was gotten annoyed at by John.'

(126) a. * ni hiləkʷ-mə-θ-ám-əs ɬ- ənˀ stáˀləs
aux happy-advC-tr-2obj-3erg det-2pos spouse
(Your wife is happy on account of you.)

b. ni hiləkʷ-mə-θ-á.-m ˀə ɬ- ənˀ stáˀləs
aux happy-advC-tr-2pas-intr obl det-2pos spouse
literally: 'You were happied for by your wife.'

That the (b) clauses are passives, as discussed above, is indicated by the verbal morphology, i.e. the transitive suffix followed by an intransitive suffix. Furthermore, the departure subject is a final 1-chomeur and is thus in the oblique case. Also, the departure object, if it is pronominal as in (118-119), is a passive person suffix.

Furthermore, there is one argument, based on transitive marking, that the (b) clauses above involve both Caus-2 advancement and passive, as represented in (127), and not an advancement directly from Caus-1, as represented in (128).

(127)

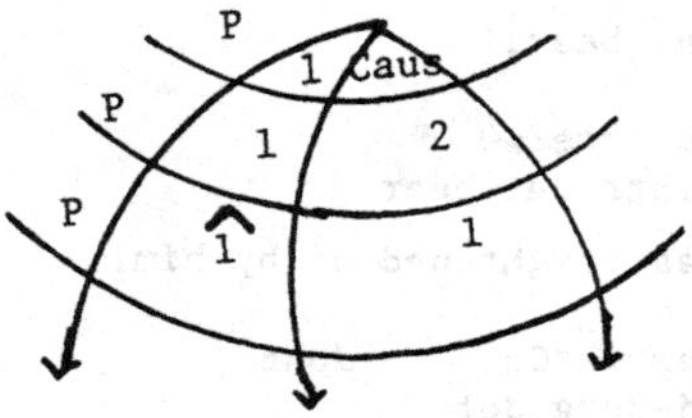

(128)

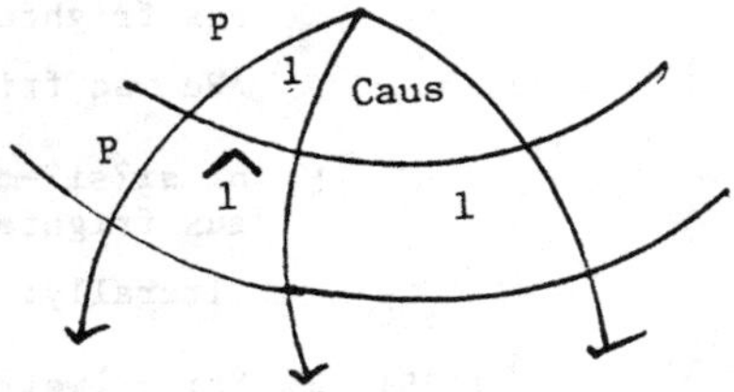

The (b) clauses, above, like other passives, have transitive marking, indicating that the departure stratum is transitive (cf. §5.5). This follows from the analysis in (127), which posits a transitive departure stratum. In (128), however, there are no transitive strata; thus there is no account of transitive marking. In the following discussion, I assume that an analysis involving both Caus-2 advancement and passive is the correct one for the (b) clauses above.

In this section, I discuss clauses with Caus-2 advancement in light of the Unaccusative Hypothesis, as proposed by Perlmutter (1978) and Perlmutter and Postal (to appear a). I give evidence that some constructions with initial causals are initially unaccusative. Finally, I show that passives of these constructions constitute a counterexample to a law proposed as a universal by Perlmutter and Postal--the 1-Advancement Exclusiveness Law.

5.7.1 The Unaccusative Hypothesis

According to the Unaccusative Hypothesis (Perlmutter, 1978 and Perlmutter and Postal, to appear a), initially intransitive clauses are of two types: those whose initial stratum is unergative, which contain a 1-arc but not 2-arc, and those whose initial stratum is <u>unaccusative</u>, which contain a 2-arc but no 1-arc. These are represented in (129-130):

(129) Unergative:

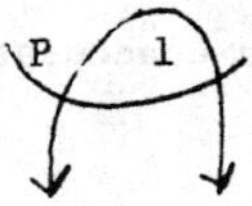

(130) Unaccusative:

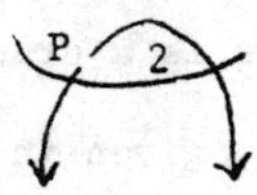

Perlmutter and Postal assert that initial unergativity vs. unaccusativity is largely predictable from the semantics of the clause. Verbs in unergative clauses are active, often willed and volitional actions, e.g. 'speak', 'walk', 'dance', and 'knock'. In contrast, verbs in unaccusative clauses are verbs of existing, happening, or undergoing, e.g. 'melt', 'fall', 'drown', and 'die'. This semantic contrast can be seen clearly in an instransitive verb such as 'fall' which appears in either initially unergative clauses, as in (131), or in initially unaccusative clauses, as in (132).

(131) John fell right on cue in the third act.

(132) John fell from the second-storey window.

While 'fall' is a volitional act in (131), it is not in (132).

It is possible for the initial object to advance to final subject, as represented in (133); this is referred to as unaccusative advancement.

(133)

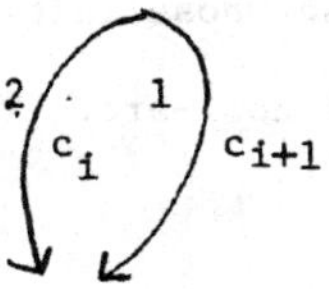

Notice that there is a crucial difference between unaccusative advancement and passive, given in (134).

(134)

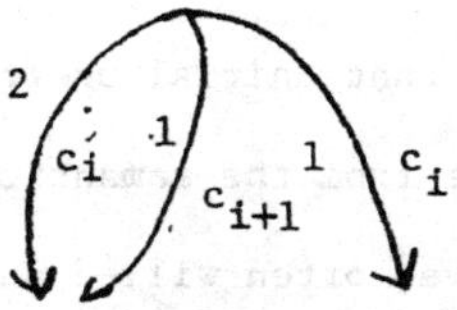

Although they both involve advancements of an object to subject, in the case of passive, the departure stratum is transitive, while in the case of unaccusative advancement, the object is in an intransitive stratum.

Perlmutter (1978) provides evidence for unergativity vs. unaccusativity from impersonal passives in Dutch. In an impersonal passive, as discussed above, a dummy inserted as an object advances to subject. Impersonal passives of initial unergatives are possible in Dutch. Perlmutter gives examples like (135-136), as represented in (137).

Dutch

(135) Er wordt hier veel geskied.
'It is skied here a lot.'

(136) Er wordt hier door de junge lui veel gedanst.

'It is danced here a lot by the young people.'

(137)

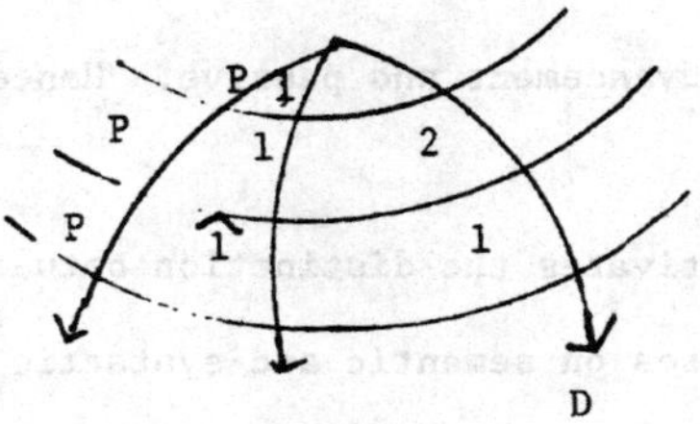

However, Perlmutter claims that impersonal passives of initial unaccusatives are not possible. The ungrammatical clauses in (138-139) are represented by the stratal diagram in (140).

(Dutch)

(138) *Er werd door de bloemen binnen een paar dagen verflenst.

'The flowers had wilted in a few days.'

(139) *Er werd door het water uit de rots gedrippeld.

'The water dripped out of the rock.'

(140) *

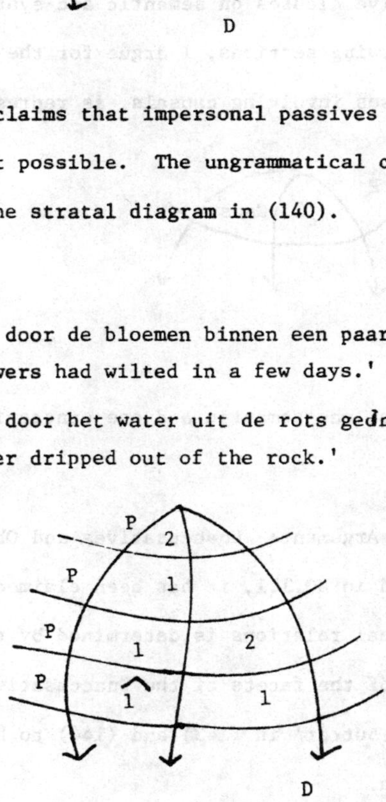

Perlmutter attributes the impossibility of impersonal passives in the case of initial unaccusatives to the fact that they would violate the 1-Advancement Exclusiveness Law. (Perlmutter and Postal, to appear a) The 1-AEX is stated informally in (141).

(141) No clause can involve more than one advancement to subject.

As can be seen in (140), impersonal passives of initial unaccusatives involve both unaccusative advancement and passive. Hence the violation of the 1-AEX.

Thus, Perlmutter motivates the distinction between two types of initially intransitive clauses on semantic and syntactic grounds.[25]

In the following sections, I argue for the initial unaccusativity of some clauses involving causals, as represented in (142).

(142)

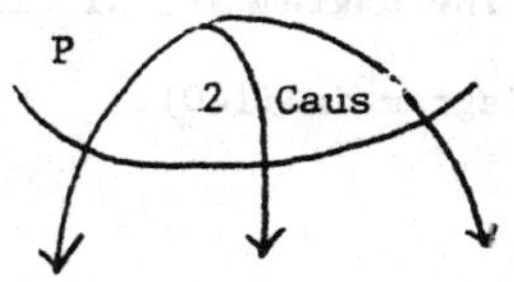

I give two arguments, one semantic and one syntactic, for the structure in (142).

5.7.1.1 A Semantic Argument: Unaccusatives and Objects of Transitives

As discussed in §0.3.1, it has been claimed that the assignment of initial grammatical relations is determined by the semantic role of the nominals. One of the facets of the Unaccusative Hypothesis is that it would allow 'the butter' in (143) and (144) to have the same initial grammatical relation.

(143) The butter melted.

(144) John melted the butter.

In each case 'the butter' is semantically the 'patient', undergoing the act of <u>melting</u>. The Unaccusative Hypothesis allows 'the butter' in (143) to be an initial object, bearing the same initial grammatical relation as 'the butter' in (144), which is the object in an initially transitive stratum.

By positing initial unaccusativity for some constructions involving causals, a similar parallelism in semantic roles can be captured. Contrast (145) and (147) with (146) and (148); the former do not involve Caus-2 advancement while the latter do.

(145) ni cən θ'ə́yˀk'ʷ-t kʷθə sqʷəméyˀ
aux 1sub startle-tr det dog
'I startled the dog.' (on purpose)

(146) ni θ'əyˀk'ʷ-meˀ-θ-ámˀš-əs kʷθə sqʷəméyˀ
aux startled-advC-tr-1obj-3erg det dog
'The dog was startled at me.' (I indirectly cause this.)

(147) ni cən c'q'ə́-t kʷθə xʷənítəm
aux 1sub surprise-tr det white man
'I surprised the white man.' (intentionally)

(148) ni c'əq'-miˀ-θ-ámˀš-əs kʷθə xʷənítəm
aux surprised-advC-tr-obj-3erg det white man
'The white man was suprised at me.' (but I was unaware of him.)

I assume that (145) and (147) are initially transitive clauses in which the 'agent' is the initial subject and the 'experiencer' is the initial object, as represented in (149).

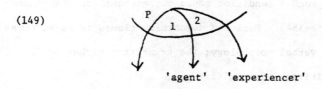

(149)

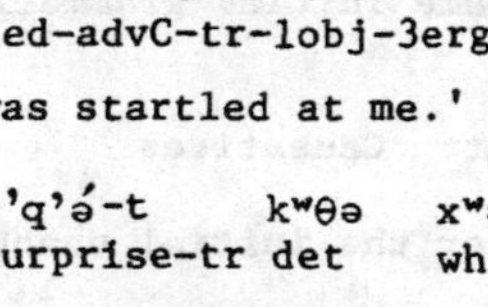

By positing an initially unaccusative structure represented in (150) for the clauses involving causals (e.g. (146) and (148)), the 'experiencer' in these clauses is also the initial object.

(150)

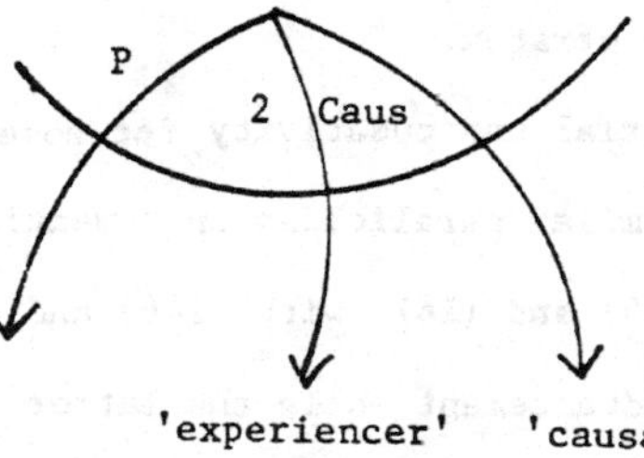

Thus, nominals having the same semantic role with respect to the same verb would be assigned the same initial grammatical relation.

5.7.1.2 A Syntactic Argument: Causatives

Syntactic evidence for the initial unaccusativity of some clauses with causals comes from Causative Clause Union (CCU) in Halkomelem. As discussed in §4.2, causatives involving CCU consist of two clauses and the predicate of the upstairs clause is -<u>st</u>, 'cause'. In addition, I argued for the following condition on CCU in Halkomelem:

(151) CCU is possible only if the downstairs clause is finally intransitive.

However, such a condition could not account for the ungrammaticality of (152-154). Here the downstairs clause is passive, as indicated by the verbal morphology; the transitive marker -<u>t</u> is followed by the intransitive suffix -<u>əm</u>.

(152) *ni q'ʷəl-ət-əm-stəxʷ-əs kʷθə səplíl ʔə ɬə sɬéniʔ
aux bake-tr-intr-cs-3erg det bread obl det woman
(He had the bread baked by the woman.)

(153) *ni q'ʷạqʷ-ət-əm-stəxʷ-əs kʷθə spéʔəθ ʔə-ƛ̓ John
aux club-tr-intr-cs-3erg det bear obl-det
(He had the bear clubbed by John.)

(154) *ni pən-ət-əm-stəxʷ-əs kʷθə sqéwθ ʔə ɬə sɬéniʔ
aux plant-tr-intr-cs-3erg det bear obl det woman
(He had the potatoes planted by the woman.)

I have represented (152) in the stratal diagram in (155).

(155)

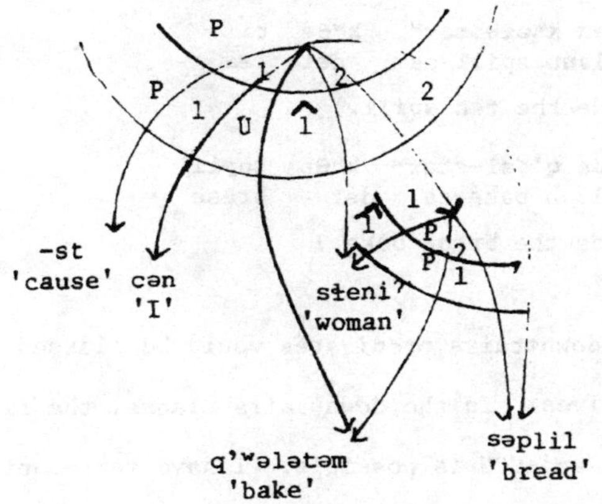

To account for the impossibility of clauses like (152-154), I formulate the following condition on CCU in Halkomelem.

(156) CCU is possible only if the final subject is the initial subject of the downstairs clause.

Thus, in (152-154), where the final subject is the initial object rather than the initial subject in the downstairs clause, CCU is not possible.

This condition on CCU taken together with the Unaccusative Hypothesis accounts for the contrast between (157-159), in which CCU is possible, and (160-162), in which CCU is not possible.

(157) ni cən ʔəɬtə́n-əstəxʷ kʷθə sqʷəmə́yʔ
aux 1sub eat-cs det dog
'I let the dog eat.' /'I fed the dog.'

(158) ni cən ʔíməš-stəxʷ kʷθə John
aux 1sub walk-cs det
'I made John walk.'

(159) ni cən ʔəmət-st-ámə
aux 1sub sit-cs-2obj
'I had you sit down.'

(160) *ni cən wəc'əƛ̓-stəxʷ kʷθə sc'ə́št
aux 1sub fall-cs det stick
(I made the stick fall.)

(161) *ni cən kʷəɬ-stəxʷ kʷθə tí
aux 1sub spill-cs det tea
(I made the tea spill.)

(162) *ni cən q'ʷəl-stəxʷ kʷθə səplíl
aux 1sub bake-cs det bread
(I made the bread bake.)

In (157-160), the downstairs predicates would be classed on semantic grounds as unergatives. In the downstairs clause, the final subject is initial subject and CCU is possible. I have represented (157) in the stratal diagram in (163).

(163)

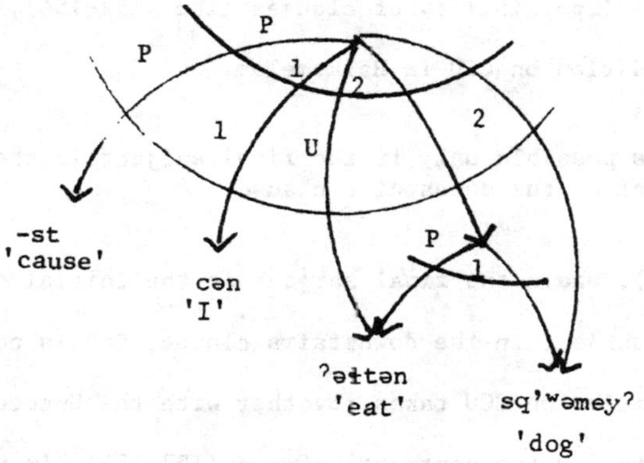

However, in (160-162), the downstairs predicates would be classed on semantic grounds as unaccusative. Since the final subject in the downstairs clause is not the initial subject, CCU is not possible. I have represented (160) in the stratal diagram in (164).

(164) *

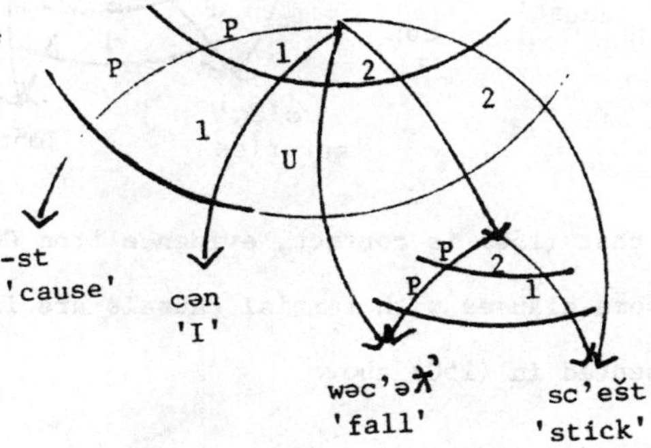

Thus, CCU in Halkomelem provides a test for distinguishing initially unaccusative from initially unergative clauses. Applying this test to the predicates occurring in clauses with causals, we find that CCU is not possible, as exemplified in (165-167).

(165) *ni cən c'əq'-əstəxʷ t^{θ}ə John
aux 1sub surprise-cs det
(I caused John to be astonished.)

(166) *ni cən hiləkʷ-stəxʷ t^{θ}ə John
aux 1sub happy-cs det
(I made John happy.)

(167) *ni cən c'iwəlˀ-stəxʷ t^{θ}ə John
aux 1sub annoy-cs det
(I caused John to be annoyed.)

This follows automatically from condition (156) if the initial intransitive strata in (165-167) are unaccusative. I have represented this analysis for (165) in (168).

(168)

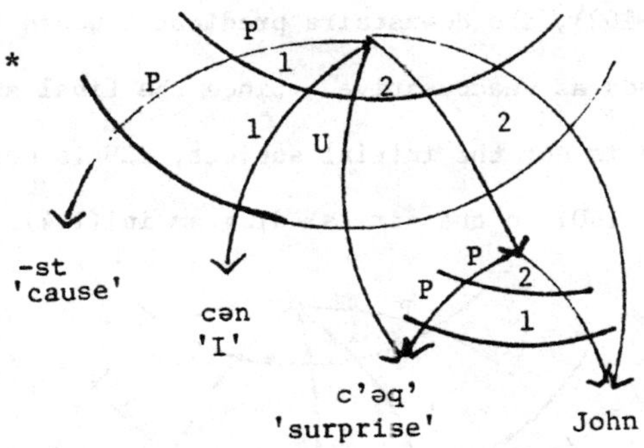

Thus, assuming that (156) is correct, evidence from CCU provides an argument that some clauses with initial causals are initially unaccusative, as represented in (150) above.

5.7.2 Passives of Caus-2 Advancements and the 1-AEX

I argued above that the 'experiencer' in clauses involving causals is the initial object in an unaccusative stratum, as represented in (169).

(169)

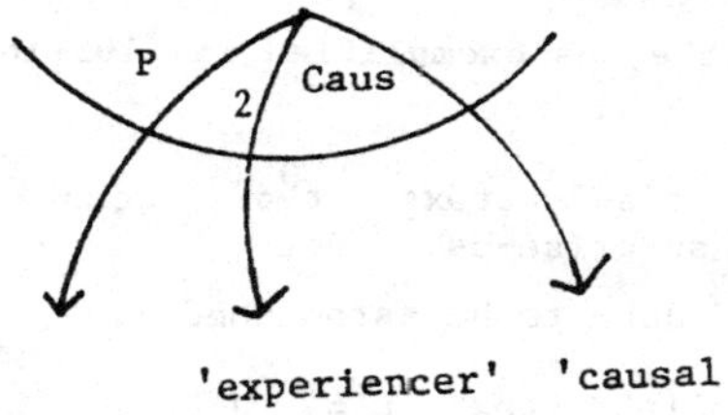

In this section, I briefly give evidence that the initial object in these constructions advance to final subject via unaccusative advancement as represented in (170).

(170)

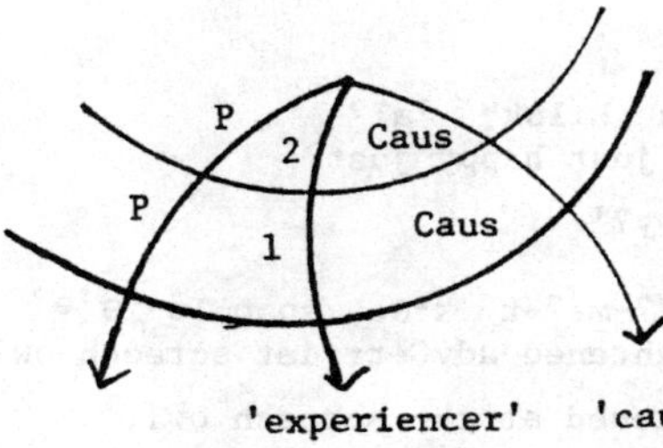

Furthermore, in clauses involving Caus-2 advancement the initial object, i.e. the 'experiencer', also advances to subject via unaccusative advancement, as represented in (171).

(171)

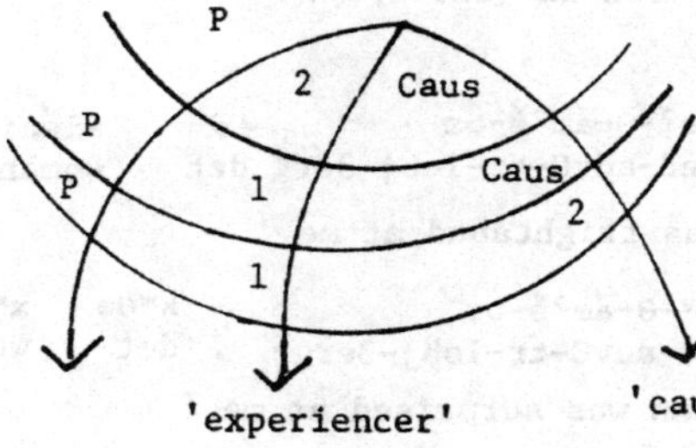

5.7.2.1 Arguments for Unaccusative Advancement

I briefly give two arguments, based on Pronominal Case and 3rd Person Agreement that the 'experiencer' in initially unaccusative clauses, as represented in (170) and (171), advances to subject.

First, as discussed in §3.1.2, when final subjects are pronominal they are in the subjective case. Final objects, on the other hand, are in the objective case. As can be seen in (172-175), 'experiencers' in initially unaccusative clauses are in the subjective case.

(172) ni cən c'ə́q'
aux 1sub surprised
'I was surprised.'

(173) ʔi ʔə č ʔu hílək^w ʔalʔ
aux int 2sub just happy just
'Are you happy?'

(174) ni cən siʔsiʔ-méʔ-t k^wθə spəpəlq^wíθ'əʔ
aux 1sub frightened-advC-tr det screech owl
'I was frightened at the screech owl.'

(175) ni ct c'əq'-mə́-t k^wθə John
aux 1plsub surprised-advC-tr det
'We were astonished at John.'

This follows from the analyses posited in (170) and (171).

Second, when the 'experiencer' is a 3rd person nominal, it is in the straight case, as seen in (176-178).

(176) ni siʔsiʔ-meʔ-θ-ámʔš-əs ɬə šɬéniʔ
aux frightened-advC-tr-1obj-3erg det woman
'The woman was frightened at me.'

(177) ni c'əq'-meʔ-θ-ámʔš-əs k^wθə x^wənítəm
aux surprised-advC-tr-1obj-3erg det white man
'The white man was surprised at me.'

(178) ni hilək^w-meʔ-θ-ámʔš-əs ɬə nə-stáʔləs
aux happy-advC-tr-1obj-3erg det 1pos-spouse
'My wife was happy for me.'

This gives evidence that it is a final nuclear term, since straight case is used only for final nuclear terms and 3rd person common noun possessors. (cf. §3.1.1). Moreover, 3rd Person Agreement (cf. §4.1.1) provides evidence that the experiencers in Caus-2 advancement clauses are final subjects. Since in main clauses there is 3rd person agreement only if the final ergative is 3rd person, the 'experiencers' in (177) and (178) are final ergatives and therefore final subjects.

5.7.2.2 The 1-AEX

In the above discussion, I have given evidence that clauses like (122-126a) above involve an initially unaccusative stratum, unaccusative advancement, and Caus-2 advancement. I repeat (122a) here as (179) and give its representation in (180).

(179) ni x̌iˀx̌eˀ-méˀ-t-əs t^{θ}ə swə́yˀqeˀ θə sɬéniˀ
aux ashamed-advC-tr-3erg det man det woman
'The man was ashamed in front of the woman.'

(180)

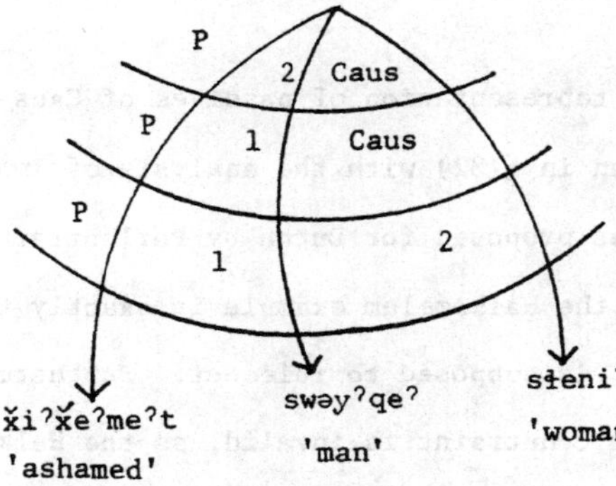

Furthermore, I gave evidence that clauses like (122-126b) involve passive as well. In (181), I repeat (122b); I give its representation in (182).

(181) ni x̌iˀxeˀ-méˀ-t-əm θə sɬéniˀ ˀə t^{θ}ə swə́yˀqeˀ
aux ashamed-advC-tr-intr det woman obl det man
literally: 'The woman was gotten ashamed in front of by the man.'

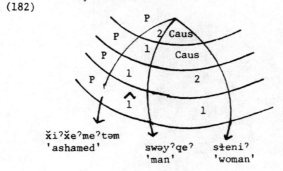

(182)

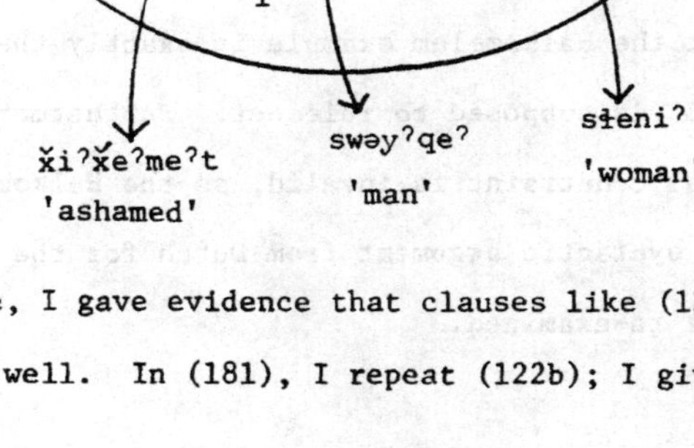

Noticeably, the structure represented in (182) violates the 1-Advancement Exclusiveness Law (cf. (141)). As discussed above, the 1-AEX rules out clauses which involve more than one advancement to subject. In the stratal diagram in (182), there are two advancements to subject; the object in the initial unaccusative stratum advances to subject via unaccusative advancement and the initial causal, which is advanced to object via Caus-2 advancement, advances to final subject via passive. Thus, clauses like (122-126b) above constitute a counterexample to the 1-AEX.[26]

Contrasting the representation of passives of Caus-2 advancement clauses given in (182) with the analysis of impersonal passives of unaccusatives proposed for Dutch by Perlmutter in (140) above, it is clear that the Halkomelem example is exactly the kind of structure that the 1-AEX is supposed to rule out. Furthermore, if the 1-AEX as a universal constraint is invalid, as the Halkomelem data suggest, then the syntactic argument from Dutch for the Unaccusative Hypothesis must be re-examined.

Footnotes to Chapter 5

[1]Galloway (1977, p. 272f) and Leslie (1979, p. 34f) treat passives as a type of verbal inflection and do not give any syntactic evidence concerning this construction. Hukari (1976b) also treats passive in this manner. He says: 'Cowichan passives appear to be subjectless transitive predicates in that they inflect for object but do not permit subject.' I discuss a more recent analysis of Hukari's (1980) in this chapter.

In other Central Salish languages, passives have been noted. Chinchor (1975) and Jelinek and Demers (ms) have given examples of Lummi passives but have assumed, without giving evidence, a Personal passive analysis. Davis (1980) gives one argument for an advancement analysis of passives in Sliammon. (cf. §5.2.2) Hess (1973) discussed passives in Lushootseed. Apparently in this language clauses with two 3rd person nominal nuclear terms are not possible; the passive is frequently used to express two nominals.

[2]The order of the two nominals in clauses like (1-5b) appears to be free, although there is some preference for having the nominal in the oblique case first.

[3]Throughout this chapter there are finally transitive clauses which are not possible for some or all speakers because of the constraints discussed in §2.7.

[4]Transitive Marking as formulated in §4.1.1 is as follows:

(i) Transitive marking is required in finally transitive clauses.

But it is also required in passives. I discuss this in §5.5 below.

[5]The intransitive markers used for passives are -<u>əm</u>, intransitive, and -<u>ət</u>, stative. The latter is used in nominalizations which do not have an auxiliary.

The passive person markers which appear before these intransitive markers (given in (55) below) are identical except for 3rd person, which appears as Ø before <u>-əm</u> but as -əw- before -<u>ət</u>.

[6]See Perlmutter (1978) and Perlmutter and Postal (to appear d).

[7]Thompson (1979b, p. 741), citing Hukari (1976b) (cf. f.n.1) seems to be implying that Halkomelem passives do not allow the departure subject to be expressed. However, as the data here show, this is not the case. He cites an interesting fact about Thompson, an Interior Salish language neighboring Halkomelem; in passives where the departure object is 3rd person, the departure subject, is expressed, but in the case of 1st and 2nd person departure objects, it is not.

[8] I use syntactic notions, i.e. departure subject and departure object, in this discussion because, as I show in §5.7, nominals playing roles other than 'agent' and 'patient' can be departure subject or object in Halkomelem passives. The Halkomelem data call into question treatments of passive which rely on semantic terminology, e.g. Leslie (1979, p. 34), and Jelinek and Demers (ms).

[9] To extract these nominals, they must be final subjects. Thus, a finally transitive clause or an antipassive clause is used rather than a passive.

[10] Also, an analysis could be possible which posits that departure subjects are final 3s via inversion (cf. Perlmutter 1979). Although it is clear that departure subjects are not 3s/2-chomeurs because they do not extract, until evidence which distinguishes final indirect objects in Halkomelem is found, this point of analysis is tentative.

[11] There is an obvious similarity of condition (15) and the condition stated on antipassives in §4.1.4.

[12] For a reply to Comrie, see Perlmutter and Postal (to appear d).

[13] I have standardized Davis' glosses and added them to parallel examples.

[14] Sliammon like Halkomelem, has a dependent passive form; cf. f.n. 5.

[15] Hukari (1980) lists only a couple of examples of this construction, so I have used data from my own fieldwork throughout this discussion. Evidentally, for all speakers, the constructions without raising are greatly preferred over those with raising. I have worked with four speakers on these constructions. I have indicated the areas of disagreement among them.

[16] For a discussion of raising within the theory of Relational Grammar, cf. Perlmutter and Postal (to appear b).

[17] According to Hukari (1980) only final subjects and departure subjects can raise. (see below) Giving one example, he claims that departure objects cannot raise. However, the speakers I worked with all agreed that departure objects could raise. Evidentally constructions like (40-41b) are no worse than constructions involving the raising of final subjects or departure objects.

[18] Apparently, raising in Halkomelem and Sliammon differ, since in Sliammon only final subjects raise, according to Davis (1980).

[19] A statement could also be formulated referring to subject without specifying level, thus implying a subject at any level. I know no evidence to distinguish this formulation from (57).

[20] There is frequently deletion of medial resonants and subsequent vowel coalescence. Thus /θamə/ + /əm/ → /θa.m/.

See Suttles (in preparation) for further discussion.

[21] This information is from M. Dale Kinkade (p.c.).

[22] In Gerdts (1979c), I presented the doubling construction as evidence against an unmotivated chomage analysis, suggesting a treatment involving reflexive passive. Hukari (1980) says:

'If [doubling] were the general pattern in [Cowichan], one might make a case for object-to-subject advancement, where the 'history' of the patient remains in the form of another suffix. . . . The fact is, however, these doubly marked constructions are rare and can hardly be taken as evidence when considering the predominant pattern.'

I take another view regarding this and other phenomena which are marginal. I claim that an analysis which can account for both the predominant and the less prevalent patterns is to be preferred over an analysis which can only handle a single pattern.

Furthermore, it should be pointed out that variation in agreement, case, etc., is frequent in many languages. A case in point, Timberlake (1976), discussing the Russian passive, notes that in Contemporary Standard Russian the departure objects is in the nominative case and determines verb agreement. In North Russian, there are three patterns for the departure object: it can be in the nominative case with or without determining agreement, or it can be in the accusative case without determining agreement.

[23] The speakers I have consulted who accept doubling all agree that (61) and (62) are somewhat worse than (63-64). I have no explanation for this.

[24] For example, in There-insertion constructions in English, There, the inserted dummy, does not determine agreement. Rather it is the nominal placed en chomage by There-insertion that determines agreement; as seen in the following:

(i) There were three drunks in the bathtub last night.

(ii) There seem to have been three drunks in the bathtub last night.

Note many younger speakers of English, myself included, frequently do not have brother-in-law agreement in these constructions in casual speech.

(iii) There's three guys at the door who say they know you.

[25]For further research on the Unaccusative Hypothesis, cf. Hubbard (1979, Özkaraköz (1980), Perlmutter (in preparation), Postal (to appear), Rosen (in preparation), and Williamson (1979).

[26]Notice that the Halkomelem data also violate various alternative formulations of the 1-AEX, e.g. the 1-Advancee Preservation Law (Watchtel 1979).

CHAPTER 6

CONCLUSION

6.0 The Results of this Investigation

This study is of value as a contribution to the description of Halkomelem syntax. In addition, there are several interesting results apropos the theory of Relational Grammar.

In the case of 3-2 and Ben-2 advancement in Halkomelem, as in many other languages, there is not a corresponding construction without advancement. In such examples, it is not unreasonable to suggest that the nominals in question do not advance to object but rather are objects at the initial level (cf. §3.3). I argue, however, that conditions on four constructions in Halkomelem--reflexives, limited control marking, antipassive, and object cancellations--distinguish initial from non-initial objects, and thus provide evidence for advancement in the cause of 3-2 and Ben-2 advancement in Halkomelem.

Second, I argue for the final intransitivity of antipassives, reflexives, reciprocals, and object cancellations in Halkomelem. These constructions, which I refer to under the cover term of object resignation, share an important feature: the object at one level is not the object at the subsequent level. Although the evidence for the exact structure of these constructions at final level is indeterminate, it appears certain that these constructions cannot be considered to be instances of a single construction. Thus, two recent analyses of final intransitivity (Postal (1977) and Aissen (to appear)) seem to be inadequate. Further research into object resignations is indicated.

Passives in Halkomelem are a third area of research with implications for the theory of Relational Grammar. Although evidence was not found, as Hukari suggests, that passives in Halkomelem involve unmotivated chomage, passives involving 1st and 2nd person departure objects were somewhat recalcitrant. Data involving raising indicated that the departure objects in Halkomelem passives were not final objects. In the case of 1st and 2nd person departure objects, however, the 1st and 2nd pronominal forms were in the objective case. I accounted for this by positing an analysis inolving impersonal passive for these constructions and by making reference to the notion acting 2 in the rule for pronominal case. Furthermore, data involving doubling, i.e., cases where both subjective and objective pronominal forms were present in the passive, could be accounted for my positing an optional rule of brother-in-law person marking, whereby the dummy in the impersonal passive optionally adopts the person of the nominal it places en chomage. Thus, Halkomelem passives with 1st and 2nd person departure objects, as with impersonal passives in other languages, can be adequately handled within the theory of Relational Grammar.

An additional Halkomelem construction which can be provided with an insightful analysis within Relational Grammar is the unaccusative. Giving evidence based on a condition on causative clause union in Halkomelem, I argued that certain initially intransitive clauses have an object but no subject, thus supporting the Unaccusative Hypothesis. However, in discussing passives of clauses involving causal to object advancement, I point out that such clauses are initially unaccusative and involve two instances of advancement of object to subject. Thus, such constructions violate a law proposed as a universal in Relational Grammar--the 1-advancement exclusiveness law.

REFERENCES

Aissen, Judith L. 1974. The Syntax of Causative Constructions. Ph.D. dissertation, Harvard University.

________. 1979. Possessor Ascension in Tzotzil. in L. Martin (ed.), Papers in Mayan Linguistics, Columbia, Mo.: Lucas Brothers, 89-108.

________. to appear a. Indirect object Advancement in Tzotzil. in Perlmutter (ed.)

________. to appear b. Valence and Coreference. in S. Thompson and P. Hooper (eds.) Transitivity.

________ and Jorge Hankamer. 1980. Lexical Extension and Grammatical Transformations. Proceedings of the 6th Annual Meeting of the Berkeley Linguisitcs Society, 238-249.

Akmajian, Adrian. 1979. Aspects of the Grammar of Focus in English. New York: G arland Publishing.

Beaumont, Ronald C. 1977. Causation and Control in Sechelt. Paper given at the 12th International Conference on Salishan Languages (ICSL), Omak, Wa.

Bell, Sarah. to appear. Advancements and Ascensions in Chamorro. in Perlmutter (ed.)

Bresnan, Joan. 1978. A Realistic Transformational Grammar. in Halle, Bresnan, and Miller (eds.) Linguistic Theory and Psychological Reality. MIT Press.

Carlson, Barry F. 1980. Two-Goal Transitive Stems in Spokane Salish. IJAL 46:1, 21-26.

Chinchor, Nancy. 1975. A Treatment of Passives and Pronouns in Lummi Matrix Sentences. in Papers from the 10th ICSL.

Chung, Sandra. 1976a. An Object-Creating Rule in Bahasa Indonesia. Linguistic Inquiry 7:1, 41-87.

________. 1976b. On the Subject of Two Passives in Indonesian. in Li (ed.)

________. 1978. Case Marking and Grammatical Relations in Polynesian. Austin: University of Texas Press.

________. to appear a. Transitivity and Surface Filters in Chamorro. Te Reo, University of Auckland.

________. to appear b. Wh-Movement in Chamorro. Linguistic Inquiry.

Cole, Peter and Jerrold Sadock (eds.) Syntax and Semantics 8: Grammatical Relations. New York: Academic Press.

Cole, Peter and S. N. Shridar. 1977. Clause Union and Relational Grammar: Evidence from Hebrew and Kannada. Linguistic Inquiry 8, 800-713.

Comrie, Bernard. 1977. In Defense of Spontaneous Demotion: The Impersonal Passive. in Cole and Sadock (eds.)

Craig, Colette G. 1977. The Structure of Jacaltec. Austin: University of Texas Press.

Davis, John H. 1974. Case and Function in a Coast Salish Language. Paper presented at the 18th Conference on American Indian Languages, Mexico City.

_______. 1980. The Passive in Sliammon. Proceedings of the 6th Annual Meeting of the Berkeley Lingusitics Society, 278-286.

Davis, Philip W. and Ross Saunders. 1973. Lexical Suffix Copying in Bella Coola. Glossa 7, 231-252.

Demers, Richard A. 1980. The Category AUX in Lummi. Paper presented at the 15th ICSL, Vancouver, B.C.

Dixon, R.M.W. 1979. Ergativity. Lanugage 55:1, 59-138.

Elmendorf, William W. and Wayne Suttles. 1960. Pattern and Change in Halkomelem Salish Dialects. Anthropological Linguistics 2.7:1-32.

Frantz, Donald G. 1971. Toward a Generative Grammar of Blackfoot. Summer Institute of Linguistics Publications, No. 34. Norman, Oklahoma: SIL of the University of Oklahoma.

_______. 1977. Antipassive in Blackfoot. in W. Cowan (ed.) Papers of The Ninth Algonquian Conference. Carleton University.

Galloway, Brent D. 1977. A Grammar of Chilliwack Halkomelem. Ph. D. dissertation, University of California-Berkeley.

_______. 1977. Numerals and Numeral Classifiers in Upriver Halkomelem. Paper presented at the Western Conference on Linguistics, Victoria.

_______. 1978. Control and Transitivity in Upriver Halkomelem. Papers from the 13th ICSL, Victoria, B.C.

Gary, Judith O. and Edward L. Keenan. 1977. On Collapsing Grammatical Relations in Universal Grammar. in Cole and Sadock (eds.)

Gerdts, Donna B. 1977. A Dialect Survey of Halkomelem Salish. M.A. Thesis, University of British Columbia.

________. 1979a. Causatives Constructions in Halkomelem. Paper presented at the 14th ICSL, Bellingham, Washington.

________. 1979b. Object Incorporation and Transitivity. Paper presented at the 43rd International Conference of Americanists, Vancouver, B.C.

________. 1979c. Passives and Transitive Marking in Halkomelem Salish. Paper presented at the Western Conference on Linguistics, Vancouver, B.C.

________. 1979d. 3-2 and Ben-2 Advancement in Halkomelem. Unpublished ms., UCSD.

________. 1980a. Antipassives and Causatives in Halkomelem. Proceedings of the 6th Annual Meeting of the Berkeley Linguistics Society.

________. 1980b. Causal to Object Advancement in Halkomelem. Papers from the 16th Regional Meeting of the Chicago Linguistic Society.

________. 1980c. On Two Surface Filters in Halkomelem. Paper presented at the Annual Meeting of the Linguistic Society of America, San Antonio.

________. 1980d. A Relational Analysis of méʔ Constructions in Halkomelem. Oral's paper, UCSD.

________. 1980e. Some Ergative Phenomena in Halkomelem. Paper Presented at the 15th ICSL, Vancouver, B.C.

________. 1980f. Subject Extraction in Halkomelem. Paper presented at the Western Conference on Linguistics, Victoria, B.C.

________. 1981a. Object Resignation and Ergativity in Halkomelem. Paper presented at the Conference on the Syntax of Native American Languages, Calgary, Alberta.

________. 1981b. Possessor Ascension and Lexical Suffixation in Halkomelem. Paper presented at the Annual Meeting of the Canadian Linguistic Association, Halifax.

________. 1981c. A Syntactic Analysis of Lexical Suffixes in Halkomelem Salish. Paper presented at the 7th Annual Meeting of the Berkeley Linguistics Society.

Gibson, Jeanne D. 1980. Clause Union in Chamorro and in Universal Grammar. Ph.D. dissertation, UCSD.

Gorbet, Larry. 1977. Headless Relatives in the Southwest: Are They Related? Proceedings of the Third Annual Meeting of the Berkeley Linguistic Society.

Hagege, Claude. 1976. Lexical Suffixes and Incorporation in Mainland Comox. Working Papers for the 11st ICSL, Seattle, Wa.

Harris, Alice. 1976. Grammatical Relations in Modern Georgian. Ph.D. dissertation, Harvard University.

Harris, Jimmy G. 1966. The Phonology of Chilliwack Halkomelem. M.A. Thesis, University of Washington.

Hess, Thom. 1968a. Directive Phrase: A Consideration of One Facet of Puget Salish Syntax. Paper given at the 3rd ICSL.

________. 1968b. The Morph /-(ə)b/ in Snohomish. Paper given at the 2nd ICSL, Seattle, Wa.

________. 1973. Agent in a Coast Salish Language. IJAL 39-2:89-94.

Hubbard, Philip L. 1979. Albanian Neapolitan Morphology: Passive, Multiattachment, and the Unaccusative Hypothesis. Linguistic Notes from La Jolla, no. 6.

Hukari, Thomas E. 1976a. Person in a Coast Salish Language. IJAL 42.4, 305-318.

________. 1976b. Transitivity in Halkomelem. Working Papers for the 11th ICSL, Seattle, Wa.

________. 1977a. A Comparison of Attributive Clause Constructions in Two Coast Salish Languages. Glossa. 11.1:48-73.

________. 1978. Halkomelem Nonsegmental Morphology. Papers for the 13th ICSL, Victoria, B.C.

________. 1979a. Diathesis and Discourse Reference in Halkomelem. Paper presented at Western Conference on Linguistics, Vancouver, B.C.

________. 1979b. Oblique Objects in Halkomelem. Papers from the 14th ICSL. Bellingham, Wa.

________. 1980. Subjects and Objects in Cowichan. Paper presented at the 15th ICSL, Vancouver, B.C.

Hukari, Thomas E., Ruby Peter and Ellen White. 1977. Halkomelem. in B. Carlson (ed.) Stealing Light. Native American Texts Series 2:3, 33-68. IJAL, University of Chicago Press.

Jacobsen, William H., Jr. 1979. Noun and Verb in Nootkan. in B. Efrat (ed.) The Victoria Conference on Northwestern Languages. Heritage Record No. 4. British Columbia Provincial Museum, 156-176.

Jackendoff, Ray. 1975. Morphological and Semantic Regularities in the Lexicon. Language 51:3, 639-671.

Jelinek, Eloise and Richard Demers. ms. Passives and the Agent Hierarchy in Coast Salish.

Johnson, David and Paul Postal. 1980. Arc Pair Grammar. Princeton: Princeton University Press.

Jones, Michael K. 1976. Morphophonemic Properties of the Cowichan Actual Aspect. M.A. Thesis, University of Victoria.

Kava, Tiiu. 1979. A Phonology of Cowichan. M.A. Thesis, University of Victoria.

Kinkade, M. Dale. 1980. Columbia Saḷish -xí, -ƛ, -túł. IJAL 46:1,33-36.

Kuipers, Aert H. 1967. The Squamish Language. Mouton.

______. 1968. The Categories Verb-Noun and Transitive-Intransitive in English and Squamish. Lingua 21:610-626.

Kuroda, S. -Y. 1976. Headless Relative Clauses in Modern Japanese and the Relevancy Condition. Proceedings of the Second Annual Meeting of the Berkeley Linguistics Society.

Langacker, Ronald and Pamela Munro. 1975. Passives and their Meaning. Language 51, 789-830.

Leslie, Adrian R. 1979. A Grammar of the Cowichan Dialect of Halkomelem Salish. Ph.D. dissertation, University of Victoria.

Li, Charles N. (ed.) 1976. Subject and Topic. New York: Academic Press.

Mattina, Anthony. 1978. Parallels Between the Colville Transitives and Pseudo-Intransitives. Proceedings of the Annual Meeting of the Western Conference on Linguistics.

McLendon, Sally. 1978. Ergativity, Case, and Transitivity in Eastern Pomo. IJAL -4:1,1-9.

Özkaragöz, İnci Z. 1980. Evidence from Turkish for the Unaccusative Hypothesis. Proceedings of the 6th Annual Meeting of the Berkeley Linguistics Society.

Perlmutter, David M. 1978. Impersonal Passives and the Unaccusative Hypothesis. Proceedings of the 4th Annual Meeting of the Berkeley Linguistics Society.

________. 1979. Working 1s and Inversion in Italian, Japanese, and Quechua.

________. 1980. Relational Grammar. in F. Moravcsik and J. Wirth (eds.) Syntax and Semantics 13: Current Approaches to Syntax. New York: Academic Press.

________. to appear. Syntactic Representation, Syntactic Levels, and the Notion of Subject. in. P. Jacobson and G. Pullum (eds.) The Nature of Syntactic Representation.

________. in preparation. Multiattachment and the Unaccusative Hypothesis: Perfect Auxiliary Selection in Italian.

Perlmutter, David M. and Paul M. Postal. 1974. Le ctures from the LSA Summer Institute.

________. 1977. Toward a Universal Characterization of Passivization. Proceedings of the Third Annual Meeting of the Berkeley Linguistics Society.

________. to appear a. The 1-Advancement Exclusiveness Law. in Perlmutter (ed.)

________. to appear b. The Relational Succession Law. in Perlmutter (ed.)

________. to appear c. Some Proposed Laws of Basic Clause Structure. in Perlmutter (ed.)

________. to appear d. Impersonal Passives and Some Relational Laws. in Perlmutter (ed.)

Postal, Paul M. 1977. Antipassive in French. Proceedings of the 7th Annual Meeting of the Northeastern Linguistic Society.

________. to appear. Some Arc Pair Grammar Descriptions. in P. Jacobsen and G. Pullum (eds.), The Nature of Syntactic Representation.

Raposo, Eduardo P. and Jeanne D. Gibson. in preparation. The Rule of Clause Union and the Stratal Uniqueness Law.

Rosen, Carol. in preparation. The Clause Nucleus in Italian: A Study in Relational Grammar. Ph.D. dissertation, Harvard University.

Saunders, Ross, and Philip W. Davis. 1975a. Bella Coola Lexical Suffixes. Anthopological Linguistics 17, 154-189.

_______. 1975b. Bella Coola Referential Suffixes. IJAL 41:4, 355-368.

_______. 1975c. The Internal Syntax of Lexical Suffixes in Bella Coola. IJAL 41:2, 106-113.

_______. n.d. The Control System of Bella Coola.

Schachter, Paul. 1977. Reference-related and Role-related Properties of Subjects. in Cole and Sadock (eds.)

Seiter, William J. 1979. Instrumental Advancement in Niuean. Linguistic Inquiry 10:4, 595-622.

Silverstein, Michael. 1976. Hierarchy of Features and Ergativity. in R.M.W. Dixon (ed.) Grammatical Categories in Australian Languages, pp. 112-171. Australian Institute of Aboriginal Studies.

Suttles, Wayne. 1969. Musqueam Notes, Unpublished teaching materials.

_______. in prep. A Reference Grammar of the Musqueam Dialect of Halkomelem.

Thompson, Laurence C. 1979a. The Control System: A Major Category in the Grammar of Salishan Languages. in B. Efrat (ed.) The Victoria Conference on Northwestern Languages. Heritage Record No. 4. British Columbia Provincial Museum, 156-176.

_______. 1979b. Salishan and the Northwest. in L. Campbell and M. Mithun (eds.) The Languages of Native America: Historical and Comparative Assessment. University of Texas Press, Austin, 692-765.

_______. ms. Control in Salish Grammar.

Thompson, Laurence C. and M. Terry Thompson. 1971. Clallam: A Preview. in J. Sawyer (ed.) Studies in American Indian Languages. University of California Publications in Linguistics 65, pp. 251-94.

_______. in press. Limited Control: A Salish Grammatical Category. Proceedings of the XLI International Congress of Americanists, Mexico City, 1975.

_______. 1980. Thompson Salish //-xi//. IJAL 46:1, 27-32.

Timberlake, Alan. 1976. Subject properties in the North Russian Passive. in Li (ed.)

________. 1979. Reflexivization and the Cycle in Russian. Linguistic Inquiry 10:1, 109-142.

________. 1980. Reference Conditions on Russian Reflexivization. Language 56:4, 777-796.

Wachtel, Tom. 1979. The Demotion Analysis of Initially Unaccusative Impersonal Passives. Papers from the 15th Regional Meeting of the Chicago Linguistic Society.

Wasow, Thomas. 1977. Transformations and the Lexicon. in P. Culicover, et. al. (eds.) Formal Syntax. Academic Press, 327-360.

Williamson, Janis S. 1979. Patient Marking in Lakhota and the Unaccusative Hypothesis. Papers from the 15th Regional Meeting of the Chicago Linguistic Society.